Making Books

Design in British publishing since

AUTHOR
COMMISSIONING EDITOR
PUBLISHER
PRODUCTION MANAGER   ART DIRECTOR
HOUSE EDITOR
PHOTOGRAPHER
COPY EDITOR
DIAGRAM DESIGNER
SCANNER OPERATOR
PICTURE RESEARCHER
ILLUSTRATOR
TYPESETTER
CARTOGRAPHER
INDEXER
TYPOGRAPHER
PRINTER
BINDER
JACKET DESIGNER

Alan Bartram

MAKING BOOKS

Design in British publishing since 1945

The British Library & Oak Knoll Press   1999

First published 1999
by The British Library
96 Euston Road
London NW1 2DB
UK
and
Oak Knoll Press
310 Delaware Street
New Castle
DE 19720
USA

British Library Cataloguing in Publication Data
A catalogue record for this book is available from
The British Library

Library of Congress Cataloging in Publication Data
Bartram, Alan
Making books: design in British publishing since 1945
/ Alan Bartram
p.   cm.
Includes bibliographical references and index
ISBN 1 884718 93 0
1. Book design – Great Britain – History – 20th century
I. Title
Z116.A3B46   1999
686'.0941 – dc21   99-29885   CIP

ISBN 0 7123 4633 3 (British Library)
ISBN 1 884718 93 0 (Oak Knoll)

Designed by Alan Bartram
Typeset in Berthold Imago Book
by Norman Tilley Graphics, Northampton
Printed in England by St Edmundsbury Press
Bury St Edmunds

Contents

Preface

When in 1995 I designed a little book on Aldus Manutius for the British Library, the editor asked the author if he had any acknowledgements he wished to make. 'Er, no, not really. It's all my own work.' This book is all my own work, too, but it is also the result of working with publishers for thirty years, and longer still working as a typographer. So the people who have unwittingly contributed to my thoughts stretch back an awfully long way. To a large extent I learnt typography from Herbert Spencer, and from my brother Harold who had been his student (as he was, simultaneously, a student of Anthony Froshaug's). But when I did freelance design for George Rainbird, Ronald Clark, and his successor there, George Sharp, probably taught me more about book design than anyone. Later conversations with Ron Costley, now at Faber & Faber, have always been illuminating, as were an exchange of letters with Rich Hendel of the University of North Carolina Press.

John Trevitt's last chapter in his revision of S H Steinberg's *Five Hundred Years of Printing* has been of great help, and should be read by anyone who wants this period broadened out in a less idiosyncratic way than my coverage. More immediately influential has been my co-author of *Typefaces for Books*, James Sutton. Our section on bookmaking in that volume was the genesis of this. John Taylor has as ever been of great help in numerous ways. Diana Allen's photocopier has played an important role, while some remarks by her on the relationship of architecture to typography have been stolen by me and worked upon.

Most directly deserving of my thanks is that selfsame BL editor mentioned above, David Way. Once again his enthusiastic understanding has been most supportive in this risky venture.

'I think you should write what you want to write, not what you think you ought to write' Alan Ross told me after looking at a tiresomely conscientious book on Apulia in 1965. In all my published books since then, including this, I have, for better or worse, followed his advice. So here are a few books which might help to balance out any prejudices in mine. I have already mentioned two: John Trevitt's revision of S H Steinberg's *Five Hundred Years of Printing* (The British Library/Oak Knoll Press, 1996); and *Typefaces for Books* by James Sutton and Alan Bartram (The British Library/New Amsterdam, 1990). Two more, both essential, are included in my examples: Hugh Williamson's *Methods of Book Design* (OUP 1956, revised edition Yale UP, 1983); and Robert Bringhurst's *The Elements of Typographic Style* (Hartley & Marks, 1992, second edition 1996; distributed in the UK by Lund Humphries). This has become the American book designer's bible, and deservedly so.

Designing Books: Practice and Theory by Jost Hochuli and Robin Kinross (Hyphen Press, 1996) is a sane, succinct and beautifully-produced book with excellent illustrations. Richard Hendel's *On Book Design* (Yale UP, 1998), again finely-produced, is particularly interesting for the approaches, described by themselves, of eight (mainly American) book designers. It demonstrates the different agenda which American designers work to (although this agenda clearly worries the book's American, but anglophile, editor).

Jan Tschichold: a life in typography (Lund Humphries/Princeton Architectural Press, 1997), Ruari McLean's revision of his 1975 classic *Jan Tschichold: Typographer*, is disappointingly designed but is full of wonderful stuff. Although, as far as I know, there has – astonishingly – yet to be a book on Hans Schmoller, a fine and well-illustrated account of his life and work can be found in *The Monotype Recorder* No.6 (new series), April 1987, edited by Gerald Cinamon.

Three books on type design are mainly, or entirely, concerned with metal types. Walter Tracy's *Letters of Credit* (Gordon Fraser/Godine, 1986) is a scholarly compilation concerning types, their design, and their designers. Although everything discussed is pre-1945, much – or most – of it remains extremely relevant today. Two further books covering this pre-filmsetting period still have their admirers. *An Atlas of Typeforms* by James Sutton and Alan Bartram (Lund Humphries, 1968) relates modern types to their historical antecedents; while Geoffrey Dowding's *An Introduction to the History of Printing Types* (Wace, 1961; reprinted 1998 by The British Library/Oak Knoll Press) is an extremely useful compact guide to the subject.

Sebastian Carter's *Twentieth-Century Type Designers* (Trefoil 1987, revised edition Lund Humphries/Norton, 1995) outlines the lives of the designers and discusses their types.

Finally, *Glaister's Glossary of the Book* (second edition George Allen & Unwin 1979, reprinted by The British Library/Oak Knoll Press, 1996) has its uses. Amongst a wealth of information highly pertinent to the subject of this present book, you can also find entries such as '*maril*: marbled inlaid leather'; '*Legend Aurea*: a collection of lives of the saints, written between 1263 and 1272'; '*book annotators*: people who write personal comments in the margins of books, either their own or those they have borrowed from public libraries' – and who Mr Glaister swipes with a quotation winging all the way from the early fourteenth century. Did you know *any* of that?

Introduction

The fate of the New Architecture lies in our own hands. It will achieve a place amongst the great architectures, only if we have a set of values which are not entirely materialistic, if we have faith in the Spirit of Mankind, if we have eyes that have learnt the power of discrimination. The age when men are eager about great work is the age when great work itself gets done. It is the impetus that is required: the will to try.

Architecture is not sinks and fitted furniture. When passion so fires the use of inert materials that they touch our deepest feelings –
that is architecture.

Those words were written in 1945, and end Ralph Tubbs's book *The Englishman Builds*, published by Penguin. They sound faintly ridiculous now, because the ideas they embody – hope and idealism – do not power our life today. But they were very strong in the austere period immediately after the war. Architects and designers, even politicians, were amongst those who saw the future with gleaming eyes.

This book sets out from that period of austerity and dreams. If we consider only the best work – as we must – from the following six decades, we see the emergence of a greater professionalism in the making of books. Tauter and more consistent relationship of pages and, if included, illustrations; skilful and conscientious editing (noticeable only if omitted); clear and elegant diagrams; outstanding botanical and other descriptive illustrations of unprecedented quality; all pictures fully integrated with the text; more and better colour; even, in the last ten years or so, rich black-and-white printing. Much of this was facilitated by the change to offset printing, the more sophisticated use of grids, and more positive use of asymmetric design. But social changes have acted against Ralph Tubbs's brave future. The visionaries of the 1940s would have been dismayed to see not only a world in which antiques are sought in preference to good modern designs, but also where newspapers devote about a third of their content solely to matters of business and finance.

The unusual conditions of that early period – war, and the end of war – seemed sympathetic to 'conviction publishing' by possibly idiosyncratic publishers. They were walking on ice. On the dry land, the larger operations which came into existence, in a world where higher profits, and shareholders, were becoming major considerations, tried to be more business-like, intently scrutinising the prospects of profitability before deciding upon publication. Such divinations have not always been more accurate than the hunches of the earlier small publisher, but they have significantly contributed to changes in the style of British publishing over the last sixty years.

In the 1940s and 1950s there was a willingness – call it a marketing ploy if you like – amongst individualistic publishers to commission eminent artists to illustrate poetry and classic – or even contemporary – novels. In 1950, for instance, Michael Joseph commissioned John Minton to illustrate *Old Herbaceous* by Reginald Arkell. Eight full-page illustrations, seven small drawings and four decorative chapter openings were all printed in a dark green second colour. An unpretentious little tale was thereby transformed (in spite of, or because of, a modest format) into a most agreeable production. The more corporate-minded firms of today hardly dare think of such a pleasing idea, nor do artists seem willing or able to do it, and such illustrations have almost entirely dropped out of fashion.

Similarly, the practice of financing a potential poor-seller by profits from successful books, as a publisher such as Victor Gollancz would do because he, personally, believed it deserved publishing even if it cost him money, or as university presses considered it their duty to do – behaviour once considered normal practice – has almost disappeared. Allen Lane subsidised the King Penguin series with profits from regular Penguins. Especially after Tschichold took them in hand they were finely produced books. Their quality gave Lane's firm prestige rather than profits. Unfortunately, it normally costs more to produce books well rather than poorly. Good printing and good paper are generally more expensive than bad. Good design will cost a little more than no design. Careful editing costs a lot in time. If photographs, maps, illustrations or artwork are required, quality has to be paid for. Good bookmaking is hard work and expensive. A book is like an iceberg. There it is, floating calmly in the bookshop, but eighty percent of it – the effort put into getting it 'bookshape' – is invisible.

Like any trade, publishing reflects the society in which it operates. Glossy colourful books on antiques, gardening or napkin folding abound in today's bookshops. Likewise, there is a market today for massive biographies laden with notes and references; publishers fill it and authors ignore Strachey's dictum to include nothing extraneous and everything relevant (enabling him to deal with four Eminent Victorians in 320 pages). There are books to expose on bookshelves or coffee tables. There is an insatiable demand for guides to The Countryside or The Heritage, lavishly illustrated in full colour. Bookshops prefer publishers to pump up novels to twice or thrice their natural format, regardless of how inconvenient they are to carry around or read at meal times, in order to create apparent 'value for money'. Bigger formats = bigger cover price = bigger profits. Ever more ambitious exhibitions have resulted in catalogues growing from an eight-page listing plus four black-and-white illustrations in the 1940s to today's erudite 540-page volumes in full colour throughout: considerably better value than catalogues of the 1960s and 1970s, which had small grey barely-recognisable illustrations. All these market-orientated ploys, one feels, have resulted in some loss of innocence in the publishing world. Strangely, although many publishers today are big businesses, this has not circumvented financial instability. The turnover that kept one man and his dog going is no longer sufficient.

Our period saw the rise of the book packager. Often scorned by 'real' publishers, they are sometimes asked to handle projects such as complicated illustrated books that a traditional publisher is not equipped for. But they also initiate publishing ideas, or concepts, themselves, and gather together writers, illustrators, cartographers, picture researchers and designers in order to sell 'the package' to a publisher, who will market the final book. One of the first and best packagers was George Rainbird, who brought real professionalism into all aspects of bookmaking. Although very much market-orientated, many fine books, excellent by any standard, were produced in this way. *The Observer* once divided publishers into Gentlemen and Players. Rainbird was certainly a Player. (John Murray was a Gentleman.)

Like the bicycle, the printed book grew out of an earlier model. Derived from hobby horse or manuscript book, they both achieved their definitive form quickly. A few maverick models were produced from time to time, but generally development consisted in refining this or that detail, new and more gears here, neater types and coloured pictures there. Only in the last thirty years have new technology and new demands resulted in serious changes: the Moulton and the mountain bike on the one hand, offset printing and filmsetting on the other. These printing developments allowed improved or quite new concepts in publishing: pictures truly integrated with text, far more and far better colour, and international co-editions. It became common for the typesetting, origination and printing operations to be carried out by different firms, often in different countries; so with the choice of the world for printing, the completed setting or even made-up pages are sent countrywide or worldwide in disk form. This division of the production process, while financially clever, can create problems, and extra work, for the designer. Today, perhaps even more than in the past, an 'overall guiding intelligence' (John Lewis's phrase) is required to ensure the result is a coherent whole.

Businesslike publishing often results in what could be called the committee concept: lavishly-illustrated books for the mass market. They clearly meet a demand, even if many of them end up being remaindered (such a fate is often built into the original budgeting). Large, awkward, beautifully-produced re-hashes of Elizabeth David, with full-colour illustrations taken from details of Italian paintings, are gifts for somebody else's coffee table (and don't spill the coffee), not for serious culinary use. There is a place for such books just as there is a place for fast food outlets or even, I suppose, building society offices. Despite their pervasive presence, these are omitted from serious books on architecture, and I have almost entirely excluded popular books from this volume. Often heavily-promoted, sometimes tied-in to a TV series, they can be imaginatively conceived and excellently produced, well printed in full colour;

but their design is not usually to my taste. They relate more closely to the marketing and advertising world than to mainstream publishing. Or so it seems to me.

Perhaps the most successful mass-market publisher – much of whose output, which is of exceptional quality, has a serious educational intent – is Dorling Kindersley; and because they are so omnipresent, I have spatchcocked a couple of examples into my sequence.

Personal preference has inevitably governed my choice of books, and in fact almost all are off my own bookshelves. If a book is poorly designed and/or poorly produced, I don't want to own it. And although many types of books are missing, I believe that, by using these examples, I have been able to describe fairly the overall changing patterns of mainstream British publishing. I hope that simplification has resulted in clarification.

I make no claim to take an Olympian overview of my subject. (In the late 1990s, there were over 100,000 new titles published in Britain every year.) Selection and views are those of a designer who learnt the rudiments of his trade in the 1950s. The principles of logic, readability and rather strict organisation, with clear presentation of disparate kinds of information, all parts relating to the whole – simple aims, often surprisingly difficult to achieve – these principles were valid then, and are valid still. I find myself unhappy with the fundamental aspects and decorative detailing of post-modernist typography. ('Well, I lay it down that a book quite unornamented can look actually and positively beautiful, if it be so to say, architecturally good' declared William Morris, even if he did not always follow this concept himself.) The twitchy PoMo characteristics: text run around pictures; ill-considered use of dropped capitals; half-tones and possibly every text page boxed around with rules, with sometimes rather fey decorative features and twiddly bits at the corners incorporated; these are a revival of practices long abandoned as impractical, unsightly, and impairing legibility. Unfortunately, designing on a computer screen has made them practical – but no less unsightly and distracting. They are intended, I suppose, to be visually enriching. Personally I find them disturbing: the publishing equivalent of the popular admiration for antiques. The historicist details unconvincingly bolted on to PoMo buildings likewise reflect uneasiness about contemporary life.

Most of the books I illustrate are British. Two or three foreign ones are included to show the disciplined approach which later affected British designs. Although benefiting greatly from the work of German designers – Jan Tschichold and Hans Schmoller – the style of British books has little in common with those of the Continent (just as French books differ from Italian, and Italian from German). American books, whose designers feel obliged to give their clients conspicuous value for money, can be recognised at a glance. Even in books intended to be published as international co-editions, the national characteristics and preferences of the originating country will always be evident. No generalised pattern in publishing can be extrapolated from one nation's story; as I try to show, all sorts of historical and social factors determine the results.

Many finely produced books will not be found here. Often, their real significance cannot be appreciated in reproduction, so, for instance, I do not show a typical Phaidon book of the 1940s (large-format monograph, coarse cloth binding, extensive plate section in brownish photogravure divorced from the text, staidly laid-out), nor a 1990s book (lavishly-illustrated, full colour, integrated, high reproduction standards, varied – often quite daring – cleanly-structured design) from this happily-resurrected firm. In their different ways, the books of both periods have strong identities, and their characteristics epitomise the comprehensive change in publishing over the last fifty years. But as so often, one needs to see the books themselves. How do you convey that a book is good to hold, has a nice format conveniently judged in relation to its bulk, has sympathetic paper, has an especially pleasant print quality, even an attractive smell? How do you indicate in two or three spreads that every detail, title page, copyright page, list of contents, headings, illustrations, notes, bibliography, index, has been carefully considered not only in itself but in relation to the whole? When I tell people I design books they think I mean just the jackets. That is not what I mean.

The careful work of the 1950s sometimes seems little appreciated. The achievements – meticulous detailing by Schmoller and others, or formal developments such as a more sophisticated use of grids – must not be allowed to decay by default. As the philosophic basis of Modernism developed, so did opportunities for WIlliam Morris's 'architecturally good' books; for, ever since the 1920s (in Germany and Holland), and the 1940s (in Britain), the principles behind architecture and typography have had much in common. Both have practical and functional needs that must be respected. While imagination is desirable, and original thinking transforming, designers' egos should be kept subordinate to the requirements of the brief. Such self-denial is often strangely difficult to accept, as I know only too well, especially as the dividing line between originality and egotism is not always easy to recognise. This conflict can be seen in many over-designed books and buildings today. Formally, there is a common concern with space, structure, logic, asymmetry, alignments, grids, purity, simplicity. Plain (often white) surfaces with rectangular holes (windows, entrances) punched through them relate to white pages with rectangular shapes (pictures, columns of text) carefully placed on them. Architecture has spatial progression as one walks through; books have linear and temporal progression as one turns over pages. In both cases, what

happened at the beginning affects (should affect) what happens later – and vice versa. Although the wilder Bauhaus typographers (Joost Schmidt for instance) were influenced by painters, the more practical typographer – especially the book typographer – is much closer to an architect than to a painter, even an abstract painter, even Mondrian. Max Bill, one of the most influential Swiss typographers, was an abstract painter (and a sculptor). But he was also an architect. So was Herbert Bayer.

It is easy enough to find incompetently-designed books today, but the best work has more structure, is more 'architectural', than books of the 1940s. And most illustrated books, even those whose design suffers from modish tricks, are better – often far better – printed. Books of straightforward text are another matter. Unfortunately, many publishers today, good publishers who publish worthwhile books, are unable to see the difference between a well-set readable text and a badly-set (but still readable) text. They have learnt only half their trade. Discomfort, even, sometimes, unreadability, displaces pleasure.

There is nothing mysterious about the requirements of good bookmaking. Good typesetting, a decent standard of printing, readability, comprehensible structure, thorough cross-referencing where helpful (especially to illustrations, if included, which need to be provided with adequate captions), consistency in editorial and visual detailing, clear signposting. These basics – all pretty obvious stuff – should be the prime aims of editor and designer working together. Although easier to list than to achieve, their lack – and in some books, despite credits to an editorial and design team, *all* are lacking – reveals the unprofessional publisher.

Generally, I have chosen to show good work rather than bad. Who wants to look at a lot of bad work, even if it is instructive?

A note on the illustrations
Generally, examples showing text design, and also artists' illustrations, are actual size or only slightly reduced. Examples showing the design structure, or the overall design of the page, are of various reductions.

There is a school of thought that believes examples of book design are often shown unnecessarily large. But text setting can only be truly judged in the size the designer intended, and all books, even those which are laxly designed, seem to undergo a magical transformation when drastically reduced. Moreover, I often discuss the writing – the words themselves. I hope in these cases the reader will read not only *my* text, but will be able to read my examples too.

1

1942! To us today, an optimistic and visionary book about the years ahead, written and published in the darkest days of the war, seems a foolhardy act of faith. This same author/architect, whom I also quote (from a different book) at the start of my introduction, later designed the Dome of Discovery at the Festival of Britain in 1951. The years 1942 to 1951 are not usually regarded as years in which a feeling of well-being flourished. Many things considered today as essential to the good life were more or less absent, even when the war had ended. Yet as an adolescent and student then I had no feeling of deprivation. Quite the contrary. None of the side-effects of too much misdirected prosperity had emerged, nor had the desire for a richer (in all senses) society been distorted into a thirst for personal enrichment. Life may have been a little sombre, but it was more relaxed and less stressful than it has now become. Stress was something found only in structures like bridges. With none of the competitive pressures later created by advanced consumer capitalism, people were happier. The few, used to living giddily, enjoying the esoteric attractions of Fitzrovia, have in their memoirs created a depressing picture of a cheerless post-war London. But away from all that, for ordinary people, who don't write memoirs, life, while a little drab, wasn't so bad. There were some benefits not appreciated at the time. Unexotic but generally healthy food; power failures, coal shortages, and a scarcity of goods in the shops, but less crime; fuming (and working) factories, mills and steelworks, but less general pollution; empty roads; undesecrated countryside; town centres blitzed by bombs but not yet by developers. One felt a new beginning could be made. Never again was there to be such a chance to create a sane and healthy society than at the end of the war. In spite of the

1

Living in Cities
Ralph Tubbs
Penguin Books 1942
174mm deep

TOWN-PLANNING AND A NATIONAL POLICY

Before he can start even preliminary designs for a town, an architect must have a clearly defined programme—that is, an outline of conditions which the plan must fulfil. Many simple requirements, such as pleasant homes and workplaces, trees and parks, cheerful markets and shopping centres, schools and playing-fields, form the basis of town-planning, but they are not the only controlling factors. National issues, as set out below, must also be considered, for on them will depend the future size and character of the town.

MOVEMENT OF INDUSTRY
Regional planners must collaborate with economists and study the many factors governing industrial changes and any possible redistribution of light industries.

DISTRIBUTION OF POPULATION
Town-planning is obviously affected by any population change. Not only is the birth-rate a factor, but any movement of population as a result of movement of industry.

USE OF THE SOIL
Agriculture must be given more consideration than before the war. The Land Utilisation Survey of Great Britain have compiled a map of land use and have analysed the quality of agricultural land. Proper use should be made of this research. It is wanton to build on good agricultural land, as some of the Trading Estates have done in the past.

COMMUNICATION
Towns must be related to a system of rail, road and air communication, to canals and to ports.

GEOGRAPHY, GEOLOGY AND METEOROLOGY
Mountainous or hilly sites, the nature of the soil and atmospheric conditions all vitally affect the development of towns.

NATIONAL PARKS
The recreational value of land of low agricultural importance must not be forgotten, and some of the moors and mountain ranges might be made into National Parks. The part of sea-coast resorts in contributing pleasure and health is important, and the present ruination of a beautiful coast-line by unconsidered development must be stopped.

28

country's near-bankruptcy, amazing things were done, from the creation of the National Health Service and the Welfare State, to the building of fifteen New Towns. That the reality did not always match the vision is beside the point. Today, money cannot be found to keep open public lavatories.

Living in Cities is not particularly well produced, nor particularly well designed. With constant changes of type measure, often over-large type, and an unhappy reliance on capitals, it is nonetheless well integrated, with a fine and varied choice of pertinent illustrations. And it is powerful and eloquent propaganda, inspiring in its optimism. Showing all the signs of being laid out by the architect/author – 'I want all this here, and I'm going to get it in somehow' – it is an early example of what can be called the TV documentary approach, with text and image truly complementing each other. Captions add a further commentary.

Both *Living in Cities* and *The Englishman Builds* (quoted earlier) have echoes of the heroic Le Corbusier style. 'What conditions are necessary for the New Architecture to flower in full perfection? ... We might well answer that they are *the very same conditions as are necessary for the regeneration of our society.*' 'Town planning cannot be divorced from a unified conception of what human life might be.' Never again, one feels, will such sentiments be so sincerely expressed.

HUMAN NEEDS
—*personal*

EARTH, SKY, TREES
—*eternal*

TECHNICAL KNOWLEDGE
—*ever changing*

LIVING ORGANISM

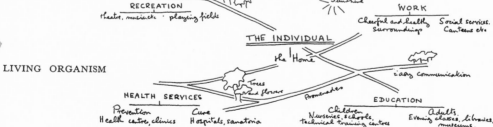

THE BASIS OF THE TOWN

29

2

The following year, 1943, Graham Sutherland was asked to illustrate a volume of David Gascoyne's poems. His five primeval and surrealist illustrations printed in black and (often) almost invisible red and blue, together with jacket/cover design in black and red only, and a title page in black only, suffer from rather poor reproduction on coated paper. The illustrations (see next spread) are tipped-in between groups of poems printed on cartridge. Although affected by wartime restrictions on quality, it is a notable venture, redolent of its period.

There was at this time an almost insatiable market for poetry, as service-men and civilians stuffed kitbags or pockets with paperbacks, to read as occasion arose, such as during endless, ever-stopping, ever-crowded, dimly-lit train journeys; waiting while the steam engines, running on poor coal, stopped to gather breath for the next push, or broke down altogether. It was but a step to embellish slightly more ambitious volumes with illustrations, and perhaps because few suitable professional illustrators were available, publishers turned to painters of their acquaintance, such as Sutherland. What they got was very different from the attractive, though often genteel, wood-engraved illustrations of the immediate pre-war period.

2
Poems 1937-1942
David Gascoyne
Poetry London Editions 1943
212mm deep

O lofty lofty lands and alien azure sky
Weigh down on her who now is no more known
As bosom or as spasm or as hot tears spilt in Time :
Who underneath the ground has turned right round
To face another, a more ashen sun.

ii   *The Moths*

There are moths shut-in below
Moths pink and black and plump
Such moths are warm with an inhuman glow
Their wings are faults of memory
These creatures have the accent of two faces marked by fate
When they are hanging strictly folded-up below.

When the moths of the flesh below are called
Up from the shadows where they wait
They rise up pink and plump
They rise up but they flap
They flap but soon are swollen tight
With odour, blindness, nudity and weight.

iii   *Brow*

The sun's come back upon the window-panes
The birds make song
And Hope invades the window-panes
Of golden-fired insurgent Morn.
Revolutions make dank mansions shake
While in the gracious light the Heroes march
And down across the blue roofs the bared heads
Of families of ancient and remorseless tyrants fall—

When Man bound to his evil fate
Is dead
Struck down by the myriad blows he merited so well,
Behold his brow take form in the calm blue on high !

20

iv *Nada*

The most beautiful most naked and most tragic splendours
The oppositions between suns and darknesses
In night's forever black protective space
The deepest ecstasy in unknown arms

All things that are no more
And yet are born in agony at dawn
See thee and lift thee up ineffable uproar
Innumerably flaming fireless sex of stars

Love's flame too flaming and too crucified
Upon the intimate blackness of our eyes
Desert of love
Organ of God.

v *The Two Witnesses*

Have pity, O harsh Lamb upon these last two
Witnesses who shall in scarlet cloak be slain and have no tomb
And take O Liberty into thy charge their red remains
For these are the two holy candle-bearers of the Lord
For they have been given power to shut the sky
For their mouths' fire has quite consumed the unjust man
For they have turned the waters into blood
But at last the Beast of the abyss
Has been sent power to deliver them
Has made war and has killed them and all their deeds has undone.

The Three Stars : *A Prophecy*

The night was Time :
The phases of the moon,
Dynamic influence, controller of the tides,
Its changing face and cycle of quick shades,
Were History, which seemed unending. Then
Occurred the prophesied and the to be

21

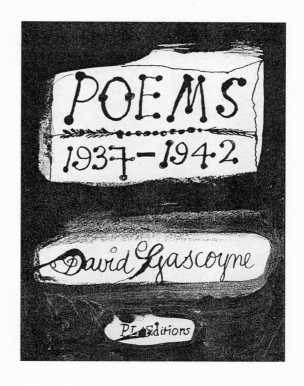

2 *Poems 1937-1942*

Over the next seven years, a remarkable batch of books was illustrated with colour lithographs printed direct from plates (that is, not as half-tones, which Sutherland's mixed-media designs were). The lithographs were commissioned from the most respected British artists of the day, and the uncompromising results were potent, emotional and inventive. Like Sutherland's designs, they depict states of mind or worlds of private mystery rather than objects from the visible world. The artists, lacking Arts Council grants, Millennium funding, or American-style art-world hype, accepted these commissions as an opportunity to earn some money; but they do, in a natural way, open up, in Lawrence Alloway's phrase, 'a long front of culture'; although what *he* meant by that was more rarefied than suggesting that artists illustrate books. He was to develop a non-hierarchical theory of visual expression in which the traditional pyramid, with fine art at the top, was abandoned. But he did not suggest, as far as I am aware, that the fine artists themselves participated in commercial or graphic design – as many artists such as Paul Nash, John Nash, Sutherland or the Bloomsbury painters had done, before the war.

The adventurous and, by today's standards, risky publishing shown here did not last long. The sort of prices the more respected artists were beginning to command, the triumph of American abstract expressionism – hardly a style adaptable to book illustration – and wide-ranging changes in society and publishing contributed to this decline. We are never likely to see *The Faber Book of Incoherent Verse Illustrated by Frank Auerbach*. But while it lasted, the vision was splendid. And all through these years, ration books were still being printed. The title of Peter Hennessy's book on the period, *Never Again*, says it all.

3

The largest group of artist-lithographed books – conceived during the war by Adprint – were the anthologies *New Excursions into English Poetry*. Adprint was the first packaging firm, although the term was not then in general use. It conceived the idea of the King Penguin series in 1939, and, amongst numerous other books, created for Collins in 1945 the New Naturalist series with their wonderful jackets by Clifford and Rosemary Ellis. These jackets, spread over thirty-seven years and nearly one hundred books, were an astonishing achievement.

The New Excursions series 'is something of an experiment and demands original work both from the anthologer and the artist, who have worked in collaboration, though there has been no attempt to give literal and pictorial illustrations of the actual poems'. There were seven books, the artists being John Craxton, John Piper, Michael Ayrton, Mona Moore, William Scott, Edward Bawden and Robert Colquhoun. The sixteen autolithographs in each volume were all printed in four colours. This first volume, *The Poet's Eye*, also included prose. Craxton exploited the medium by overprinting not only colours but even white over a colour. Deeply romantic, with echoes of the Samuel Palmer/Sutherland vision, often reflecting his then preoccupation with the shepherd/dreamer/poet image, his illustrations display genuine originality and poetry (see next spread). The little black-and-white motifs scattered throughout the text succeed wonderfully. But as with all seven books in the series, many illustrations are turned on their side, which is especially disturbing as this is not always immediately apparent. Such a cavalier approach is generally frowned upon today as not being reader-friendly.

3

The Poet's Eye
Geoffrey Grigson
Frederick Muller 1944
203mm deep

GEORGE CRABBE 1754-1832

36. SEASIDE FEN

THE ditches of a fen so near the ocean are lined with irregular patches of a coarse and stained lava; a muddy sediment rests on the horse-tail and other perennial herbs, which in part conceal the shallowness of the stream; a fat-leaved pale-flowering scurvy-grass appears early in the year, and the razor-edged bull-rush in the summer and autumn. The fen itself has a dark and saline herbage; there are rushes and *arrow-head*, and in a few patches the flakes of the cotton-grass are seen, but more commonly the *sea-aster*, the dullest of that numerous and hardy genus; a *thrift*, blue in flower, but withering and remaining withered till the winter scatters it; the *saltwort*, both simple and shrubby; a few kinds of grass changed by their soil and atmosphere, and low plants of two or three denominations undistinguished in a general view of the scenery;—such is the vegetation of the fen when it is at a small distance from the ocean; and in this case there arise from it effluvia strong and peculiar, half-saline, half-putrid, which would be considered by most people as offensive, and by some as dangerous; but there are others to whom singularity of taste or association of ideas has rendered it agreeable and pleasant.

36

55. SONNET

The azur'd vaulte, the crystall circles bright,
The gleaming fyrie torches powdred there,
The changing round, the shyning beamie light,
The sad and bearded fyrcs, the monsters faire:
The prodiges appearing in the aire,
The rearding thunders, and the blustering winds,
The foules, in hew, in shape, in nature raire,
The prettie notes that wing'd musiciens finds:
In earth the sav'rie floures, the mettal'd minds,
The wholesome hearbes, the hautie pleasant trees,
The sylver streames, the beasts of sundrie kinds,
The bounded roares, and fishes of the seas:
    All these, for teaching man, the Lord did frame,
    To do his will, whose glorie shines in thame.

JOHN MILTON 1608-1674

56. VISIONS OF THE MOON

I

. . The horned moon to shine by night
    Amongst her spangled sisters bright . . .

II

. . Unmuffle ye faint stars, and thou fair Moon
    That wontst to love the travailer's benizon,
    Stoop thy pale visage through an amber cloud,
    And disinherit Chaos, that reigns here
    In double night of darkness, and of shades . . .

54

III

. . Why sleepst thou, Eve? now is the pleasant time
    The cool, the silent, save where silence yields
    To the night-warbling bord, that now awake
    Tunes sweetest his love-labour'd song; now reigns
    Full orb'd the Moon, and with more pleasing light
    Shadowy sets off the face of things—in vain,
    If none regard; Heav'n wakes with all his eyes . . .

IV

. . And in her pale dominion checks the night . . .

V

. . Now came still Ev'ning on, and Twilight gray
    Had in her sober livery all things clad;
    Silence accompanied, for beast and bird,
    They to their grassy couch, these to their nests,
    Were slunk, all but the wakeful nightingale;
    She all night long her amorous descant sung;
    Silence was pleas'd: now glow'd the firmament
    With living sapphires: Hesperus that led
    The starry host, rose brightest, till the Moon
    Rising in clouded majesty, at length
    Apparent Queen unveil'd her peerless light,
    And o'er the dark her silver mantle threw . . .

55

3 *The Poet's Eye*

4

Poems of Sleep and Dream
Carol Stewart
Frederick Muller 1947
203mm deep

4

Robert Colquhoun was an experienced printmaker when he illustrated *Poems of Sleep and Dream*, and it shows. Although his sleep seems more troubled by nightmares than dreams, this is probably the most successful book of the New Excursions series. Not only is lack of typographic finesse less apparent but, more important as a piece of bookmaking, the illustrations are better integrated with the text area, rather than slopping around on the page. All except four are portrait-shaped (and so upright on the page) or ambiguous. The images are powerful and inventive, and their scale well-judged for the format. Colquhoun's experience has enabled him to translate his personal

PERCY BYSSHE SHELLEY 1792–1822

FRAGMENT

I went into the deserts of dim sleep—
That world which, like an unknown wilderness,
Bounds this with its recesses wide and deep.

W. J. TURNER 1889–1946

SLEEP

Sleep is not so merciful
So sorrowful as death
Which taketh all
All quieteth.
Yet Sleep, enchanting breath
Less than a sigh,
Lays a faint, funeral wreath
On life.

With fluttering eye
In dream the soul departeth
Far thro'. night's halls to ramble
With ghostly death
In strife;
But each dark portal
Seals, guarding breath,
Sleep, like a sentinel.

49

vision into pure printmaking language, with a vigorous and confident use of black, and subtle use of colour. The strong and somewhat two-dimensional style sits happily with the type.

Each volume in this series cost 10s 6d. To get for this price sixteen original four-colour lithographs by some of the most respected artists of the day, printed direct from the plates, not photographically reproduced as half-tones, seems today rather good value.

Present their shapes; while fantasie discloses
　Millions of *Lillies* mixt with *Roses.*
Then dream, ye heare the Lamb by many a bleat
　Woo'd to come suck the milkie Teat:
While *Faunus* in the Vision comes to keep,
　From rav'ning wolves, the fleecie sheep.
With thousand such enchanting dreams, that meet
　To make sleep not so sound, as sweet.

JOHN MILTON 1608–1674
from
PARADISE LOST

These lull'd by Nightingales imbraceing slept,
And on thir naked limbs the flourie roof
Showrd Roses, which the Morn repair'd. Sleep on,
Blest pair; and O yet happiest if ye seek
No happier state, and know to know no more.

WILLIAM BLAKE 1757–1827
THE ANGEL

I dreamt a Dream! what can it mean?
And that I was a maiden Queen,
Guarded by an Angel mild:
Witless woe was ne'er beguil'd!

And I wept both night and day,
And he wip'd my tears away,
And I wept both day and night,
And hid from him my heart's delight.

So he took his wings and fled;
Then the morn blush'd rosy red;
I dried my tears, & arm'd my fears
With ten thousand shields and spears.

20

5

One of the last and best books illustrated by original lithographs was *A Season in Hell*. Not only are the eight three-colour illustrations of high quality, but the book as a whole seems more professionally worked out. Keith Vaughan's early experience in advertising and print gave him a feeling for bookmaking, and after the war he designed many of John Lehmann's books, including jackets and bindings. He was presumably responsible for the typography here, where the original French text is run alongside the English translation throughout, even on the title page.

Today, working their computers, some authors try to design their own books. Vaughan, as artist/designer, knew what he was doing. Greatly influenced by Sutherland's Gascoyne illustrations [2], his designs also form section titles; but they are beautifully printed (by The Baynard Press) on the same sheets as the text – which was printed separately by Shenval. They fall where required without having to be inelegantly and expensively tipped in.

5
A Season in Hell
Arthur Rimbaud
John Lehmann 1949
216mm deep

A SEASON IN HELL

TRANSLATED BY NORMAN CAMERON

WITH DRAWINGS BY KEITH VAUGHAN

AND THE ORIGINAL FRENCH TEXT BY

ARTHUR RIMBAUD

PUBLISHED IN LONDON BY

JOHN LEHMANN

1949

UNE SAISON EN ENFER

'Il dit: "Je n'aime pas les femmes: l'amour est à réinventer, on le sait. Elles ne peuvent plus que vouloir une position assurée. La position gagnée, coeur et beauté sont mis de côté: il ne reste que froid dédain, l'aliment du mariage, aujourd'hui. Ou bien je vois des femmes, avec les signes du bonheur, dont, moi, j'aurais pu faire de bonnes camarades, dévorées tout d'abord par des brutes sensibles comme des bûchers . . ."

'Je l'écoute faisant de l'infamie une gloire, de la cruauté un charme. "Je suis de race lointaine: mes pères étaient Scandinaves; ils se perçaient les côtes, buvaient leur sang. Je me ferai des entailles par tout le corps, je me tatouerai, je veux devenir hideux comme un Mongol: tu verras, je hurlerai dans les rues. Je veux devenir bien fou de rage. Ne me montre jamais de bijoux, je ramperais et me tordrais sur le tapis. Ma richesse, je la voudrais tachée de sang partout. Jamais je ne travaillerai . . ."

'Plusieurs nuits, son démon me saisissant, nous nous roulions, je luttais avec lui! Les nuits, souvent, ivre, il se poste dans les rues ou dans des maisons, pour m'épouvanter mortellement. "On me coupera vraiment le cou; ce sera dégoutant." Oh! ces jours ou il veut marcher avec l'air du crime!

'Parfois il parle, en une façon de patois attendri, de la mort qui fait repentir, des malheureux qui existent certainement, des travaux pénibles, des départs qui déchirent les coeurs. Dans les bouges ou nous nous enivrions, il pleurait en considerant ceux qui nous entouraient, bétail de la misère. Il relevait les ivrognes dans les rues noires. Il avait la pitié d'une mère méchante pour les petits enfants. Il s'en allait avec des gentillesses de petite fille au catéchisme. Il feignait d'être éclairé sur tout, commerce, art, médecine. Je le suivais, il le faut!

'Je voyais tout le décor dont, en esprit, il s'entourait: vêtements, draps, meubles; je lui prêtais des armes, une autre figure. Je voyais tout ce qui le touchait, comme il aurait voulu le créer pour lui. Quand il me semblait avoir l'esprit inerte, je le suivais, moi, dans des actions étranges et compliquées, loin, bonnes ou mauvaises: j'étais sûre de ne jamais entrer dans son monde. A côté de son cher corps endormi, que d'heures des nuits j'ai veillé,

'He says: "I do not love women. Plainly, love must be re-invented. All that women can do is to wish for an assured position. Position once achieved, heart and beauty are set aside. Nothing is left but cold disdain, the food of marriage nowadays. Or else I see women who have the tokens of happiness, of whom I myself might have made good comrades, devoured from the first by brutes with the sensibilities of chunks of wood . . ."

'I have heard him boasting of infamy, making a magic spell of cruelty: "I am of a distant race. My forefathers were Scandinavian. They pierced their sides and drank their own blood. I will make gashes all over my body. I will tattoo myself. I wish to become as hideous as a Mongol. You shall see, I will howl in the streets. I wish to become utterly mad with rage. Never show me jewels: I would crawl and writhe on the carpet. I like to have my treasures stained all over with blood. I shall never work!"

'On several nights his demon seized me, and we would roll on the ground together, while I struggled with him. Often at night when he was drunk he would lie in wait in streets or houses, in order to scare me to death. "I am bound to have my throat cut," he would say. "That will be disgusting." And then there were the days when he liked to walk about with an air of crime!

'Sometimes he speaks, in a sort of tender jargon, of death that brings repentance, of all the miserable people there must be in the world, of painful labours and heartrending partings. In the hovels where we used to get drunk he would weep as he watched those around us, poverty's cattle. He would lift up drunkards from the black streets. He had a wicked mother's pity on little children. He would go about with the pretty airs of a little girl at Sunday school. He pretended to be expert in all subjects, commerce, art, medicine. I followed him, I have to!

'I could see the whole setting with which in imagination he surrounded himself: clothing, stuffs, furniture. I lent him a coat of arms, another face. Everything that touched him I could see as he would have wished to create it for himself. When he seemed listless in spirit, I would follow him a long way through strange and complicated activities, good or evil. I was sure that I would never enter his world. Beside his dear sleeping body I have watched

Following Sutherland, Keith Vaughan incorporated hand-drawn lettering. Deeply emotional, almost overwrought – like the text – the subtlety and richness of these designs is increased by using a very fine screen in some areas of black, creating effects of crayon and wash. Rather than drawing direct on the plates, Vaughan probably drew each of the three colours individually on paper, to be photographed down onto the plates. Nonetheless, having no meaningful existence until all three colours had been printed together, in this book, these are original lithographs, not four-colour reproductions.

This splendid volume brings to an end a unique period in British publishing.

5 *A Season in Hell*

6

During the latter half of the 1940s, Keith Vaughan and Michael Ayrton were joined by John Minton (famously), Edward Burra, Anthony Gross, Barnett Freedman and other notable artists, to illustrate books more traditionally (and economically) in black and white. Despite continuing 'authorised economy standard' restraints, humdrum typesetting and poor quality paper, these productions have a character unique to this period. The anodyne books of today lack such individuality.

The most prolific, and the best, of these black-and-white artists is John Minton, without doubt. His fluent illustrational style, always recognisable, is surprisingly adaptable: melodrama in *Treasure Island*; dream-like romanticism in *The Wanderer*; idyllic Mediterranean pastoralism in Elizabeth David's books.

The gutsy illustrations for *Treasure Island* sit happily amongst the well-designed pages. This volume is one of the Camden Illustrated Classics, published by Paul Elek, with illustrations by Anthony Gross, Edward Burra, Keith Vaughan, William Scott and others, all designed by Peter Ray – an early example in British publishing of a named typographer. The title page and chapter openings in *Treasure Island* are a brave departure from the norm found in British books hitherto.

6

Treasure Island
Robert Louis Stevenson
Paul Elek 1947
230mm deep

Chapter V

The last of the blind man

My curiosity, in a sense, was stronger than my fear, for I could not remain where I was, but crept back to the bank again, whence, sheltering my head behind a bush of broom, I might command the road before our door. I was scarcely in position ere my enemies began to arrive, seven or eight of them, running hard, their feet beating out of time along the road, and the man with the lantern some paces in front. Three men ran together, hand in hand, and I made out, even through the mist, that the middle man of this trio was the blind beggar. The next moment his voice showed me that I was right.

"Down with the door!" he cried.

"Ay, ay, sir!" answered two or three, and a rush was made upon the "Admiral Benbow," the lantern-bearer following, and then I could see them pause, and hear speeches passed in a lower key, as if they were surprised to find the door open. But the pause was brief, for the blind man again issued his commands. His voice sounded louder and higher, as if he were afire with eagerness and rage.

"In, in, in!" he shouted, and cursed them for their delay.

Four or five of them obeyed at once, two remaining on the road with the formidable beggar. There was a pause, then a cry of surprise, and then a voice shouting from the house:—

"Bill's dead!"

But the blind man swore at them again for their delay.

"Search him, some of you shirking lubbers, and the rest of you aloft and get the chest," he cried.

I could hear their feet rattling up our old stairs, so that the house must have shook with it. Promptly afterwards, fresh sounds of astonishment arose, the window of the captain's room was thrown open with a slam and a jingle of broken glass, and a man leaned out into the moonlight, head and shoulders, and addressed the blind beggar on the road below him.

"Pew," he cried, "they've been before us. Someone's turned the chest out alow and aloft."

"Is it there?" roared Pew.

"The money's there."

42

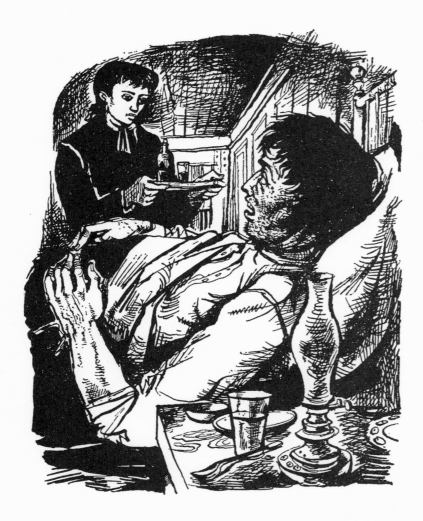

"A week at least," said I.

"Thunder!" he cried. "A week! I can't do that: they'd have the black spot on me by then. The lubbers is going about to get the wind of me this blessed moment; lubbers as couldn't keep what they got, and want to nail what is another's. Is that seamanly behaviour, now, I want to know? But I'm a saving soul. I never wasted

good money of mine, nor lost it neither, and I'll trick 'em again. I'm not afraid on 'em. I'll shake out another reef, matey, and daddle 'em again."

As he was thus speaking, he had risen from bed with great difficulty, holding to my shoulder with a grip that almost made me cry out, and moving his legs like so much dead weight. His words, spirited as they were in meaning, contrasted sadly with the weakness of the voice in which they were uttered. He paused when he had got into a sitting position on the edge.

"That doctor's done me," he murmured. "My ears is singing. Lay me back."

Before I could do much to help him he had fallen back again to his former place, where he lay for a while silent.

"Jim," he said, at lenth, "you saw that seafaring man to-day?"

"Black Dog?" I asked.

"Ah! Black Dog," says he. "*He's* a bad 'un, but there's worse that put him on. Now, if I can't get away nohow, and they tip me the black spot, mind you, it's my old sea-chest they're after, you get on a horse—you can, can't you? Well, then, you get on a horse and go to—well, yes, I will!—to that eternal Doctor swab, and tell him to pipe all hands—magistrates and sich—and he'll lay 'em aboard at the 'Admiral Benbow'—all old Flint's crew, man and boy, all on 'em that's left. I was first mate, I was, old Flint's first mate, and I'm the on'y one as knows the place. He gave it me to Savannah, when he lay a-dying, like as if I was to now, you see. But you won't peach unless they get the black spot on me, or unless you see that Black Dog again, or a seafaring man with one leg, Jim—him above all."

"But what is the black spot, captain?" I asked.

"That's a summons, mate. I'll tell you if they get that. But you keep your weather-eye open, Jim, and I'll share with you equals, upon my honour."

He wandered a little longer, his voice growing weaker, but soon after I had given him his medicine, which he took like a child, with the remark, "If ever a seaman wanted drugs, it's me," he fell at last into a heavy, swoon-like sleep, in which I left him. What I should have done had all gone well I (•) not know. Probably I should have told the whole story to the doctor, for I was in mortal fear lest the captain should repent of his confessions and make an end of me. But as things fell out, my poor father died quite suddenly that evening, which put all other matters on one side. Our natural distress, the visits of the neighbours, the arranging of the funeral,

Robert Louis Stevenson

Treasure Island

Introduction by H. M. Burton

drawings by John Minton

CAMDEN CLASSICS . PAUL ELEK . LONDON

It says much for Minton's skill that he is able to move successfully from the blood-and-thunder of *Treasure Island* to the romantic beauty of *The Wanderer (Le Grand Meaulnes)*. This was also published by Elek, although not as one of the Camden Classics series. Anthony Froshaug's design is even more determinedly reacting against tradition. The title page is distinctly odd and may raise eyebrows, but the text pages, with good margins, are set in Bodoni whose thicks and thins are a perfect companion for Minton's illustrations (see next spread). These are small on the page and of irregular shape, and full of atmospheric devices – long shadows, romantic lighting, twisting roads, fallen cartwheels, rich vegetation, distorted perspective – classic Minton idioms here used with mysterious success.

Printed on somewhat flimsy paper – we are still in 1947 – this is nonetheless a beautiful production, equal in its way to *A Season in Hell*. I am not aware of any other book designed by Froshaug, who is better known for smaller-scale work: stationery, exhibition leaflets and catalogues (much influenced by early Tschichold), and as an inspiring and influential teacher at the Central School.

7
The Wanderer (Le Grand Meaulnes)
Alain-Fournier
Paul Elek 1947
210mm deep

Alain-Fournier   Translated
by Françoise
Delisle

The Wanderer . Le Grand Meaulnes

Illustrated
by John
Minton
and with an
Introduction
by Bonamy
Dobrée

Paul Elek . London . 1947

We had reckoned too soon on the coming of spring. On Monday evening we decided to do our home work immediately after four as in the summer and, to get a better light, we dragged two big tables into the playground. But the sky became suddenly cloudy; a drop of rain fell on an exercise-book; we hastened to go in. And we silently watched, out of the large windows of the big classroom now so dark, the flight of the clouds in the grey sky.

Then Meaulnes, who was at the window with us, one hand on the handle, could not refrain from saying, as if he were angry to feel so much regret rise up in him: 'Ah! the clouds rolled along better than this when I was on the road, in the Fair Star cart.'

'On what road?' asked Jasmin.

But Meaulnes made no reply.

'As for me,' I said, to create a diversion, 'I should have loved travelling that way in a carriage, with the rain pouring down, sheltered under a big umbrella.'

'And reading all the while during the journey, as if you were indoors,' added another.

'It was not raining and I had no longing to read,' replied Meaulnes. 'I thought only of looking at the countryside.'

But when in his turn Giraudat asked him of what country he spoke, Meaulnes again kept silent. And Jasmin said: 'I know . . . Always that famous adventure! . . .'

He had said these words in conciliatory and important tones, as if he was himself a little in the secret. It was trouble lost; his advances met with no response; and as night was falling, every one raced off through the cold downpour, his overall wrapped over his head.

The rain continued until the following Thursday. And that Thursday was even gloomier than the last. The whole countryside was bathed in a sort of icy mist as in the worst days of winter.

Millie, led astray by the beautiful sun of the week before,

had had the washing done, but there could be no question of hanging it out to dry on the garden hedges, nor even on lines in the lumber-rooms, as the air was so damp and cold.

Discussing the matter with M. Seurel, she conceived the idea, as it was Thursday, of spreading the washing in the classrooms and of heating the stove red-hot. Meals were to be cooked on the stove to dispense with fires in the kitchen and in the dining-room, and we were to spend the day in the top-form classroom.

At first – I was so young! – I regarded this novelty as a treat. A dreary treat! . . . All the heat of the stove was taken by the washing; it was extremely cold. In the playground a fine wintry rain fell softly and endlessly. Yet it was there that at nine o'clock in the morning, bored to death, I discovered Admiral Meaulnes. Through the bars of the tall gate against which we silently rested our heads, we looked towards the top of the village and watched a funeral procession which had come from remote parts of the country and had stopped at the Cross-Roads. The coffin, brought on an ox wagon, was lowered and placed on a flagstone at the foot of the tall cross where the butcher, one night, had noticed the bohemian's sentries! Where was he now, the young captain who could so well fake the boarding of a ship? . . . The vicar and the choir boys, as was the custom, walked up to the coffin and their mournful chants reached us. This, as we knew, would be the only sight the whole day, which would pass like muddy water along the gutter.

'And now,' said Meaulnes suddenly, 'I am going to pack. I must tell you, Seurel: I wrote to my mother last Thursday asking her to let me complete my studies in Paris. I am leaving to-day.'

He continued looking towards the village, his hands against the bars, level with his face. No use asking if his mother, who was rich and indulged all his whims, had allowed this one. No use either to ask why he suddenly wanted to go to Paris! . . .

But certainly there was regret in him, and fear at leaving this dear land of Sainte-Agathe from which he had set out marquis even though you're only a pot-boy like me, and you will descend to the fancy-dress ball, since that is the good pleasure of these little gentlemen and of these little ladies.'

He added, in the tone of a quack at a fair, with a final bow: 'Our friend Maloyau, of the kitchen department, will present the character of Harlequin and your humble servant that of tall Pierrot. . . .'

Voyage de Monsieur Perrichon, and many of Molière's plays, all acted under canvas, often in the most primitive kind of tent. Molière and his 'illustre Théâtre' were a troupe of that kind.

At the yearly fair these strolling players may often be just a man and his wife, or a small party travelling with a few performing animals. The word *bohémien* is often applied to such actors and showmen with contempt, as in English is the word *gipsy*. Yet again it is used indifferently with *saltimbanque* for real gipsies who travel in caravans and make a trade of wicker chairs, brooms, etc.

But the grand style of *bohémiens*, the strolling actors travelling in caravans, are looked upon as wonderful people surrounded with glamour. They used to fascinate me as a child, and all the town was astir when they came, most people feeling the same fascination. After the play we children would go prowling round their caravans, a land of mystery. Yet, however welcome these people were in our little town – where they brought joy and mirth – one knew that at the back of people's minds was a certain amount of mistrust. One felt that people were purposely over-polite, displaying an exaggerated courtesy, the result of their unconscious distinction between the honest, nice, and gentlemanly *bohémiens* and those who might not be. And indeed one often went to school (as I did) with the other type of *bohémien;* children of sellers of wicker chairs or small peddlers, etc.

From all this it is clear that to translate the word *bohémien* by *gipsy* is wrong when applied to people not of gipsy race, yet *gipsies* must be used whenever one wants to show contempt or mistrust. Of course the word can never mean here the Bohemian of Bohemian life, of Murger and Montmartre's style; it means these strolling comedians, still a part of French life of people of Alain-Fournier's generation, though now that most little towns boast a theatre these troupes have a tendency to disappear, to be replaced by more modern touring companies. *Note by Translator.*

64

7 *The Wanderer (Le Grand Meaulnes)*

Chapter XIV

He entered another door and found himself in a dining-room lit by a hanging lamp. There also fun was on, but fun for the children. Some of these, seated on hassocks, were busy turning over the pages of albums open on their knees; others, squatting on the floor in front of a chair were gravely engaged in displaying pictures on the seat; others, again, near the fire said nothing and did nothing but listen to the hum of the fête audible throughout the great house.

One door of this dining-room was wide open. In the next room could be heard the piano being played. Meaulnes, inquisitively, put his head in. It was a sort of drawing-room parlour; a woman or a young girl, with a brown cloak thrown over her shoulders and her back turned, was very softly playing tunes of round games and nursery rhymes. Close to her, on the sofa, six or seven little boys and girls sat in a row as in a picture, good as children are when it grows late, and listened. Only now and again one of them, using his wrist as prop, lifted himself up, slid down to the ground, and passed into the dining-room: then one of those who had finished looking at the pictures came to take his place.

After the ball where everything was charming but feverish and mad, where he had himself so madly chased the tall Pierrot, Meaulnes found that he had dropped into the most peaceful happiness on earth.

Noiselessly, while the girl played on, he went back to sit in the dining-room, and opening one of the big red books scattered on the table, he absent-mindedly began to read.

Almost at once one of the little boys crouched on the floor came up to him, and catching hold of his arm, climbed on his knee to look over; another settled on the other side. Then began a dream like his old dream. His mind could dwell on the fancy that he was married and in his own home during a beautiful evening and that this lovely unknown person playing the piano, close to him, was his wife.

72

8

A very different artist-illustrated book is what must be one of the last of its kind, published in 1963. The surrealist and very un-English images, drawn in crayon on rough textures, are reproduced in line. Rolf Brandt was a painter (brother of Bill the photographer) and the strength of imagination tells.

Production values have greatly improved since the constraints put upon wartime and postwar books. I worry about the typography though, presumably by the usually esteemed Berthold Wolpe. Why turn over one small word on page 27? Verse has shape as well as sound; the measure could easily have been broken.

8
The Earth Owl
Ted Hughes
Faber and Faber 1963
207mm deep

Cactus-Sickness

I hope you never contract
The lunar galloping cact-
-us, which is when dimples
Suddenly turn to pimples,
And these pimples bud—
Except for the odd dud—
Each one into a head with hair
And a face just like the one you wear.
These heads grow pea-size to begin
From your brows, your nose, your cheeks and your
    chin.
But soon enough they're melon-size,
All with mouths and shining eyes.
Within five days your poor neck spreads
A bunch of ten or fifteen heads
All hungry, arguing or singing
(Somewhere under your own head's ringing).
And so for one whole tedious week
You must admit you are a freak.

And then, perhaps when you gently cough
For silence, one of the heads drops off.
Their uproar instantly comes to a stop.
Then in silence, plop by plop,
With eyes and mouth most firmly closed,
Your rival heads, in turn deposed,

27

Three, possibly four, turnovers on page 15 could similarly have been taken back; and – quite astonishingly – longer lines are justified, creating erratic word spacing. This is only a 48-page book (including prelims and eleven illustrations). A few minutes' attention to the proofs could have sorted all this out. And why those *slightly* larger initial letters? They do nothing except irritate.

Clearly, the time has come to turn to typographic niceties.

8 *The Earth Owl*

Moon-Horrors

When he has dined, the man-eating tiger leaves certain signs.
But nothing betrays the moon's hideous number nines.
Nobody knows where they sleep off their immense meals.
They strike so fatally nobody knows how one feels.
One-eyed, one-legged, they start out of the ground with
    such a shout
The chosen victim's eyes instantly fall out.
They do not leave so much as a hair but smack their chops
And go off thinner than ever with grotesque hops.

Now the shark will take a snack by shearing off half a swimmer.
Over the moon presides a predator even grimmer.
Descending without warning from the interstellar heavens
Whirling like lathes, arrive the fearful horde of number
    sevens.
Whatever they touch, whether owl or elephant, poet or
    scientist,
The wretched victim wilts instantly to a puff of purple mist
And before he can utter a cry or say goodbye to kith and kin
Those thin-gut number sevens have sucked him ravenously in.

Mosquitoes seem dreadful, for they drink at a man as he sleeps.
Night and day over the moon a far craftier horror creeps.
It is hard to know what species of creature you would have
    to be
To escape the attentions of the moon's horrible number three.

15

9

Postwar typesetting standards varied considerably. Books such as the large-format Phaidon monographs, with far more pretension than this little one, and which were otherwise carefully produced, had much inferior setting than that seen here. This is generally rather good, certainly better than in the Penguin that follows. Word spacing is pleasantly tight, and full points are not followed by large disrupting gaps. Although the Times Roman of the next example is leaded one point, the taller ascenders and much longer descenders of Bembo, even set solid as here, make this text more readable.

Chapter headings are acceptable if unexceptional. While their relationship to the subheads is happy, one might question that of subheads to running heads: are the latter relatively so important? The small cap chapter numbers are slightly letterspaced; this attention would have improved the other headings too, even if, in the full cap headings, only to give optically-even spacing.

In certain circles, the use of bold in normal bookwork is anathema (still). Schmoller for instance avoided it in the complicated hierarchy required in the Pevsner Guides. Although they were not available until the nineteenth century, and so were never used by the great Renaissance or classical printers, bolds should not be despised. Their careful use can provide an extra level of heading, or typographic colour to an otherwise grey page – which this is, a little.

The book was 'produced in complete conformity with the authorised economy standard'. Despite this, the overall effect is more attractive than many comparable books today.

9

The National Ballet
Arnold L Haskell
Adam & Charles Black 1947
217mm deep

CHAPTER III

TOWARDS A NATIONAL BALLET

I. BALLET IN DANGER

THE problem in ballet has never been the supply of dancers, and this was specially so in the case of England where girls of all shapes and sizes found their way to the dancing schools. The need has always been to find a strong directing force possessed of a knowledge of the component arts and of absolute artistic integrity. There are twenty *potential* Nijinskys for one Diaghileff. Where there are state-subsidised institutions with a strong tradition the position is different, and in the interim between good directors the ballet can mark time without running the risk of disintegration. Vsevolojsky gave the Imperial Ballet new life, Teliakovsky lowered its reputation, but it continued unshakable.

Economically speaking, the Diaghileff Ballet was never a sound proposition and relied entirely on the subsidies of its wealthy patrons. With his great prestige that was possible in spite of many close shaves and a major disaster in 1921 with *The Sleeping Princess*. No one else could hope to follow on those lines. It became a fixed belief that ballet was an art for the wealthy that could not possibly pay, though Pavlova had proved conclusively to the contrary. This wish to run things *à la* Diaghileff without his individual touch (I use the word in both its senses) was a considerable handicap to any enterprise. It is one of the main reasons for the decadence of Russian post-Diaghileff ballet. The waste of money through faulty planning was appalling, and if a patron did put up the money, he attached conditions that had little to do with art.

Three groups of people, working independently and at the same time co-operating in a spirit that is only possible with the much-abused British temperament, formed the beginnings of British ballet proper, largely on overdrafts and promises and totally without the support of those wealthy patrons who professed to love the ballet. It should be placed on record that the Wells, the Camargo, the Ballet Club were started and run by professionals and, on the other side of the footlights, by the general public; they owed nothing to any Maecenas.

The first spectacular effort was that of the Camargo Society, founded in 1930 by P. J. S. Richardson and the present writer. The Camargo was a management without a company, a shop-window without a store, so that first it is necessary to study the groups that it used.

II. MARIE RAMBERT

Marie Rambert had been a pupil of Jacques Dalcroze and was chosen by Diaghileff to teach the principles of eurythmics to the Russians. She soon became an enthusiastic convert to classicism and a pupil of Cecchetti. She started a London studio and there formed a group of pupils, brought up on the classics. Her method differed from that of the majority of teachers in that she made the ballet-stage the goal of her teaching, concentrating on the development of stagecraft and personality. Her pupils were no doubt destined for the Diaghileff Ballet, but when he died she kept her little group intact and its members were animated by the spirit of a company.

Marie Rambert was the first by her teaching to put the English girl on a level with the Russians, psychologically speaking. She broke down the reserve and the old school principle of not shining if it were possible to remain hidden in the team. She stung her girls into becoming *solistes* and they showed countless others that it could be done. She has done great things, but that especially must be remembered. One saw a plump schoolgirl enter her studio doors; a term later she came out as an attractive personality. Rambert's 'babies' held the stage many years before de Basil's and before the Wells had revealed any personalities.

As early on as 1930 she gave a highly successful matinée at the Lyric, Hammersmith, that was far more creative than any pupil show. Among those young dancers were some who were destined to play a major role in our story, all were pioneers—Pearl Argyle, Diana Gould, Prudence Hyman, Andrée Howard, Maud Lloyd, Elizabeth Schooling, Frederick Ashton, Harold Turner and William Chappell; all of them dancing under the then serious handicap of English names. Later, Karsavina and Woizikovsky paid these young dancers the unique compliment of appearing with them for a season.

district where your family is held in honour. One must try, however, not to take these things too melodramatically. We live but once; we owe nothing to posterity; and a man's own happiness counts before that of anyone else. My father's tastes happen to have lain in a direction which commended him to his fellows. Had his nature driven him along lines that failed to secure their sympathy, or even their approval, I should have been the last to complain. The world is wide! Instead of coming here, one could have gone somewhere else.

V

BLUMENEGG

AFTERNOON, and warmer than usual. Fön shifts about in irresolute, vagrant puffs of heat; the sky, shortly before sunrise, had been flaring red, copper-coloured, from end to end. This is the ardent and wayward but caressing wind under whose touch everything grows brittle and inflammable; when in olden days all cooking had to be suspended and fires extinguished; when whole villages, for some trifling reason, were burnt to the ground; it was during Fön weather that Tiefis and Nüziders, and several in the Rhine valley, were annihilated within the memory of our fathers.[1] The peasants, unfamiliar with real heat, go about gasping. . . .

While crossing our cemetery to revisit the grave, now vanished, of a little brother of mine—he died unbaptized, and the Catholics were kind enough to make room for him here—it struck me how poetic are the German designations for such sad spots, *Friedhof* and *Gottesacker*, when contrasted with our soul-withering "churchyard" or "graveyard" or "burial-ground." The people hereabouts contrive to invest with a halo of romance even that most unromantic of objects, the common potato, by calling it *Erdapfel*, or *Grundbirne*. And the names of the ruined castles that strew this region, Schattenburg, Sonnenberg, Rosenegg, and so forth, were surely invented by a race that had a fine feeling for such things.

Or Blumenegg—which happens to be nothing but a translation of Florimont, the Rhæto-Roman name of this locality.

[1] The Fön, if it then existed, may be responsible for the destruction by fire of so many of the prehistoric Swiss lake settlements.

If you follow the main road to Ludesch, you will pass through a fir wood and then come to the Lutz bridge. Do not cross the stream; keep on this side, and walk along the water. After a few hundred yards you will arrive at the "Schlosstobel" (the old "Falster"; also called "Storrbach") which rushes past the foot of Blumenegg castle. Not many years ago it descended in a wild flood, uprooting trees and covering the ground with a hideous irruption of shingle, which will remain for some little time. On the Schlosstobel's other side you enter a forest called Gstinswald; part of it used to belong to our family. Here, at the entrance of the wood, stood a landmark; a picture attached to a tree, in memory of a man who was drowned at this spot while endeavouring to cross the rivulet during some spate of olden days. It was a realistic work of art, depicting both Heaven and earth. This was the subject: down below, a watery chaos, a black thundercloud out of which buckets of rain descended upon the victim whom you beheld struggling in the whirlpool of waves, while his open umbrella floated disconsolately in the neighbourhood; overhead, on the other side of the thundercloud (it had taken on a golden tinge of sunshine half way through) the Mother of God with a saint or two, gazing down upon the scene with an air of detachment which bordered on indifference. The picture is no longer there; and nothing remains of its tree save a mouldy stump.

From this point you can climb direct to the castle. We preferred to wander awhile up the Gstinswald which clothes the right flank of the Lutz river, in order to see what has happened to that mysterious and solitary peasant-house which lay on a grassy slope in the forest. It is still there, but those skulls of foxes and badgers and other beasts, nailed by its occupant to a certain wooden door—skulls that held a fascination for us children—are gone. And what of the snowdrops? This, and a little hillock near Ludesch, were the only places where they could be found; tiger-lilies grew elsewhere; *Primula auricula* only at the Hanging Stone; cyclamen only at Feldkirch (where they were discovered in the middle of the sixteenth century by Hieronymus Bock); the cypripedium orchid (*calceolus Divæ Virginis*), the lady's slipper, at two other places; stag's horn moss, *vulgo* "Fuchsschwanz," at four or five: we knew them all! but flowers were dropped, when butterflies began. From this farmhouse you have an unexpected view upon the summit of the Scesaplana, and by far the best time to come here is after a summer shower, when a procession of

10
Together
Norman Douglas
Penguin Books 1945
182mm deep

For the rest, such days of heavy-lidded atmospheric brooding are rare in Siren land.

They are clear-eyed and caressing as a rule, these summer breezes; caressing and cleansing; they set all the shining leaves a-tremble and scatter town-memories and the fumes of musty learning. How the bizarre throng of water-witches and familiars grows uneasy in that brave light, and wan—how they fade away, like the ghosts they are!

II

Uplands of Sorrento

WITH the exception of Capri, which is the only spot within a hundred miles of Naples where a foreigner is reasonably well treated, no accommodation in the septentrional sense of the word can be found in Siren land save at Sorrento and Sant' Agata, the idea being that 'foreigners must first come' before anything can be done to welcome the few that flee into these solitudes from the din and confusion of that fair land whose frontier-station bears the ominous name of Chiasso (noise). Massa is rich and populous, but contains not a single hotel or even restaurant; it is a community of peasant-proprietors who live, some of them, in fine country houses built in pre-Bourbon days by Spanish and Neapolitan grandees— indeed, it is one of the surprising things in this district to see mouldering structures with ample courtyards, arched galleries, and noble escutcheons over their gates, now inhabited by mean-looking folk whose manners, at least, are still in harmony with their dwellings. Massa is full of them, but even the humblest village can boast

of one or two. The terrors of a century of Bourbonism reduced this country to direst distress. Capri, after the discovery of the Blue Grotto, began to thrive in spite of its sovereigns, but the mainland portions are only just now recovering from the blight. Neapolitans have grown rich again and seek the fine air of the hills as of yore, while the inhabitants themselves bring much money from New York; and from Argentina, where a good half of them are periodically employed in selling potatoes to the Spaniards, who apparently eat nothing else. 'Good people' they call them, because they are easily gulled in the matter of weights and measures.

One consequence of this revival is that the price of land is rising once more and new houses are being built. This would be satisfactory, were it not that the style of architecture has changed for the worse. That harmonious medley of small vaulted chambers with their vine-shaded loggia in front, so becoming to this climate and charming to look upon, has been displaced by hideous *palazzi* constructed with iron beams, asphalt, and roofing tiles— things formerly unheard of. No person with a sense of the fitness of things will ever fall in love with these new dwellings, although they are built, as the architects will tell you, according to the latest *regola d'arte*. When a Southerner discourses upon *regola d'arte*, he is generally up to some mischief.

Even the colossal hand-made house-keys of the olden days, now replaced by weedy cast-iron abominations, were not without a certain austere beauty: there was a smack of Saint Peter about them. And they had their uses, too. Three years ago a wealthy landowner, returning home at night, was attacked by two ruffians with knives. Having no ordinary weapon of defence, not even a walking-stick, he began to wield his house-key with such dexterity that one of his assailants was brained on the spot, while the other crawled into the fields, where he was

11
Siren Land
Norman Douglas
Penguin Books 1948
182mm deep

10 and **11**
Two Penguins. *Together*, 1945, pre-Tschichold. *Siren Land*, 1948, post-Tschichold – but only just. It is apparent that he had been able to work on the title page, prelims, margins, chapter headings, running heads, type size and leading, but had yet to create his demands for setting standards. Word spacing is loose, and unspaced em dashes are used instead of spaced en dashes. But the title page is all Tschichold: elegant, simple, clean, with letterspaced capitals (see overleaf). Perversely, the title page for *Together* has letterspaced lower-case for the title, but unspaced capitals. Text pages have insufficient leading, double quotes, four full points widely spaced, huge spaces after full points – all to be forbidden by Tschichold. And how much pleasanter is the chapter opening for *Siren Land*, and its relationship to the running heads.

NORMAN DOUGLAS

Together

"*And he said unto me, Son of man,
can these bones live?   And I answered,
O Lord God, thou knowest.*"
EZEKIEL xxxvii. 3.

PENGUIN BOOKS

HARMONDSWORTH MIDDLESEX ENGLAND
245 FIFTH AVENUE NEW YORK U.S.A.

SIREN LAND

BY NORMAN DOUGLAS

PENGUIN BOOKS

WEST DRAYTON · MIDDLESEX

CHILDREN AS ARTISTS

by
R. R. TOMLINSON

Senior Inspector of Art to the
London County Council

The KING PENGUIN *Books*
LONDON *and* NEW YORK
1944

Romney Marsh

ILLUSTRATED

AND DESCRIBED

BY

JOHN PIPER

PENGUIN BOOKS

1950

12 and **13**
Two King Penguins, Allen Lane's 'prestige' series. *Children as Artists*, 1944, pre-Tschichold; *Romney Marsh*, 1950, clearly designed by Tschichold although he returned to Switzerland in December 1949, as a result of the devaluation of the pound. But his work was effectively done.

As his replacement he suggested Hans Schmoller, whose obsessive pursuit of perfection meant that the standard was never allowed to slip for twenty-five years.

These two books speak for themselves. The earlier one is clumsily designed with irritating and superfluous details on the title page (what purpose does the 'by' serve here?) and heavy, insufficiently-leaded text, poorly set (see overleaf). The delicacy of the Romney Marsh title page (here, 'BY' is essential, for meaning and layout) with choice decoration and rules, reflects the elegance of the well-leaded text.

being one of the fundamental things of human experience, can no more be defined than can life itself—or time, or love, or any other basic principle or passion. Those who cherish the three Greek ideals—the good, the true, and the beautiful—identify art with the beautiful. Others mystify matters by quoting Keats's celebrated dictum: Beauty is Truth, Truth Beauty. But the very statement that art is concerned with beauty has itself been challenged. Such an authority as the late Roger Fry once said, 'The word "beauty" I try hard to avoid', and Max I. Friedländer in his recent book on *Art and Connoisseurship* appears to find a similar difficulty in the use of the word 'beauty'; for he says, 'Since beauty in nature and that which has value in art are divergent, we feel inclined to avoid the expression "beauty" in judging art'.

The attributes which are so appealing in the unsophisticated work of children are their integrity, frankness and inevitability, and those who admire their drawings most, refer to them as being charming rather than beautiful. It cannot be claimed that their work is skilfully expressed, neither is it desirable that it should be so; for a child's means of expression is found to be adequate for the occasion by those with sympathy and understanding.

The author therefore proposes to confine himself to describing the artistic training of children in the past and the present, and to speculating (with some misgivings) on future developments and possibilities. He has chosen his illustrations from as wide a range and area as possible; and with a view to as varied an art content and spirit as possible. For one must look at children's drawings to understand them. The written word cannot replace or reproduce their spirit. Whether the little people who have done the pictures shown in this book are worthy of the title of artists, the reader must decide for himself.

The similarity between the unsophisticated work of children today in all civilised countries and that of primitive people leads to the conclusion that the means

4

and modes of expression in both graphic and plastic forms are inherent in the human race. The recapitulation theory, the belief that the development of the child follows somewhat the same course as the history of the race, may or may not have been conclusively vindicated, but it seems true that in dealing with children we are dealing with little primitive people. The term 'primitive' is used with reference to two distinct groups. It is used by the ethnographer to describe uncivilised people, and by the art historian to denote the early stages of a well defined school of painting. When used in the latter sense it is most commonly applied to the Italian school at the time of Cimabue and Giotto. Primitives of both groups, however, resemble children in one essential respect: in their artistic urge to explore with zeal entirely new paths untutored and unaided.

To enable us to gain some knowledge of the principles which underlie the evolution of Art, it is advisable to study the work that has been produced by the primitive peoples of the first group. One fact of great importance that can be gleaned from this study is that a great deal of artistic expression owes its birth to attempts at realism —attempts faithfully to reproduce nature. The fact that æsthetic laws and the laws of nature are intimately connected may be responsible for this instinctive association. The study and understanding of both are essential to the equipment of the educationist, of the teacher, and indeed of all who have the welfare of children at heart.

Space will not permit of further consideration here of this important relationship in the evolution of art. Those seeking further information will, however, find much to help and guide them by a close study of primitive art and the history of art generally. They are referred for this purpose to such helpful works as *Evolution in Art* by Dr. A. C. Haddon, *Primitive Art* by L. Adam (a Pelican book), *Decorative Patterns of the Ancient World* by Sir Flinders Petrie and the guide books to the Ethnographical Sections of the British Museum, published by the Museum authorities.

5

12
Children as Artists
R R Tomlinson
Penguin Books 1944
179mm deep

not so easy to make a fortune now as a sheep farmer on the Marsh, the Romney Marsh breed still has a great name outside as well as inside the country, especially in New Zealand and Australia. Isolated shepherds' huts – always of much the same pattern, of one room with a gabled tiled roof and with a chimney at one end – are prominent everywhere. Cobbett was excited when he saw the sheep on his Rural Ride across the Marsh from Appledore to Hythe in September 1823. He calls them 'very pretty and large. The wethers, when fat, weigh about twelve stone, or one hundred pounds. The faces of these sheep are white; and indeed the whole sheep is as white as a piece of writing paper. The wool does not look dirty and oily like that of other sheep.'

At present the sheep farming here is on the decline. This, the best of grazing land, is also among the best arable, and much of it was ploughed up during the Hitler war, and more has been ploughed since. There is very little loss of beauty, if any; for burgeoning root crops and waving cornlands on these lowlands have as much beauty, and look as personal to the neighbourhood, as the lush grasslands.

Romney Marsh is a generic name, but was never the only name, and is still not the only map-name, of the levels between Hythe and Rye that are bounded on the landward side by the low hills behind the Military Canal. The area includes Romney Marsh proper (nearly 24,000 acres), Walland Marsh, Denge Marsh and Guldeford Level (together, about 22,600 acres) – the last, with East Guldeford village and the vanished village of Broomhill, in Sussex.

There is so much doubt about the origin and development of the whole area, and so many important points have not been settled (and many points now are questioned that had long been thought to be settled), that the statement of a few isolated facts about which there are not many remaining doubts is necessary.

Probably there was never a time when the whole area was covered by the sea at low tide; that is, not a recent geological

10

time. In early historical times there was a great bay of the Channel at Romney and a smaller bay by West Hythe and Lympne, extending as a narrow arm of sea to Appledore and Rye by the line of the present Military Canal; while wooded peninsulas between Appledore and Fairlight and islands at Oxney, Rye and Winchelsea divided other arms of the sea that flowed inland at high tide, the sea never receding far enough at low tide to leave the flooded areas 'in any state but that of a soft loose residuum through which the rivers wound their way'. (Holloway.) So that the old cliffs to the west and north of the present-day Marsh were only in places true sea cliffs, and the area was riddled with enormous tidal creeks and unhealthy marshes. The Romans used Portus Lemanis, which was probably under Lympne, by Stutfall Castle, as a port (it is mentioned in the Antonine Itinerary). The picturesque ruins of the castle – low broken walls – lie scattered up the cliffside towards Lympne, across the Royal Military Canal. Most authorities credit the Romans with the first bold reclamation scheme. This scheme was the building of the Rhee Wall from Appledore to Romney, and the Dymchurch Wall along the east coast, which first enclosed and defined what is still Romney Marsh proper. It seems fairly certain that there was already a measure of shingle protection (possibly of the present Chesil Beach kind) where the Dymchurch Wall now stands; and that the marshes grew up inside the protecting shingle – with much assistance from man. Outside the area, by the eighth century Romney was an island at high water, with a wide strip of land extending towards Hope.

Much discussion has gone on, and still goes on, about the probable early courses of the Limen, or Rother river. It may have changed its course twice and it has certainly changed it once. Before the eleventh century it may have flowed out at Hythe – or rather, West Hythe – the Saxon-named renewal of the Roman Portus Lemanis. Certainly from the eleventh to the sixteenth centuries it flowed out at Romney, adopting roughly the present

11

13
Romney Marsh
John Piper
Penguin Books 1950
179mm deep

14 and **15**

Here, and on the next spread, are two more King Penguins, showing Tschichold's inventive but restrained use of decorative lettering on the title page. (Schmoller, although not averse to this, rarely if ever used it on standard Penguins.) It is obvious from these examples that every book was given careful individual attention. Each had its own characteristics, and therefore each was given its own solution.

14
A Prospect of Wales
Kenneth Rowntree and Gwyn Jones
Penguin Books 1948
179mm deep

A PROSPECT OF

𝕎𝕒𝕝𝕖𝕤

—

A SERIES OF WATER-COLOURS
BY KENNETH ROWNTREE
AND AN ESSAY BY
GWYN JONES

PENGUIN BOOKS

LONDON

With these words of Arthur Machen's I am neither willing nor able to compete. I turn instead to that crumpled blanket of the South Wales industrial valleys in which I was born. It is in many men's mouths to call them ugly, and there's an end on't. But the dividing hills are oftentimes most beautiful, with their turf and bracken laid on scarps of unyielding Pennant Grit. No greater contrast of man-made and nature was ever laid in closer pattern. The curlews cry within ten minutes' walk of many a pithead; from moorland lakes one counts the steam-wreathed stacks. Inky rivers run their immemorial course, now between meadows, now between coal-tips, through beechy glades and defiles of slag. Long snaky chains of houses lie in the valley bottom or along its lower ledges; sometimes they reach out in grey isolation along the bitten hillsides. The railway and the road keep with the river. Gaunt, undoubtedly, with the gauntness of an old collier's face, tough in fell and hard of bone, the views over much of this toil-racked country are extraordinarily impressive: whether one looks up past Blaen Cwm from opposite Hendderwen to the death of the Rhondda Valley in the blue-green uplands; or from the bleak waste of Cefn Golau along the upper Rhymney or Sirhowy; or best of all from the old pilgrim-haunt of Penrhys, or from Bwlch across Cwmparc, to the hacked and gashed panorama of the Rhondda Fawr. Indeed, for this last I should claim in defiance of all authority (and all preciosity) that it is one of *the* views of Wales.

The effective history here is of more recent date than the remote and legend-haunted glories of Dyfed and Gwent. It may be read without a book, in the valley bottoms themselves, in the glow of molten metal and the dark magnificence of pitheads, in the hands of men and the faces of

their women. If in the North we sense a kingly atmosphere of sword and spear, here in the South the awareness is of a hard swopping of punches. If the type there is Llywelyn the Last Prince, here it is rather Jimmy Wilde, the Tylorstown Terror. And if one grins at the comparison, how right the grin is; for this is a district which has kept its grin through all that spoliation, depression and neglect

could do to it. The clannishness of the North has here yielded to a warm gregariousness; blood 'from the old big vein' stirs faster in a mongrel brew. The North found its mountains ready-made; in the South they grow them, great navy-blue masses of slag and slack. Witness Bargoed, which has raised on its own navel so monstrous a tip that the sun illumines its western flank at three in the afternoon, and deserts the eastern a minute later.

What do they know of Wales who only Snowdon know? It has always roughed my heel, and I trust it ever shall, to find seekers after the 'truly picturesque' by-pass the industrial region of South Wales with an assurance that

Who am I to quarrel with the use of ″
instead of *inches* on page 19 of *A Book
of Scripts*?

A BOOK OF SCRIPTS

by Alfred Fairbank

Penguin Books

15
A Book of Scripts
Alfred Fairbank
Penguin Books 1949
179mm deep

(Plates 42 and 43). A number of the English writing masters were contemptuous, aggressive, and vain, issuing challenges and allowing their portraits and excessive praise to appear in their books; but their devotion to their craft and recognition of their eminent predecessors and even of their contemporaries are compensating qualities. Joseph Champion in his *The Parallel* writes that 'Mr. Edward Cocker, a voluminous author, led on by lucre, let in an inundation of copy-books and these followed by others, either vile imitators or pirates in PENMANSHIP, had almost rendered the art contemptuous, when col. *John Ayres*, a disciple of Mr. *Topham's*, happily arose to check this mischievous spirit (which was about the year 1690) and he actually began the reformation of LETTERS, and introduced the mixed round hands, since naturalised and improved amongst us: he was indefatigable and wrote all hands, more especially the law-hands finely; nor is it any diminution of our CHARACTERS who survive him, to own that the colonel was our common father, who so magnificently carried the glory of *English* PENMANSHIP far beyond his predecessors'.

Colonel John Ayres, who produced eleven copy-books between 1680 and 1700 (Plate 46), has wrongly been given credit for the introduction of the italic hands in England; he introduced the French Italienne-Bastarde or 'A la Mode Round-hand'. Two important French writing-books, doubtless well known to English writing masters, were Lucas Materot's *Les Œuvres* (Avignon, 1608) and Louis Barbedor's *Les Écritures Financière,*

facile a jmiter pour les femmes.

FIG. 5. Lucas Materot's *Lettre facile à imiter pour les femmes.*

et Italienne-Bastarde (Paris, 1647). Materot is described by Bickham as the Darling of the Ladies because of the elegant Italian script presented as 'Lettre facile à imiter pour les femmes'. Champion says of Barbedor that 'his performances were peculiarly daring, free and grand', and certainly the brilliant flourished displays of his large folios seem almost to take calligraphy into the sphere of non-functional abstract art (Plate 40). Other influences, bearing on Ayres and his immediate successors and freely acknowledged, were the Dutch Masters, and particularly van den Velde (Plate 37) and Perlingh.

Although the round hand is a development of the Italian hand, a distinction in eighteenth-century nomenclature was made: *e.g.* an anonymous copy-book titled *Young Clerks Assistant* (1733) shows the Italian to be a narrower and lighter letter than the round hand, though otherwise closely related, and to be intended for the Ladies, whilst the round hand was for the Young Clerks and was plainly a business hand.

The development of the round hand was advanced by the considerable school of penmen called forth by commercial necessity during the early years of the eighteenth century; significant members were George Shelley, Charles Snell, Ralph Snow, Robert More, John Clark, and George Bickham (Plates 47 to 49). When, in 1710, George Shelley secured the position of Master to the Writing School of Christ's Hospital there were over four hundred pupils. Bickham's *Universal Penman*, issued in parts, contains not only 212 engraved plates, $16\frac{1}{4}'' \times 10\frac{1}{4}''$, but presents the scripts of twenty-five penmen. English sea-borne trade was expanding, and handwriting and accounting had gained a new significance as Dutch commerce declined in importance. The leadership in writing had passed in the seventeenth century from the Italians to the French and Dutch, but the English running hand (taught often by writing masters who also taught 'accompts') now began to follow English exports

19

→ 15 ←

ANOTHER week over – and I am so many days nearer health, and spring! I have now heard all my neighbour's history, at different sittings, as the housekeeper could spare time from more important occupations. I'll continue it in her own words, only a little condensed. She is, on the whole, a very fair narrator, and I don't think I could improve her style.

In the evening, she said, the evening of my visit to the Heights, I knew, as well as if I saw him, that Mr Heathcliff was about the place; and I shunned going out, because I still carried his letter in my pocket, and didn't want to be threatened, or teased any more.

I had made up my mind not to give it till my master went somewhere; as I could not guess how its receipt would affect Catherine. The consequence was, that it did not reach her before the lapse of three days. The fourth was Sunday, and I brought it into her room, after the family were gone to church.

There was a man servant left to keep the house with me, and we generally made a practice of locking the doors during the hours of service; but on that occasion, the weather was so warm and pleasant that I set them wide open; and to fulfil my engagement, as I knew who would be coming, I told my companion that the mistress wished very much for some oranges, and he must run over to the village and get a few, to be paid for on the morrow. He departed, and I went upstairs.

Mrs Linton sat in a loose, white dress, with a light shawl over her shoulders, in the recess of the open window, as usual. Her thick, long hair had been partly removed at the beginning of her illness; and now she wore it simply combed in its natural tresses over her temples and neck. Her appearance was altered, as I had told Heathcliff, but when she was calm, there seemed unearthly beauty in the change.

The flash of her eyes had been succeeded by a dreamy and melancholy softness: they no longer gave the impression of looking at the objects around here; they appeared always to gaze beyond, and far beyond – you would have said out of this world. Then, the paleness of her face – its haggard aspect having vanished as she recovered flesh – and the peculiar expression arising from her mental state, though painfully suggestive of their causes, added to the touching interest which she awakened; and – invariably to me, I know, and to any person who saw her, I should think – refuted more tangible proofs of convalescence and stamped her as one doomed to decay.

A book lay spread on the sill before her, and the scarcely perceptible wind fluttered its leaves at intervals. I believe Linton had laid it there, for she never endeavoured to divert herself with reading, or occupation of any kind; and he would spend many an hour in trying to entice her attention to some subject which had formerly been her amusement.

She was conscious of his aim, and in her better moods, endured his efforts placidly, only showing their uselessness by now and then suppressing a wearied sigh, and checking him at last, with the saddest of smiles and kisses. At other times, she would turn petulantly away, and hide her face in her hands, or even push him off angrily; and then he took care to let her alone, for he was certain of doing no good.

Gimmerton chapel bells were still ringing; and the full, mellow flow of the beck in the valley came soothingly on the ear. It was a sweet substitute for the yet absent murmur of the summer foliage, which drowned that music about the Grange, when the trees were in leaf. At Wuthering Heights it always sounded on quiet days, following a great thaw or a season of steady rain – and, of Wuthering Heights, Catherine was thinking as she listened; that is, if she thought, or listened, at all; but she had the vague, distant look I mentioned before, which expressed no recognition of material things either by ear or eye.

'There's a letter for you, Mrs Linton,' I said, gently inserting it in one hand that rested on her knee. 'You must read it immediately, because it wants an answer. Shall I break the seal?'

'Yes,' she answered, without altering the direction of her eyes.

16
Wuthering Heights
Emily Brontë
Penguin Books 1965
181mm deep

Emily Brontë

WUTHERING HEIGHTS

EDITED BY

DAVID DAICHES

✳

PENGUIN BOOKS

Cumberland and Westmorland

BY

NIKOLAUS PEVSNER

★

PENGUIN BOOKS

---

16 and **17**
Schmoller brought his own style to
Penguins, or developed it, as if he had
been preparing himself for this job
throughout his earlier career. While
different in detail from Tschichold's style,
his was based on all the same fundamental principles and standards, and
concern for the smallest detail. There were
those at Penguin who swore he could
distinguish between a Garamond full point
and a Bembo at two hundred paces.

A title page is a decorative device,
which also provides bibliographic
information; it is not an advertisement
or a selling tool shouting across the bookshop. Hence the restraint of these two
Schmoller designs. The effect is achieved
by careful choice of capitals, lower case,
italic; minimal decorative devices;
immaculate spacing; good judgement
(and the support of a sympathetic
publisher).

CUMREW

5050

ST MARY. 1890 by *George Dale Oliver*. It is bad architecture with its busy rock-facing, its NW tower, and its C13 detail but round-headed chancel arch. – PLATE. Cup of 1615. – MONUMENT. Defaced effigy of a Lady, early C14. A puppy by her pillow.

CAIRN, on Cumrew Fell, 2 m. E of the B6413. This great cairn is still some 70 ft in diameter and 8 ft high. It was partially excavated in the C19, when a number of cremation burials in urns were found.

CUMWHITTON

5050

ST MARY. Thin W tower, round-arched doorway, keyed-in nave window to the S, smaller arched aisle windows to the N. The chancel lancets are of course later. The inside reveals quite a different story. The aisle E window, probably *ex situ*, is Anglo-Saxon, small and double-splayed. In the S wall (outside) is a small length of Norman zigzag. The N arcade of three bays is of *c.*1200: round piers and arches with one step and one slight chamfer. – FONT. Plain octagonal bowl, dated 1662. – SCULPTURE. Part of a Maltese-cross-head, regarded by Collingwood as Norman. – PLATE. Chalice, late C16 or later.

HOLME HOUSE. 1778. The standard five-bay type with a pedimented doorway. But the graceful decoration of the frieze below the pediment reveals the date.

DACRE

4020

ST ANDREW. Norman W tower, rebuilt in 1810. But the unmoulded arch to the nave must be genuine. Late C12 chancel with doorway with thin shafts (one waterleaf and one crocket capital) and long round-arched windows. Those of the E end are C19. The aisles are Perp externally, but the arcades date from the early C13. They differ from one another, and the N arcade is earlier, because the arches here have slight chamfers, while in the S arcade they have normal chamfers. The piers are mostly round on the N, all octagonal on the S. But the responds are all four semicircular. – COMMUNION RAIL. Late C17; with twisted balusters. – SOUTH DOOR. The lock and key were given by Lady Anne Clifford; cf. the initials and the date 1671. – SCULPTURE. Two parts of cross-shafts, one

with intricate trails with naturalistic detail and a human-faced quadruped. This appears to be C9. – The other is dated by Collingwood second quarter of the C10 and has from top to bottom a quadruped looking back, two figures hand in hand, another quadruped, and Adam and Eve with the tree. It is all very lively and not at all monumental. – PLATE. Cup and Cover Paten, formerly gilt, with a band of ornament, 1583;* Paten, 1674. – MONUMENTS. Effigy of a Knight, cross-legged. – Edward Hasell, 1708. Cartouche with putto heads in an architectural frame with segmental pediment. – Edward Hasell † 1825. By *Chantrey*, 1830. White marble. Kneeling female figure by an urn on a base. Relief. – CURIOSUM. The four corners of the original churchyard are marked by four bears, perhaps from the former gatehouse of Dacre Castle. On two of them squat lynxes.

DACRE CASTLE. An early C14 pele tower on its own with two 29 strong square and two more buttress-like diagonal angle projections. The SW buttress contains the garderobe. In the NW projection is the staircase. The large windows with their mullion and transom crosses are of *c.*1700. The battlements are unusually well preserved. The basement consists of two tunnel-vaulted chambers. On the main floor is the hall, with a pretty *lavatorium* with a trefoil-pointed arch and a twelve-petalled drain like that of a piscina. Above the hall is the solar, called the King's Chamber. In 1354 a licence for a chapel in the castle was granted.

(ROSE BANK. Partly 1689, partly 1773. MHLG)

DUNMALLET HILLFORT, *see* Pooley Bridge, Westmorland, p. 284.

DALEGARTH HALL *see* BOOT

DALEMAIN
1¼ m. E of Dacre
4020

Sir Edward Hasell, steward of Lady Anne Clifford, bought the estate in 1680. His son gave the house its exceedingly fine Georgian E front. The same family is still at Dalemain. The house is oblong and has a narrow inner courtyard. The E front and the sides are essentially of *c.*1740–50. They are faced with

* The Rev. K. H. Smith tells me that the cup originally belonged to George, third Earl of Cumberland, and was given to the church by Lady Anne Clifford.

17

Cumberland and Westmorland
Nikolaus Pevsner
Penguin Books 1967
181mm deep

The text detailing is equally sensitive. The simple invention for the chapter opening of *Wuthering Heights* is remarkably effective. The continuous text of a novel contrasts with the complexity of the Pevsner Guide, but here, too, nothing has been left to chance. There is a subtle use of caps and small caps, and a combination of both for the building names. En dashes help to point up the small cap headings within the text. Hanging indents display the building names, centred headings display the place. The italic figures in the margin are map references, roman figures are illustration references. And it all looks so natural, as if it just happened without any struggle at all.

one of Johnson's, telling against their own prejudice, – though its symmetry be as of thunder answering from two horizons.

From *Praeterita*, I, § 251

¶ 76
RUSKIN'S STYLE

Although my readers say that I wrote then better than I write now, I cannot refer you to the passage [1] without asking you to pardon in it what I now hold to be the petulance and vulgarity of expression, disgracing the importance of the truth it contains. A little while ago, without displeasure, you permitted me to delay you by the account of a dispute on a matter of taste between my father and me, in which he was quietly and unavailingly right. It seems to me scarcely a day since, with boyish conceit, I resisted his wise entreaties that I would re-word this clause, and especially take out of it the description of a sea-wave as 'laying a great white table-cloth of foam' all the way to the shore. Now, after an interval of twenty years, I refer you to the passage, repentant and humble as far as regards its style, which people sometimes praised, but with absolute reassertion of the truth and value of its contents, which people always denied.

From *Val d'Arno*, Lecture VII, § 171

¶ 77
PROJECTS, (c. 1883)

The emotions of indignation, grief, controversial anxiety and vanity, or hopeless, and therefore uncontending, scorn, are all of them as deadly to the body as poisonous air or polluted water; and when I reflect how much of the active part of my past life has been spent in these states, – and that what may remain to me of life can never more be in any other, – I begin to ask myself, with somewhat pressing arithmetic, how much time is likely to be left me, at the age of fifty-six, to complete the various designs for which, until past fifty, I was merely collecting materials.

Of these materials, I have now enough by me for a most interest-

1. *The Stones of Venice*, Vol. I, ch. XXX.

ing (in my own opinion) history of fifteenth-century Florentine art, in six octavo volumes; an analysis of the Attic art of the fifth century B.C., in three volumes; an exhaustive history of northern thirteenth-century art, in ten volumes; a life of Turner, with analysis of modern landscape art, in four volumes; a life of Walter Scott, with analysis of modern epic art, in seven volumes; a life of Xenophon, with analysis of the general principles of Education, in ten volumes; a commentary on Hesiod, with final analysis of the principles of Political Economy, in nine volumes; and a general description of the geology and botany of the Alps, in twenty-four volumes.

Of these works, though all carefully projected, and some already in progress, – yet, allowing for the duties of my Professorship, possibly continuing at Oxford, and for the increasing correspondence relating to *Fors Clavigera*, – it does not seem to me, even in my most sanguine moments, now probable that I shall live to effect such conclusion as would be satisfactory to me; and I think it will therefore be only prudent, however humiliating, to throw together at once, out of the heap of loose stones collected for this many-towered city which I am not able to finish, such fragments of good marble as may perchance be useful to future builders; and to clear away, out of sight, the lime and other rubbish which I meant for mortar.

From *Deucalion*, I, Introduction, §§ 1–3

¶ 78
GROWING OLD

Among the many discomforts of advancing age, which no one understands till he feels them, there is one which I seldom have heard complained of, and which, therefore, I find unexpectedly disagreeable. I knew, by report, that when I grew old I should most probably wish to be young again; and, very certainly, be ashamed of much that I had done, or omitted, in the active years of life. I was prepared for sorrow in the loss of friends by death; and for pain, in the loss of myself, by weakness or sickness. These, and many other minor calamities, I have been long accustomed to anticipate; and therefore to read, in preparation for them, the confessions of the weak, and the consolations of the wise.

18
Ruskin Today
Kenneth Clark
Penguin Books 1967
197mm deep

18
This Ruskin anthology is a simpler problem than the Pevsner Guide, but Schmoller makes it look simpler than it is. Lesser hands would have unnecessarily given headings and source greater prominence; here, the often quite complicated reference is discreetly undisplayed, while the restrained extract titles and numerals are quite sufficient for their purpose. Footpath signs rather than motorway signs. A neat and appropriate use of paragraph and section marks adds a touch of colour, as do the larger initial caps beginning each extract. These, without drawing attention to themselves, are, unlike Wolpe's for the Ted Hughes poems [8], large enough to make their effect.

The whole design philosophy shows respect for readers, unlike many books today. As with the Pevsner Guides, the typography appears to have grown of its own accord.

The cleansing and revitalising effects of France and the Mediterranean have long played an important part in the British character. Before looking at a seminal pair of books on this subject, it is instructive to examine Minton's illustrations to *Time Was Away* of three years earlier. To send a British artist at the height of his neo-romantic period to a Mediterranean island may seem perverse, but Corsica has strangely dramatic landscapes. Minton's drawings, which include eight four-colour lithographs, capture both this drama and the lassitude of the small towns. (His use of overprinting in those lithographs, using the same four colours throughout, was extraordinarily varied and inventive, far more so than Craxton's in *The Poet's Eye*.) Alan Ross later thought his text may have over-emphasised the island's seediness, but the different parts of Europe were still, in 1947, in their different ways, recovering from the war, and his descriptions seem sharply evocative of that time. A much-praised, wider-ranging book lacks this condensed poetic acuteness when a contemporaneous journey is described. Both Ross and Minton exploited the virtues of spontaneous reaction. Their book, a period piece, is an early taste of the 'exotic' Mediterranean life, at this time difficult for British people to experience due to restrictions on foreign travel. Lehmann's imaginative project, enabling the right writer and right artist to go at the right time to the right place, produced a considerably more inspired book than did the Spender/Hockney journey through China in 1982.

19

Time Was Away
Alan Ross
John Lehmann 1948
237mm deep

FACES WITHOUT FUTURE

THE APATHY, the staring idleness of the children, the lack of ambition in the men is the result of centuries without economic conflict. The island is a well out of which the means of life can be drawn as required—wine, fruit, salt, birds, honey, fish. There is no need for any organisation in acquiring them, and beyond what is actually necessary for moderate living, there is no point in acquiring any more.

Possessions breed their own responsibilities and after having been bled of their material prosperity by one occupying power after the other, no one has the interest to start over again. So after doing his military service, and perhaps spending a year or so on the Continent to save up some money, the Corsican comes home and lives on whatever he can buy with his savings—a shop, an inn, a few acres of cultivated land. There is little industry and the land practically works itself, so freed from worry he has the rest of his life in front of him to exist, to play cards and to sleep. And so the young men of ambition leave home for good.

The proud, fiery, individual violence appears to have been drained from the national character, perhaps by cross-breeding, perhaps by the slump in energy after the abandonment of the lost cause of independence. The failure to achieve that is a sort of hump in the middle of Corsican history; after it everything flops back on to a listless plain.

All the specialised natural products—crayfish, olive oil, chestnuts, briar, timber, coupled with various drugs—are clumped together at Ajaccio or Bastia and shipped off by merchants for sale at high prices in the south of France, and the inland districts of the island are left with nothing. As a result, and to further the exportation of everything, the peasants inland live very simple, primitive lives, eating roughly and very little, drinking only a glass or so of coarse wine a day, and with no amenities of life—no drainage, no comforts, no normal imports to redress the balance of their exports. Instead, the money is saved and a few weeks' negotiation brings in enough to last the rest of the year.

Yet the lines of communication are there, and the faint infiltrations of urban life—Dubonnet advertisements stuck on peasants' cottages, Shell petrol signs, flashy café hoardings, photographs of film stars

46

SIMON AND JEAN PAUL

CARGÉSÉ

As a coherent piece of bookmaking, *Time Was Away* lacks finesse. Done without thought or foreknowledge of how they were to appear on the page, Minton's drawings (some drawn on the spot, some worked-up later in the hotel room) show several changes of scale and style. Many (even including the colour lithographs) are of landscape format. All this created problems for Keith Vaughan when he came to design the book. There is a certain rag-bag effect, echoing the episodic and impressionist text. But sometimes ordinary considerations of fine bookmaking need to be ignored. Formal imperfections are often found in great works of art. Minton, the thorough professional, was perfectly capable of producing illustrations to fit pre-ordained shapes; but here, in this vivid record of a three-week tour, he was working as one of the last great artist-illustrators.

CARGÉSÉ

19 *Time Was Away*

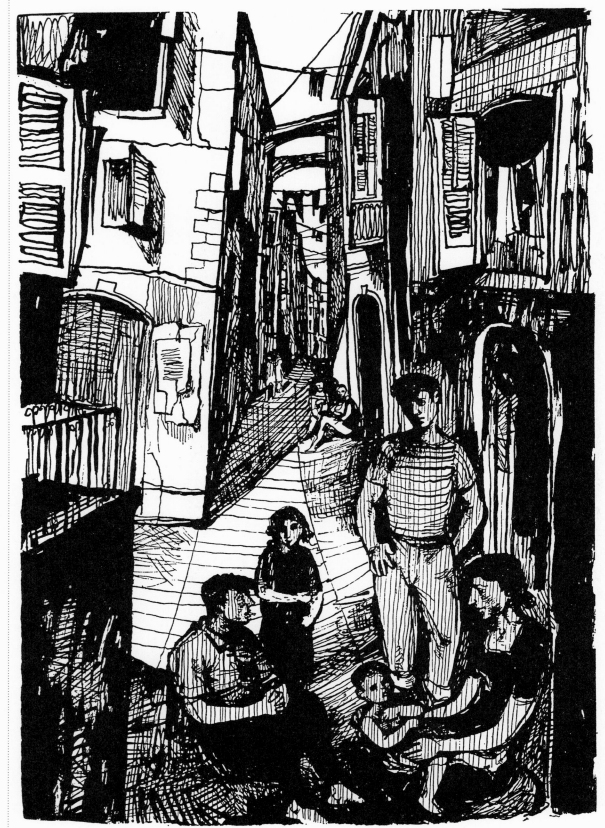

BASTIA—STREET SCENE

20
French Country Cooking
Elizabeth David
John Lehmann 1951
198mm deep

21
French Country Cooking
Elizabeth David
Penguin Books 1959
181mm deep

20 and **21**

Elizabeth David's *French Country Cooking* was originally published by John Lehmann in 1951, and by Penguin in 1959. It followed her *A Book of Mediterranean Food* (1950) which, crucially appearing when post-war austerities were about to become dim memories, and foreign travel was becoming more feasible, revolutionised not only British food but British life. Nothing could be further removed from the current spate of TV-linked, heavily-promoted, 'leisure activity' cookery extravaganzas, crammed with full-colour photographs of what (optimistically) the final dish might look like.

Elizabeth David's books were serious. They included background information and quotations from (amongst others) Henry James, Gertrude Stein, Norman Douglas, Arnold Bennett, and assorted gourmets and cooks. They were a sensible size and practical. They were illustrated, not with glamorous colour photography, but (far more attractively) with black-and-white line drawings by – who else? – John Minton. The very smell of Mediterranean or French country life wafted from these books. It has been claimed that Elizabeth David has changed British life more than any other woman this century. Is it too much to suggest that Minton's drawings may have played a part in this? Her *Italian Food* of 1954 (Penguin 1963) was disappointingly illustrated in a heavy-handed way by Renato Guttoso, who entirely lacked Minton's evocative poetry.

Penguin edition

FISH

Lobster

" During the early summer months, lobsters are in prime condition, and may be bought either alive or dead. As they are very tenacious of life, and indeed will live on till their substance is utterly wasted, it is clearly better to buy them alive, taking care not to kill them till just before cooking. The heaviest are the best; and if the tail strikes quick and strong, they are in good condition, but if weak and light and frothing at the mouth are exhausted and worthless. In like manner, when buying a boiled lobster put your finger and thumb on the body and pinch it; if it feels firm, and the tail goes back with a strong spring, the lobster—if heavy and of a good colour—is a desirable specimen."

These instructions are given by the cookery expert of *Spons Household Manual,* published in the 'eighties. Nowadays lobsters, except for restaurants, are nearly always bought ready cooked, but, while nobody can be blamed for avoiding participation in the martyr's death they die, the fact remains that a freshly cooked lobster prepared in one's own kitchen makes a very much better dish than one cooked by the fishmonger. It may be of some solace to know that Mr. Joseph Sinel, who made experiments on behalf of the R.S.P.C.A., came to the conclusion that a lobster put into cold water which is slowly brought to the boil collapses and dies painlessly when the heat reaches 70°. For grilling, the lobster can be killed instantaneously by the insertion of a skewer into the spinal cord, which is to be found at the joint between the tail shells and the body; or you can probably arrange with an obliging fishmonger to supply you with a half-boiled lobster which you can then split in two and bake in the oven or under the grill.

51

The Lehmann editions were well-enough designed, but it is instructive to compare them with Schmoller's versions, which used the same illustrations. These Penguins, in a slightly smaller format, were given true section titles rather than a frontispiece to each section; more notable are the subtle typographic changes: italic for headings instead of capitals, carefully letterspaced small caps for recipe names rather than italic, the use of a row of asterisks instead of a rule, and a general refinement of spacing and leading. Small changes, but they give not only greater elegance, but delight.

SALADS

Tomates Provençales en Salade

Take the stalks off a large bunch of parsley; pound it with a little salt, in a mortar, with 2 cloves of garlic.

Cut the tops off good raw tomatoes; with a teaspoon soften the pulp inside and turn them upside down so that the water drains out. Fill the tomatoes up with the parsley and garlic mixture. Serve them after an hour or two, when the flavour of the garlic and parsley has permeated the salad.

Tomato Salad with Cream

Put the required number of whole tomatoes into boiling water to remove the skins. Arrange them in a shallow salad bowl or silver dish.

Pour over them a dressing consisting simply of fresh cream into which is stirred a little salt and a tablespoon of chopped tarragon or fresh sweet basil.

A splendid accompaniment for a cold or, for that matter, a hot chicken.

Salade Armènienne

You will need ½ lb. of mushrooms, a couple of rashers of bacon, garlic, parsley, pimentos, celery, olive oil and a glass

M   177

Salads

* * * * * * * * * * * * * * * * * * *

TOMATES PROVENÇALES EN SALADE

Take the stalks off a large bunch of parsley; pound it with a little salt, in a mortar, with 2 cloves of garlic and a little olive oil.

Cut the tops off good raw tomatoes; with a teaspoon soften the pulp inside, sprinkle with salt, and turn them upside down so that the water drains out. Fill the tomatoes up with the parsley and garlic mixture. Serve them after an hour or two, when the flavour of the garlic and parsley has permeated the salad.

TOMATO SALAD WITH CREAM

Put the required number of whole tomatoes into boiling water to remove the skins. Arrange them in a shallow salad bowl or silver dish.

Pour over them a dressing consisting simply of thick fresh cream into which is stirred a little salt and a tablespoon of chopped tarragon or fresh sweet basil.

A splendid accompaniment for a cold or, for that matter, a hot chicken.

163

Tschichold's involvement with British publishing is easily explained. With the war over, and a general feeling of renewal, Allen Lane saw the need to get his Penguins sorted out. This entailed sorting out British book production generally. There was no better person for this job than Tschichold.

The success of Half-Point Schmoller's reign over twenty-five years seemed to derive from his personal passion for quality. Significantly, both men were German. Their typographic sensibility counterbalanced the dogmatic German character. No British typographer had the finesse, the ruthlessness or the obsession to carry out the job. It is unfortunate that Schmoller's retirement was followed by various far-reaching changes: the swallowing up of Penguin by a large nebulous conglomerate, a loss of direction, a general collapse of standards (not only at Penguin), a decision to take a more aggressive marketing stance (Penguin's earlier success had encouraged a host of rivals).

None of this was initially helped by the helter-skelter changes in printing technology. Typesetting systems were particularly affected, although once understood, and properly used, they could actually improve standards. Unfortunately the computer systems which appeared next enabled anyone, including those with no typographic training, to set type. If crude results become familiar, then the norm, it is difficult to convince anyone that this new norm is not good enough.

In conception, design and printing, illustrated books have improved overall. But it is rare today for a book consisting of text only to even approach the standards set by Tschichold and Schmoller. Pre-war publishers such as Chatto and Windus, Faber and Faber, Jonathan Cape, relying heavily on the skills of a printing industry which was to be severely disrupted, had produced sound if unremarkable-looking books; but it was the quantity of books produced by Penguin that, almost willy-nilly, raised the general standard throughout the industry after the war. Or was it mere coincidence that the years 1950-70 saw what was possibly the most civilised period of British book design and production for almost two hundred years?

22
Methods of Book Design
Hugh Williamson
Oxford University Press 1956
244mm deep

One would hope that books on book design are themselves well-designed and well-produced. A notable example is shown here. Well-printed on creamy-white Basingwerk Parchment, and with a cloth binding, its appearance inspires confidence. Chapter heads and subheads are clearly and simply displayed, and there is a minimum of fuss throughout. Such reference books need to provide an easy and direct method of access to the information buried in them, and Williamson has two solutions. First, a very comprehensive contents list, including all the sub-headings. Second, an original glossary/index providing a quick answer to the simpler queries. Well-designed editorially and visually, the book is still in print. The appearance of this revised edition, again designed by its author, somehow lacks the quality of the original. Symptomatic of the times, perhaps?

9

Principles of text design

Text composition must both *appear* to be legible and *be* legible.[1] The casual glance must first be attracted to the printed words, and then must be invited to travel along the lines. Any oddity or ambiguity that may catch at the reader's eye or interrupt the rhythm of reading is best avoided.

A person equipped with determination and adequate eyesight can read almost anything without conscious difficulty; up to a certain point, bad printing is not incapable of being read. Printing which is bad beyond this point is too bad to read, and is therefore not worth carrying out. The limit is rarely if ever passed, but is all too often approached. The production of certain newspapers is an example; some of the type-faces used for the text are spindly and deformed: the spacing of the text and the arrangement of headings is sometimes inept to an extreme: the use of worn matrices causes hair-lines to appear between the letters: and parts of letters and marks of punctuation often fail to appear on the paper. But people put up with it—indeed, they hardly notice; the newspapers are often read by indifferent light on moving buses and trains, and in crowds where the reader has to hold the paper much too close to his nose.

Reading without conscious difficulty is not the same as reading without strain. Some children read avidly and surreptitiously after going to bed, by the dim light of an electric torch, or in the gathering shadows of a summer evening. The child may notice no difficulty; but a few years of this kind of eye-strain are certain to aggravate defects of vision. The eye-strain inflicted on older readers by bad typography, perhaps too slight to be noticed at the time, may cause headaches and a gradual deterioration of the sight. Type which is too small or too large, too closely set or too widely spaced, undoubtedly blunts the pleasure of reading, and tends to discourage all but the enthusiast.

Legibility, then, is the aim. It may be defined as the capacity of a text to be read, by the reader for whom and in the circumstances for which it is intended, with ordinary speed and accuracy and without undue effort.

[1] In his 'A psychological study of typography' Burt points out that text is not always as legible as it looks to the reader.

It is impossible to prove at what point a printed text ceases to be legible according to this definition, or even whether one text is more legible than another. There are no generally accepted principles according to which legibility may be secured without fail. The typographer's only guides are his eyes; and he cannot always test his specifications for text composition by sustained reading, but must judge their effect by looking at one or two specimen pages. He can sharpen his judgement only by evaluating every example of text setting that comes within arm's length, and thus keeping his eyes sensitive to detail and proportion.

Very little has been proved about legibility, and this is one reason why tradition in the style of text setting retains its influence. The advantages of such radical alterations as the use of sans-serif types for sustained reading can only be asserted in face of the disagreement of most readers and typographers.

The unpopularity of even so small a change as the omission of serifs suggests that every printed detail may have some value to the reader. The details of a page which is to be printed can be varied to a considerable degree; each type-face has its peculiarities of serif, stress, weight, set, fitting, and size on the body, and each fount in the series can be set in a number of different measures and spaced differently both horizontally and vertically. Quite apart from this, ink of various degrees of black may be used on papers of a variety of shades, and there are other variables which are dealt with in other chapters. It is by a careful adjustment of all the variables of the text page to each other, under the guidance of a practised and sensitive eye, that legibility is achieved.

The design of the text page is the chief task of the book designer; not only this chapter but six of those which precede it and nine of those which follow deal more or less directly with this task. This chapter only describes some principles governing the choice of text area and the arrangement of type within it; the next chapter is concerned with details of arrangement, and the chapter after that with decorative typography, which to some extent affects the text page.

§ 78 · TEXT AREA

The dimensions of the text area are of course influenced by those of format and margins, but are too important to be determined finally by such influences. The margins are in fact only the extra space on the page round the text, and if they have already been planned they may have to be altered to suit the text area.

For purposes of design, the text area may be defined as the space occupied by lines of text and by the headline if there is one. The headline usually occupies enough space to count as an extra line; the page number, useful in dates (6/6/92 = 6.vi.92 = 6 June 92) and in text where a comma or parenthesis might otherwise have been used.

Wednesday / August 3 / 1977
Tibetan Guest House / Thamel / Kathmandu
Victoria University, Toronto / Ontario
he/she hit him/her

Dashes,
Slashes
and Dots

The other slash mark on the font is a solidus or fraction bar, used to construct fractions such as ³⁄₃₂. The solidus generally slopes at close to 45° and kerns on both sides. The virgule, not the solidus, is used to construct *level* fractions, such as $2\pi/3$. (Notice, for instance, the difference in slope and kerning between the two slash marks in the type specification 8/9½.)

5.2.6   *Use a dimension sign instead of a serifed x when dimensions are given.*

A picture is 26 × 42 cm; studs are 2 × 4 and shelving is 2 × 10 inches; North American letter paper is 8½ × 11.

5.2.7   *Use ellipses that fit the font.*

Most digital fonts now include, among other things, a prefabricated *ellipsis* (a row of three baseline dots). Many typographers nevertheless prefer to make their own. Some prefer to set the three dots flush ... with a normal word space before and after. Others prefer ... to add *thin* spaces between the dots. Thick spaces (M/3) are prescribed by the Chicago Style Manual, but these are another Victorian eccentricity. In most contexts, the Chicago ellipsis is much too wide.

Flush-set ellipses work well with some fonts and faces but not with all. At small text sizes – in 8 pt footnotes, for example – it is generally better to add space (as much as M/5) between the dots. Extra space may also look best in the midst of light, open letterforms, such as Baskerville, and less space in the company of a dark font, such as Trajanus, or when setting in bold face. (The ellipsis generally used in this book is part of the font and sets as a single character.)

In English (but usually not in French), when the ellipsis occurs at the end of a sentence, a fourth dot, the period, is added and the space at the beginning of the ellipsis disap-

pears.... When the ellipsis combines with a comma..., an exclamation mark, or question mark, the same typographical principle applies. Otherwise, a word space is required both fore and aft.

5.3   PARENTHESES

5.3.1   *Use the best available brackets and parentheses, and set them with adequate space.*

The parentheses of the Renaissance and early Baroque were pure line, like the virgule (/) and the long dash (–). They were curved rules, with no variation in weight – and they were loosely fitted, with plenty of space between them and the text they enclosed. Centaur is one of the few twentieth-century faces that have reasserted this Renaissance style, and Monotype Van Dijck is one of the few historical recuttings that are faithful on this important point of detail.

A few other recent faces, such as Trump Mediäval, have been designed with parentheses based on pen-drawn Renaissance forms. Others still, such as Hermann Zapf's Melior and Karl-Erik Forsberg's Berling, have parentheses distinctively their own, that are clearly evolved from these particular letterforms. But on many twentieth-century text fonts, the parentheses are stock eighteenth-century swelled rules. In company with a neoclassical alphabet, such as Baskerville, these parentheses look fine. With letters of most other kinds, they are out of place.

Analphabetic
Symbols

(abc) (abc)

Centaur and Trump, above. Baskerville and Melior, below.

(abc) (abc)

In older German typeface classifications, *Antiqua* means roman and *Mediäval* means Renaissance – because Italian Renaissance architects and scribes revived and updated the romanesque and Carolingian forms of the Middle Ages. *Trump Mediäval Antiqua,* or Trump Mediäval roman, in spite of its name, grows out of late Renaissance forms.

23
The Elements of Typographic Style
Robert Bringhurst
Hartley & Marks 1992
229mm deep

23

It is interesting how little disagreement there is on sound typographic practice, between Tschichold, Schmoller, Williamson, and the author of this recent book on typography – especially as typographers are notoriously cantankerous. The Canadian author is also a poet – and it tells. He is mysteriously able to touch on elementary points by metaphor and simile, while still entertaining informed readers. A different solution to the problem of access is offered, with a battery of chapter heads, side-heads, sub-heads and cross-heads, clearly differentiated and ordered both typographically and by the numbering system. The relatively narrow margins of this unusually tall format are still able to accommodate not only headings but notes, references and some illustrations. Other illustrations are well built into the text width, with sans serif captions. In this well-thought-out book, writing and design have gone hand-in-hand. It affirms that, despite all the new technology, most of the well-established principles, largely governed by concerns for legibility and readability, still hold.

24

The design of poetry has its own problems. Line lengths within poems often vary considerably, and in a collection each poem will take a different form. What to do? Should poems (and their titles) be centred within a notional text area? If, as is often the case, the title is centred over the longest line, which could appear anywhere in the poem, it could look lost. Or should all poems and their titles be ranged left within the text area? If so, should the ranging line vary from page to page, depending upon the shape of the poems on that page? Can extra-long lines be accommodated by breaking the notional measure, extending into the margin, or do they have to be taken over? If so, by how much should they be indented? How are these to be differentiated from lines *intended* to be indented?

(If a poetic quotation appears within text, centring the poem on the longest line – the generally accepted solution – is usually unsatisfactory, since the principle is disguised by variations in line length, and it can look especially awkward if two poems appear on the same page. Often the best way is to indent by the same amount as the paragraph openings; or simply range left.)

Schmoller has opted for the centred principle, but with a wide outer margin. He has, however, adjusted each page: poems and titles are centred on the folio, but this is allowed to move left or right (see overleaf). The adjustment is so subtly done that one is only aware of it if, wondering how all poems sit happily in the page width, one compares folio positions very carefully.

He has had to turn over some lines, and I am surprised that the long lines, as in Wolpe's design for Ted Hughes [8], are justified, again producing irregular word spacing. And the first line on page 398 has a hyphenated word. Why?

The first running head on the spread would be less confusing if it named the author of the first poem; which, on page 12, is *Breton* not *Sidney*, and on page 398 is *Hardy* not *Housman*. Nonetheless, his general detailing is, as usual, very refined, with titles, subtitles and verse divisions neatly handled, and the first word of each poem delicately emphasised by larger initial and small caps.

The slightly complex list of contents shows equal sensitivity and clarity, with poet and his dates well displayed. Titles are differentiated from first lines; titles supplied by the editor are in square brackets; titles of works from which the extract is taken are in italic.

Contents

xv

24
The Penguin Book of English Verse
John Hayward
Penguin Books 1956
181mm deep

Thus with many a pretie oath,
Yea and nay, and faith and troth,
Such as silly shepheards use,
When they will not love abuse.
Love, which had beene long deluded,
Was with kisses sweet concluded:
And *Phyllida* with garlands gay,
Was made the Lady of the May.

SIDNEY

from *ASTROPHEL AND STELLA*

LOVING in truth, and faine in verse my love to show,
    That she (deare she) might take some pleasure of my paine:
    Pleasure might cause her reade, reading might make her
        know,
    Knowledge might pitie winne, and pitie grace obtaine,
I sought fit words to paint the blackest face of woe,
    Studying inventions fine, her wits to entertaine:
    Oft turning others leaves, to see if thence would flow
    Some fresh and fruitfull showers upon my sunne-burn'd
        braine.

But words came halting forth, wanting Inventions stay,
    Invention Natures child, fled step-dame Studies blowes,
    And others feete still seem'd but strangers in my way.
Thus great with child to speake, and helplesse in my throwes
    Biting my trewand pen, beating my selfe for spite,
    Foole, said my Muse to me, looke in thy heart and write.

        ★

    WITH how sad steps, ô Moone, thou climbst the skies,
        How silently, and with how wanne a face,
        What, may it be that even in heav'nly place
        That busy archer his sharpe arrowes tries?

    Sure if that long with *Love* acquainted eyes
        Can judge of *Love*, thou feel'st a Lovers case;
        I reade it in thy lookes, thy languisht grace
        To me that feele the like, thy state descries.

12

Then ev'n of fellowship, ô Moone, tell me
    Is constant *Love* deem'd there but want of wit?
    Are Beauties there as proud as here they be?

Do they above love to be lov'd, and yet
    Those Lovers scorne whom that *Love* doth possesse?
    Do they call *Vertue* there ungratefulnesse?

['JUST EXCHANGE']

MY true love hath my heart and I have his,
By just exchange one for another geven:
I holde his deare, and mine he cannot misse,
There never was a better bargaine driven.
    My true love hath my heart and I have his.
My heart in me keepes him and me in one,
My heart in him his thoughts and sences guides:
He loves my heart, for once it was his owne,
I cherish his because in me it bides.
    My true love hath my heart, and I have his.

['FAREWELL WORLD']

LEAVE me ô Love, which reachest but to dust,
And thou my mind aspire to higher things:
Grow rich in that which never taketh rust:
What ever fades, but fading pleasure brings.

Draw in thy beames, and humble all thy might,
To that sweet yoke, where lasting freedomes be:
Which breakes the clowdes and opens forth the light,
That doth both shine and give us sight to see.

O take fast hold, let that light be thy guide,
In this small course which birth drawes out to death,
And think how evill becommeth him to slide,
Who seeketh heav'n, and comes of heav'nly breath.
    Then farewell world, thy uttermost I see,
    Eternall Love maintaine thy life in me.

13

AFTERWARDS

WHEN the Present has latched its postern behind my tremu-
    lous stay,
  And the May month flaps its glad green leaves like wings,
Delicate-filmed as new-spun silk, will the neighbours say,
  'He was a man who used to notice such things'?

If it be in the dusk when, like an eyelid's soundless blink,
  The dewfall-hawk comes crossing the shades to alight
Upon the wind-warped upland thorn, a gazer may think,
  'To him this must have been a familiar sight.'

If I pass during some nocturnal blackness, mothy and warm,
  When the hedgehog travels furtively over the lawn,
One may say, 'He strove that such innocent creatures should
    come to no harm,
  But he could do little for them; and now he is gone.'

If, when hearing that I have been stilled at last, they stand at
    the door,
  Watching the full-starred heavens that winter sees,
Will this thought rise on those who will meet my face no more,
  'He was one who had an eye for such mysteries'?

And will any say when my bell of quittance is heard in the
    gloom,
  And a crossing breeze cuts a pause in its outrollings,
Till they rise again, as they were a new bell's boom,
  'He hears it not now, but used to notice such things?'

HOUSMAN

TELL me not here, it needs not saying,
  What tune the enchantress plays
In aftermaths of soft September
  Or under blanching mays,
For she and I were long acquainted
  And I knew all her ways.

On russet floors, by waters idle,
  The pine lets fall its cone;
The cuckoo shouts all day at nothing
  In leafy dells alone;
And traveller's joy beguiles in autumn
  Hearts that have lost their own.

On acres of the seeded grasses
  The changing burnish heaves;
Or marshalled under moons of harvest
  Stand still all night the sheaves;
Or beeches strip in storms for winter
  And stain the wind with leaves.

Possess, as I possessed a season,
  The countries I resign,
Where over elmy plains the highway
  Would mount the hills and shine,
And full of shade the pillared forest
  Would murmur and be mine.

For nature, heartless, witless nature,
  Will neither care nor know
What stranger's feet may find the meadow
  And trespass there and go,
Nor ask amid the dews of morning
  If they are mine or no.

THOMPSON

from CONTEMPLATION

THE river has not any care
Its passionless water to the sea to bear;
The leaves have brown content;
The wall to me has freshness like a scent,
And takes half-animate the air,
Making one life with its green moss and stain;
And life with all things seems too perfect blent
For anything of life to be aware.

25

Miscellanies of verse *and* prose present somewhat similar problems to those of poetry anthologies. Here, they are neatly solved. A strong spine – not unlike Schmoller's – is created by centring short rules (actually light blue/grey) between the items, and centring running heads and folios. This spine secures both the text extracts, justified to quite a wide measure, and the erratic-length lines of poetry, stabilising what might otherwise be a rather loose-looking page. The references are unobtrusively handled.

This miscellany also included a wide range of well-chosen engravings, woodcuts and lithographs, of various (uninsured and often amusing) disasters. Well printed on laid paper, this imaginatively conceived, witty, finely-executed book rises well above its origin, which was merely a celebration of the 150th anniversary of an insurance company. Such subtle low-key publicity would be unlikely today.

ON RISK

any greater strain on himself and his men than was all in the day's work of polar exploration. Nothing more business-like could be imagined. On the other hand, our expedition, running appalling risks, performing prodigies of superhuman endurance, achieving immortal renown, commemorated in august cathedral sermons and by public statues, yet reaching the Pole only to find our terrible journey superfluous, and leaving our best men dead on the ice. To ignore such a contrast would be ridiculous: to write a book without accounting for it a waste of time.

A. CHERRY-GARRARD *The Worst Journey in the World*

We have suffered various oppression,
But mostly we are left to our own devices,
And we are content if we are left alone.
We try to keep our households in order;
The merchant, shy and cautious, tries to compile a little fortune,
And the labourer bends to his piece of earth, earth-colour, his own colour,
Preferring to pass unobserved.
Now I fear disturbance of the quiet seasons:
Winter shall come bringing death from the sea,
Ruinous spring shall beat at our doors.
Root and shoot shall eat our eyes and our ears,
Disastrous summer burn up the beds of our streams
And the poor shall wait for another decaying October.

T. S. ELIOT *Murder in the Cathedral*

So if a son that is by his father sent about merchandise do sinfully miscarry upon the sea, the imputation of his wickedness, by your rule, should be imposed upon his father that sent him: or if a servant, under his master's command transporting a sum of money, be assailed by robbers and die in many irreconcil'd iniquities, you may call the business of the master the author of the servant's damnation. But this is not so: the King is not bound to answer the particular endings of his soldiers, the father of his son, nor the master of his servant: for they purpose not their deaths when they purpose their services. SHAKESPEARE *Henry V*

8

25
On Risk
Atlas Assurance Company 1958
246mm deep

GENERALITY

But as when many and great wrecks befall,
The great sea tosses bench, ribs, yard, and prow,
And masts and floating oars; and gilded poops
Come drifting to the shores of all the world,
That men may see and by that warning shun
The wiles, the might, the treachery of waters,
Nor let themselves at any time be lured
With the sly magic of a smiling sea.

LUCRETIUS *De Rerum Natura*

Dangers are no more light if they once seem light, and more dangers have deceived men than forced them; nay, it were better to meet some dangers half-way, though they come nothing near, than to keep too long a watch upon their approaches; for if a man watch too long it is odds he will fall fast asleep. BACON *Instauratio Magna, 1623*

It has been predicted, and it certainly is to be hoped, that by improvement in the education and industrial training of manual labourers, rendering them more discreet; by improvement in the arts, rendering processes and engines more safe; and by moral, religious, and physical training of intellectual labourers, rendering them less liable to mental aberrations and suicides, violent deaths may be somewhat reduced.   *The Insurance Guide's Handbook 1857—dedicated especially to Insurance Agents*

Caesar should be a beast without a heart
If he should stay at home today for fear:
No Caesar shall not; Danger knows full well
That Caesar is more dangerous than he.
We hear his lions litter'd in one day,
And I the elder and more terrible,
And Caesar shall go forth.   SHAKESPEARE *Julius Caesar*

9

Books with a mass of editorial content need careful and sympathetic design. The five volumes of Virginia Woolf's *Diaries* are exemplars of editing. While the footnotes are extensive, none are superfluous, and they are grouped so that several references may be collated into one note in a reader-friendly form. A hanging indent ensures easy access to note numbers. Virginia Woolf's helter-skelter prose is happily simulated by typographic detail, and later additions are neatly inset. Month and year are indicated in running heads, day and date by restrained italic quite sufficiently displayed, editorial linking commentary is given a different voice from Virginia Woolf's text by the use of italic.

Elegant and reticent typography in harmony with discreet editing make enjoyable a text which must have presented enormous problems.

26
The Diary of Virginia Woolf
Vol V 1936-1941
Edited by Ann Olivier Bell
Hogarth Press 1984
235mm deep

MAY 1939

repeat the fact that my head is a tight wound ball of string. To unwind it, I lie on my Heal chair bed & doze of an evening. But the noise worries me. The 2 houses next door are down; we are shored up. There are patches of wall paper where there used to be hotel bedrooms. Thus the Southampton Row traffic gets at me; & I long for 37 Mecklenburgh Sq: but doubt if we shall get it. Pritchard is negotiating with the Bedfords.[1] A talk about the future with John. He is harassed by the lean year. Cant live in London on £500 minus his mothers interest &c. 37 is a large seeming & oh so quiet house, where I could sleep anywhere. But it dont do to dwell on it. & there would be the horror of the move in August.

Day Lewis came one day; thrust in on the wake of Elizabeth. A stocky sturdy man. truculent. a little like Muggins 40 yrs ago, as I think George called Malcolm Macnaghten. "Priestley lolling on the beach" was discussed.[2] I made him laugh by repeating that word. I wish *should it be lōl ling or lolling?* I could repeat more words. Boswell did it. Could I turn B. at my age? "I'm doing films for the gas people . . . I live a purely country life. A rather too arty home. Devonshire." I infer some rupture with the Bugger Boys.

Boswell at Sissinghurst. Gwen walking through the Bluebell woods, speaking of her youth—a little to justify herself. Had been advertiser to a scent shop. had done welfare work. Her daughter Jiccy meets a prostitute outside the Berkeley whom she has deliv[er]ed. "Must just speak to Bessy" she says to the youth who's treating her—"Its her beat." G. a little shocked.[3] And I liked the soft cream & yellow flowers on the sunny grass & the bend stooping like a picture. And the thread of bright blue bells: & Vita in her breeches.

We are going to Brittany by the way after Whitsun. A whole 2 weeks rambling. Now that'll fill my dry cistern of a head. But this is nothing

1. Although the Woolfs' lease of 52 Tavistock Square ran until 1941, the din and disturbance caused by the adjacent demolitions compelled them to move. On 9 May they saw over and resolved upon 37 Mecklenburgh Square, and their solicitor-tenant Mr Pritchard—who agreed to move with them—attempted (unsuccessfully in the event) to persuade their landlords, the Duke of Bedford Estates, to accept the early surrender of their current lease.
2. Elizabeth Bowen came to tea with VW on 3 May; they were joined by the poet Cecil Day Lewis (1904-72), who was currently writing the script for a projected documentary film on colliers for the British Commercial Gas Association. The High Court judge Sir Malcolm MacNaghten (1869-1955) had been at Eton and Cambridge with George Duckworth. The Woolfs saw J. B. Priestley's play *Johnson Over Jordan* at the Saville Theatre on 4 May.
3. The Woolfs had gone to Sissinghurst on 8 May *en route* from Rodmell to London. Gwen St Aubyn's daughter Jessica (b. 1918) is (1983) mystified by this story.

like so bad as The Years. A nun writes to invite me to stage a meeting of Outsiders in Hyde Park. I stop to answer her. Gertler tonight.[4]

Thursday 25 May

A queer little note to run off in a hurry: L. is bargaining for 37 M. Sq upstairs: I'm packing. We're off: & very likely I shant write much more in this now so tidy studio. Tidied for Ben to work in. I must pack upstairs. Brittany & Rodmell for 3 weeks.

Party last night. G. Keyneses: Eth Wn & her underworld friend. Ben Nicolson.[5]

Interrupted by parties come to see the house. The first day its in the agents hands. Shall we end our lives looking in that great peaceful garden; in the sun? I hope so.

On the afternoon of 25 May the Woolfs drove to Rodmell for Whitsuntide, and on 5 June crossed the Channel to Dieppe for a motor tour of Normandy and Brittany. They visited Les Rochers, *Mme de Sévigné's château near Vitré, and continued to Vannes and round the Brittany peninsula to Dinan and Bayeux. (Their itinerary is briefly recorded by* LW *(Diary, LWP, Sussex); the notebook to which* VW *refers does not survive). They returned to Monks House on 19 June and to Tavistock Square on Thursday 22 June.*

Friday 23 June

Back to London again after 4 weeks. Two spent driving about Brittany. I kept notes in a little square ruled pocketbook in my bag; a good method perhaps, if carried out in London; but I doubt if its worth sticking them here. Perhaps a few, for like pressed leaves they somehow bring back the whole forgotten hedge. So soon forgotten in bulk. The London uproar at once rushes in. Okampo today; John; then I must go to Penman. We have 37 M[ecklenburgh] S[quare]: & this is still unlet.[6]

4. For the nun's letter, see MHP, Sussex, LVP (Books). VW had asked Gertler to dine as she 'was anxious to get your account of the way [Roger Fry] struck younger painters.' (*VI VW Letters*, no. 3501.) See also *Moments of Being*, p. 85: 'May 15th 1939. . . . Last night Mark Gertler dined here and denounced the vulgarity, the inferiority of what he called "literature"; compared with the integrity of painting.'

5. The Woolfs' dinner guests were Maynard Keynes's younger brother the surgeon and bibliophile Geoffrey Langdon Keynes (1887-1982) and his wife Margaret, *née* Darwin. Elizabeth Williamson, her friend Leonie Leontineff (?), and Benedict Nicolson—to whom VW was to lend her 'studio' while she was away—came in afterwards.

6. Victoria Ocampo (1880-1979), the wealthy Argentine founder and publisher of the literary review *Sur*, was an extravagant admirer of VW, whom she met in 1934 (see

This encyclopedia presents a different problem of co-ordination, and also of co-operation between author, house editor, illustrators, picture researcher and designer. It is one in a Shell series produced by George Rainbird for various publishers. George Sharp was Art Director. Diagrams, graphs, illustrations, photographs, editing, typesetting and printing are all of the exceptionally high standard characteristic of this packager. It is doubtful if such overall professionalism would have been seen in a book of this kind – or would even have been available – before the 1960s or 1970s.

Books like this require a well-considered hierarchy of headings, but the simpler this can be kept the better. Here are bold headings, sub-heads also in bold but preceded by an en dash and, unlike the first rank, without a line space above. (Baskerville's unusually strong bold is useful here.) Sub-sub-heads are in small caps and occasionally in italic. Additionally, inserted amongst the regular alphabetical entries are major topics running for several pages. These are identified by headings in a toned strip at the head of each page.

Cross-references are thorough. Many tables and equations are incorporated in the text, and there are numerous photographs, illustrations, graphs and diagrams. All these have to be jigsawed together. This requires care: without an orderly arrangement, strictly controlled by grids and alignments, the clarity essential to such reference books could be lost. This is book engineering.

27

The Shell Encyclopedia of Sailing
Edited by Michael W Richey
Produced by The Rainbird Publishing
Group for Stanford Maritime 1980
280mm deep

Performance and yacht design

Performance and yacht design

Why does one boat sail faster than another? What is the best course to windward? How much does the crew contribute to yacht performance? How close to windward can a given boat sail? How can boat performance be measured or predicted?

To inquire meaningfully into questions like these it is necessary to acquire some understanding of the basic principles governing yacht motion and the forces involved.

– resistance and performance

At first sight a sailing boat appears to bear a close family resemblance to a ship. It is a characteristic of all hulls, which are supported by water-buoyancy force – discovered by Archimedes some 22 centuries ago – that their resistance takes a sharp upturn as soon as the so-called relative speed $V_S/\sqrt{L}$ exceeds only a little more than unity. This effect, due to rapid increase in the wave-making resistance, puts an effective brake on the maximum speed, which in the case of displacement craft rarely exceeds $1.4\sqrt{L}$. It has long been understood that designers cannot hope to continue indefinitely the speed improvement of these monohull yachts by increasing thrust, i.e. sail power, alone. However, it may be argued, that 'to really improve a boat's performance, one must be able to reduce resistance'. This obvious, commonsense inference, apparently well-substantiated by fig. 1, and accepted as an axiom in ship science, is not applicable without qualification to sailing craft, except in the case of a yacht sailing upright and down-wind.

In the early 1930s K. S. M. Davidson proved, in his now well-known paper 'Some experimental studies of the sailing yacht' (*Techn.Mem.* No 130, Stevens Institute of Technology, Hoboken, N.J.), an almost paradoxical point: overall boat performance can be improved when hull resistance is increased. Fig. 2a and 2b illustrate the point. The measured resistance curves of the two 6-metre boats given in fig. 2a indicate that the yacht *Jack* had lower resistance when sailing upright in the range of useful speeds than the older *Jill*. As might be expected, *Jack*'s racing records in running conditions were better than that of the rival boat, but she proved to be distinctly inferior to *Jill* in close-hauled ability. It was generally agreed that the failure of the newer boat *Jack* could not be attributed to faulty sails or to incompetent handling; a number of different sails had been tried and various experienced sailors had raced her.

Subsequent calculation of close-hauled speeds in terms of speed made good to windward – based on model tests in the towing tank and shown in fig. 2b – confirmed the observed performance differences of the full-scale yachts, which were quite conspicuous.

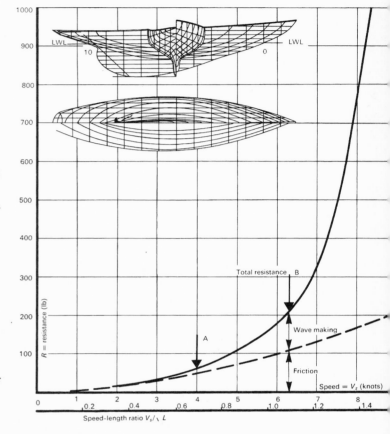

Thus, these tests seem to dispose of any idea that the upright resistances could be regarded as a sufficient indication of the overall performance of a yacht hull under sail. When the poorer performer of two boats, Davidson argued, has slightly more sail area (as in the case of *Jack*) and appreciably lower upright resistance over much of the useful speed range, it is evident that other factors must be at least as important as the upright resistances: the differences must lie in the hulls. But where, in the first place, should these differences be sought?

– sailing-yacht mechanics

The answer to the question just posed was given, many years before Davidson's paper was written, by F. W. Lanchester. In his book *Aerodynamics*, vol. 1 (London 1907), he made an outstanding contribution, by his contemporaries' standard, to understanding the mechanics of windward sailing. According to him, '. . . the problem of sailing-yacht mechanics resolves itself into an aerofoil combination in which the aerofoil acting in the air (a sail)

and that acting under water (a keel, fin, o dagger plate) mutually supply each other reaction.

'The result of this supposition is evident that the minimum angle at which the boa can shape its course relative to the wind is sum of the under and above water gliding angles.'

Introducing contemporary sailing termi ogy, 'the gliding angles' are equivalent to so-called aerodynamic and hydrodynami angles ε_A and ε_H, defined in fig. 3, which presents Lanchester's concept in diagram matic form. The problem is usually simpl by looking down from above the boat and considering separately:
1. the aerodynamic forces (3a);
2. the hydrodynamic forces (3b);
3. the equilibrium of sail and hull forces (

Fig. 3 shows a dinghy sailing upright (or nearly upright) to windward and driven b single sail. The forces on a boat come from two sources: apparent wind V_A action on sail, and hydrodynamic action resulting f

Fig. 1 (opposite) *Resistance characteristics of a heavy displacement keelboat, sailing upright in smooth sea: New York 32 LOA 45.50 ft (13.87) LWL (L) 32.26 ft (9.83 m), beam 10.58 ft 3.22 m), draught 6.56 ft (1.99 m), displacement*

11.38 tons (25 000 lb or 11 567 kg). It is seen that, in order to obtain maximum speed V_S close to $1.4\sqrt{L}$ (where speed V_S is in knots and the hull length L in feet), sails must provide driving force = resistance of about 800 lb

Fig. 2 (below) *Comparison of the 6-Metre boats Jack and Jill : (a) upright resistance; (b) calculated close-hauled speeds in terms of V_{mg} and V_s (for a definition of these terms see fig. 7)*

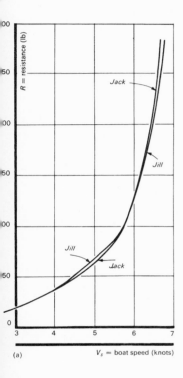

(a) V_s = boat speed (knots)

(b) Speed (knots)

Fig. 3 *Sailing-yacht mechanics: (a) aerodynamic forces on sail; (b) hydrodynamic forces on hull c) equilibrium of sail and hull forces. CE = centre of effort; CL = centreline; D = drag; ε_A = aerodynamic angle; ε_H = hydrodynamic angle;*

F_H = *heeling force; F_R = driving force; F_S = hydrodynamic side force; F_T = total aerodynamic force; L = lift; λ = angle of leeway; R = resistance; R_T = total hydrodynamic force; V_A = apparent wind; V_S = course sailed*

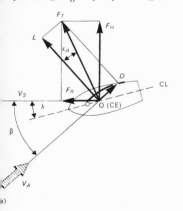

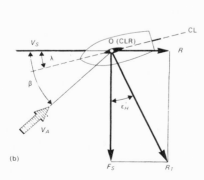

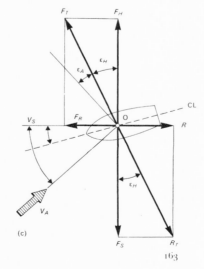

163

more easily handled sail. Smaller craft were often rigged with one or two standing lugs, and the sails were occasionally fitted with a boom, which might indicate an eastern origin; most commonly they were used in combination with dipping lugs as the mizzen of two- and three-masted luggers.

The archetype of French luggers, the *chasse-marée*, was tremendously canvased; one with three masts might carry two topsails above the fore and main standing lugs and one above the mizzen. To ameliorate the disability when yards were to windward these were slung on alternate sides of the masts.

The north European lugsail appeared in a great variety of shapes and rig arrangements. Some lugs were cut broad and shallow; others tall and narrow. Jibs were set in some types on a long bowsprit. A standing-lug mizzen might be sheeted over a sheave at the end of a stern outrigger of more than half the length of the hull. There were luggers in which the combined length of bowsprit and stern outrigger exceeded the length of the hull. A boat's rig could be varied with the season and occasion: winter rig; summer rig; and, for craft in localities where there was enthusiasm for racing, regatta rig. In many rigs the lug was tacked down to the stem, or beyond it on a short downward-inclined metal bowsprit (bumpkin). In other rigs the tack of the sail was far enough aft for a bowline to be rigged. In a few types a descendant of the Viking *beitáss* (*see* Square rigs *above*) was used, a bearing-out spar latterly known as a foregirt. Sometimes a spritsail was used as a mizzen; sometimes a leg-of-mutton sail.

– balanced lug

This is a lugsail with its foot laced to a boom. Both boom and yard project forward of the mast, to which neither is secured, when the sail is hoisted. It is in fact a dipping lug to which a boom has been fitted; but this was never done in Europe outside the Mediterranean, where it was fairly usual in the Adriatic and Aegean. It was the rig of the Italian fishing lugger and the coasting-trade *trabacola*, often in preference to the lateen. The *trabacola* had two masts and a triangular headsail, or jib, set from a long bowsprit. The Greek lugger was generally similar in character.

Whereas the jib was clearly imported into the Mediterranean from northwest Europe, there can be little doubt that the balanced lug came from the East: directly from the Chinese junks, according to a suggestion made by Dr Joseph Needham in his *Science and Civilisation in China*, vol. 4 (London and New York 1962).

The Chinese form of the balanced lug, with yard and boom and numerous closely spaced battens, is assumed, though no evidence can be offered, to be the descendant of a tall, narrow, battenless square sail, which, in the

Galway Blazer II, *a modern two-masted Chinese-rigged yacht which, with Bill King, completed a single-handed circumnavigation in 1972.*

Eastern manner, would have had a boom. The sail would then have become a balanced lug of the Mediterranean kind. The unique contribution of the Chinese to sail techniques was to attach a series of battens across the sail, a remarkable invention stiffening the sail and bringing exceptional qualities not only aerodynamically but, thanks to a style of rigging evolved nowhere else, particular advantages

in handling (*see* CHINESE RIG). Adapted for modern materials, the Chinese type of lug is being used by a number of experienced modern yachtsmen, in preference to the Bermudian mainsail and jib: a tribute to the rig's innate qualities.

See also CHINESE RIG; MASTS AND RIGGING; PERFORMANCE AND YACHT DESIGN; YACHT RACING

194

ising
fore-and-aft strake supporting the thwarts
a small boat.

oach
he outward curve in the side or foot of a sail.

olling hitch *see* ROPEWORK: Bends and
tches

opework
he term is used comprehensively here to
clude rope itself, and bends, hitches, and
lices.

rope
or a long time rope was measured by its
rcumference in inches or its diameter in
illimetres. Nowadays the latter is all but
niversal. Technically the term rope denotes
rdage greater than 2 in (51 mm) in circum-
rence. Cordage smaller than this is referred
as small stuff. Cordage is manufactured
om natural fibres such as manila, sisal,
mp, and cotton, or man-made fibres such
nylon, polythene, and polyester (Terylene,
acron, Tergal).
he strength of a rope of natural fibre is due
tirely to the friction between the relatively
ort fibres when the rope is stressed. In
ntrast, that of a man-made-fibre rope
mes from the inherent strength of the ma-
rial of which it is made, each filament ex-
nding throughout the length of the rope.
nese facts produce the significant difference
the manner in which different types of rope
rt when overstressed. The broken ends of a
tural-fibre rope fall dead when the rope
rts; those of a man-made-fibre rope be-
ve like the broken ends of a taut spring
at breaks under excessive tension. Special

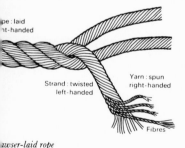

pe : laid
ht-handed

Strand : twisted
left-handed

Yarn : spun
right-handed

Fibres

awser-laid rope

re, therefore, is needed when handling man-
ade-fibre ropes liable to part under tension.
he traditional construction of a rope in-
lves twisting a sliver of fibres, usually right-
nded, to form a rope yarn; twisting a
mber of rope yarns in the opposite sense to
m a rope strand; and twisting a number of
ands (usually three) in the same sense as

that of the fibres to form the rope. The alternate twisting of fibres, yarns, and strands
ensures that the form of the rope is preserved.
Three-stranded right-handed rope is called
hawser-laid rope. Man-made-fibre rope is
quite often plaited, a form designed to prevent twists, reduce kinkage, and to prevent
accidents should such a rope part when under
tension.

Fibre rope is usually supplied in coils. When
breaking out a new coil, and indeed when
handling rope at all times, care is necessary to
avoid forcing out kinks such that the rope
may become permanently distorted and
weakened. The best method is to sling the coil
clear of the deck or ground on a swivel and to
uncoil from the outer end of the rope. Any
leads through which a rope may pass should
be smooth and the angle of lead, that is the
angle between the standing and hauling parts
of the rope, should be as near 180° as possible.
If the angle of lead is less than about 50° a
bad nip results and this may distort and
weaken the rope permanently. If practicable
the part of a stressed rope lying in a fairlead
should be parcelled with burlap or similar
material, to prevent damage from chafing.
When a rope is rove through a sheave it is
important that the sheave is sufficiently large
to ensure that the rope is not unduly distorted. A good practical rule is to use a sheave at
least nine times the diameter of the rope rove
through it; for example, a rope of 1-in
(25 mm) diameter should not be used in a
sheave of less than 9 in (229 mm) in diameter.

All ropes should be protected from saltwater
and dust. Crystals of salt or particles of grit
lodged between the fibres of a rope may cause
damage by abrasion when the rope is subsequently under stress. Dampness and heat
are damaging to natural-fibre ropes so that
rope lockers should be well ventilated, and
such ropes should be dry before stowing for a
long period. Ropes of man-made fibre do not
deteriorate through dampness and they are
not affected by mildew as are natural-fibre
ropes. Neither do they absorb moisture or lose
their strength. They can, however, harden
and become brittle through prolonged ex-
posure to sunlight.

A rope should always be coiled in the same
direction as that in which the strands are laid.
A right-handed rope (in which the lay runs
from right to left, when held vertically)
should, therefore, be coiled clockwise when
looking down on the coil. When coiling a
rope that is secured to a cleat or bitts, the coil
should be started from the part of the rope
secured in order to prevent kinks forming.

The tension in a rope at the point of parting
is known as the breaking stress. This depends
upon the size, material, and condition of the
rope. For example, in manila rope the breaking stress B, in tonnes, is given by the formula:

$$B = \frac{2D^2}{300}$$

where D is the diameter of the rope in milli-
metres.

The British Standards Institution recom-
mends a factor of safety of not less than 6
when using new natural-fibre ropes for lifting
purposes. The factor of safety is the ratio
between the breaking stress and the safe
working load. Using this recommendation a
manila rope of diameter 20 mm (the breaking
stress of which is taken as 2 tonnes) should not
be used to lift a weight exceeding one-third of
a tonne. Nylon and polyester ropes can be
used to 90 per cent of their breaking stress,
although this should not be repeated too
often, especially where a splice is involved.
Knotting has a marked effect on the strength
of a synthetic-fibre ropes – a bowline, for
example, can reduce the strength by as much
as 40 per cent. The comparative strengths of
similar ropes made of various synthetic and
natural fibres are given in Table I. Synthetic
fibre ropes, because of their strength and
durability, have almost entirely replaced
those made of natural fibres in yachts for
running rigging and warps. Table II illustrates the reduction in rope strength due to
wetting; the strengths of a range of synthetic-
fibre ropes are listed in Table III (pp.198–9).

*Table I: Comparative strengths (kg) of 3-stranded,
24-mm diameter ropes*

Nylon	12 000
Polyester (high-tension)	9 140
Polypropylene	7 600
Manila	4 570
Hemp	4 277
Sisal	4 060

*Table II: Dry and wet impact strengths of 10-mm
diameter cordage*

MATERIAL	WEIGHT (kg)	
	DRY	WET
Nylon	223	182
Hemp	73	55
Sisal	55	36
Manila	50	32

Rope is often vitally important to safety; it is
also an expensive item of equipment, and it
should be used intelligently. Rope should be
examined frequently to ensure that there are
no abrasions: it is unwise to take undue risk
with faulty cordage. The end of a rope should
be prevented from unlaying by means of a
whipping, or, with synthetics, heat-sealing. A

195

77

If ever you have to cut a Lime – not for logs, since Lime wood smells rather unpleasant in the fire – it ought to be worth experimenting with the fibre of the inner bark, which is 'white, moyst, and tough, serving very well for ropes, trases, and halters' (Gerard). Ropes of lime bark used to be woven in Devon and Cornwall and in Lincolnshire (125).

A small plant may have a hundred local names. Since trees give timber, and timber is sold and is an essential of life, the names of one species do not vary a great deal. Turner, in the second part of his *Herbal* (1562), wrote of the 'Lind tre'. Lyte called it Linden or Linden tree. 'Line' was common in the sixteenth century. 'Lin' survived in Yorkshire, 'Line' in Lincolnshire, 'Lind' in Scotland. 'Whitewood' has been recorded in Worcestershire and 'Pry' was an old Essex name. Linnaeus – Carl Linné – owed his family name, very aptly for a botanist, to the tall Lime, or Linden, which guarded the family home.

XXII. Malvaceae

1. Musk Mallow. *Malva moschata* L.   92, H 34

Thrusting its pink flowers (sometimes they are white) and its delicately cut leaves out of the grass along a road, the Musk Mallow is among the prettiest of all English plants – pretty as *Sidalcea* – and it does well, and looks well, in gardens. Musky it is. You do not notice the smell out of doors, but take the flowers into a warm room, and the musk soon becomes obvious.

2. Common Mallow. *Malva sylvestris* L.   102, H 40 3. Dwarf Mallow. *Malva neglecta* Waler.   90, H 25

Local names. BILLY BUTTONS, Som; BREAD AND CHEESE, Dor, Som; BREAD AND CHEESE AND CIDER, Som; BUTTER AND CHEESE, Dev, Som; CHEESE-CAKE FLOWERS, Yks; CHEESE FLOWER, Som, Wilts, Suss; CHUCKY CHEESE, Som; CUSTARD CHEESES, Lincs; FAIRY CHEESES, Som, Yks; FLIBBERTY GIBBET, Som; FRENCH MALLOW, Corn; GOOD NIGHT AT NOON, Som; HORSE BUTTON, Donegal; LADY'S CHEESE, Dor; LOAVES OF BREAD, Dor, Som.

MALLACE, Dev, Som, Hants, I o W, Bucks; MALLOW-HOCK, Som; MARSH-MALLICE (by confusion with the name of *Althaea officinalis*), Dev, Som, Shrop, Lakes, N'thum; MAWS, Notts, N'thum, Scot; OLD MAN'S BREAD AND CHEESE, Som; PANCAKE PLANT, Som, Lincs; RAGS AND TATTERS, Dor, Som; ROUND DOCK, Som; TRUCKLES OF CHEESE, Som.

108

These two Mallows are very much a species of waste and wayside; but rather than the gay flowers, it was the disk of nutlets which caught the fancy, the 'knap or round button, like unto a flat cake' (Gerard), and like a cheese. Children still eat these disks or 'cheeses', as they are known from Cornwall to the Border (cf. the name *fromages* in France). Crisp and slimy, they taste not unlike monkey-nuts.

Like the Marsh Mallow and the Tree Mallow, the Common Mallow is

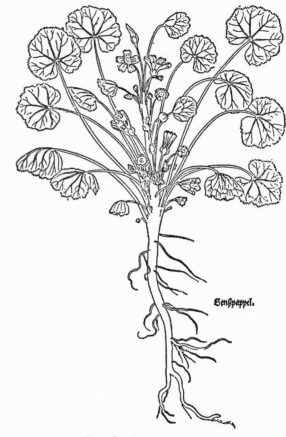

15 Dwarf Mallow *Malva sylvestris*

109

28

An Englishman's Flora
Geoffrey Grigson
Paladin 1975
196mm deep

28

The presentation of complex information requires close attention to detail. It receives it here. Plant groups are effectively displayed, in bold, without dominating the page. Standard English names, generic names in Latin, and the formula indicating its distribution (not *height*, as the uninitiated might assume) are followed by a list, often very long, of local names. The use of roman, italic, or small caps, sorts all this out admirably.

The small caps used for local names are not letterspaced. This is wise, as such treatment in what is effectively continuous text can make the type look thin and spidery.

The book is illustrated throughout by woodcuts from various sixteenth-century herbals. There is a pleasing relationship between these and the text, even though this is entirely twentieth-century in treatment.

small leaves $\frac{1}{4}$ inch long; the pale pink flowers have a funnel-shaped corolla. Bog Pimpernel inhabits damp peaty places, and wet, mossy banks and bogs, especially in western England, Wales and Ireland. The third species is *A. foemina* Mill. a blue-flowered Pimpernel difficult to distinguish from some colour forms of *A. arvensis.*

Glaux maritima L. (Sea Milkwort) another small, creeping herb, has succulent, overlapping leaves and sessile, pinkish flowers less than $\frac{1}{4}$ inch across; the flowers have no corolla, and the coloured calyx bears rounded lobes. The species is restricted to salt-marshes, sea-cliffs and muddy places near tidal estuaries. Another maritime member of the family is *Samolus valerandi* L. (Brookweed), locally frequent in wet, sandy or marshy ground; it is an erect herb, 2–12 inches high, with rosettes of obovate leaves, and flowering stems bearing alternate leaves and racemes of minute, white flowers.

———

Gentianaceae The Gentian Family

A cosmopolitan family of herbs usually with opposite, undivided, sessile leaves, and 4- or 5-merous flowers. The lobes of the persistent corolla are twisted around one another in bud, and the stamens are inserted in the corolla-tube; the pistil is solitary with a simple or divided stigma. The capsule splits longitudinally at maturity dispersing numerous small seeds. *Gentianaceae* contains many species grouped into more than 60 genera, 5 of which occur in the British Isles.

Centaurium minus *Moench* (fig. 123)   COMMON CENTAURY

An annual herb with a rosette of obovate or oblanceolate leaves, $\frac{1}{2}$–2 inches long and prominently 3- to 7-nerved from the base. One or more, erect, leafy flowering stems, 1–18 inches high, and branched in the upper part, arise from the rosette. The flowers are almost sessile and arranged in dense, repeatedly forked cymes; the narrow, cylindrical, pink corolla-tube, about $\frac{1}{4}$ inch long, is produced into 5 spreading lobes, and the stamens are inserted near the mouth of the tube. The capsule is longer than the deeply divided calyx.

Common Centaury is frequent in most areas of Britain, on sand-dunes, and in dry or damp, grassy places and open woods, especially on chalky soils; it is widely distributed in Europe and the Mediterranean region. *C. pulchellum* (Sw.) Druce, frequent in some coastal districts of southern England and Ireland, but rather rare in non-maritime areas, is usually a smaller plant than *C. minus*, bearing stem leaves only, and small, bright pink, star-like flowers on short pedicels. The genus *Centaurium* is also represented in Britain by 4 rare, coastal species.

Blackstonia perfoliata (L.) Huds. (Yellow-wort), locally frequent in southern England, on chalk downs and on banks near the sea, may be found growing with *Centaurium minus*; it extends to northern Eng-

Fig. 123. COMMON CENTAURY
(*Centaurium minus*).

land and southern Ireland. Yellow-wort is a greyish-green herb 6–18 inches high, producing opposite leaves, united around the stem (perfoliate), and 6- to 8-merous flowers about $\frac{1}{2}$ inch in diameter with bright yellow petals shortly joined at the base.

Gentianella campestris *L.* (fig. 124)   FIELD GENTIAN

A slender biennial herb with leafy flowering stems 1–10 inches high, branched in the upper part; the broadly lanceolate leaves are about 1 inch long, and the terminal and axillary, 4-merous flowers are borne on pedicels up to $1\frac{1}{2}$ inches long. The deeply divided calyx consists of 2 broad, outer lobes overlapping 2 narrow, pointed, inner lobes; the pale bluish-mauve corolla, about $\frac{2}{3}$ inch in diameter, has a cylindrical tube $\frac{1}{2}$–1 inch long, and 4 spreading lobes each with a conspicuous, basal fringe of hairs. The narrow capsule terminates in 2 persistent stigmas.

29

British Wild Flowers
Patricia Lewis
Eyre and Spottiswood 1958
(The Kew Series)
185mm deep

29

The innumerable approaches to plant identification indicate the complexity of the subject. The introduction to this book states: 'In addition to strictly scientific works [comprehensive in content and austere in style], there is an almost unlimited variety of popular guides to British plants, usually designed to avoid the difficulties of botanical terminology … The present work might fairly claim to be a compromise between these two types.'

It certainly avoids any taint of popularism in its approach, although the writing is clear, accessible and – so far as is possible with this subject – jargon-free.

The typography has a simplicity similar to that of the previous example. Text is compact and decently set, with well-thought-out headings which order the different information in a straightforward way without fuss or gimmickry. Well printed on a smooth off-white cartridge, with a good format that is pleasant to

handle, attractive cleanly-drawn line illustrations and fifteen extremely elegant paintings in well-printed colour, this is a very pleasing production.

There is a positive attempt to help the reader in the arrangement of the *Key to Genera* (see overleaf). Some preliminary device – whatever form it takes – is the essential means of entry into such books. Here, its treatment is sensible and logical, if a little unimaginative.

F. LEAVES ALTERNATE OR SPIRALLY ARRANGED, SIMPLE

Stems climbing or twining:
  Flowers conspicuous, white or coloured:
    Flowers funnel-shaped, solitary, white or pink:
      Calyx hidden by large, conspicuous bracts   **Calystegia** p. 268

      Calyx not hidden by conspicuous bracts   **Convolvulus** p. 267

    Flowers not funnel-shaped, in branched clusters, usually mauve or purplish   **Solanum** p. 269

  Flowers inconspicuous, greenish:
    Stipules inconspicuous or absent; fruit a scarlet berry **Tamus** p. 326
    Stipules conspicuous, membranous; fruit a dark brown nutlet   **Polygonum** p. 307

Stems not climbing or twining:
  Flowers forming a capitulum (Daisy and Thistle Family):
    Flowers with all or some of the florets blue or purple:
      Flowers uniformly bright blue; stems exuding latex when broken   **Cichorium** p. 242

      Flowers not uniformly bright blue; stems not exuding latex:
        Leaves very broad, heart-shaped or kidney-shaped; involucre with hooked bracts   **Arctium** p. 236

        Leaves not very broad:
          Leaves with prickly margins   **Cirsium** p. 238

          Leaves without prickly margins:
            Leaves thick, fleshy; salt-marsh plants   **Aster** p. 220

            Leaves not thick or fleshy; plant of dry ground   **Erigeron** p. 221

    Flowers without blue or purple florets:
      Leaves thick, fleshy; flowers golden-yellow   **Inula** p. 223

      Leaves not thick or fleshy:
        Central florets ('disk'-florets) tubular:
          Flowers yellow, yellowish or brown:
            Flowers bright yellow; ray-florets conspicuous:
              Flower-heads in dense panicles or clusters   **Solidago** p. 218

              Flower-heads in loose, open panicles or solitary:
                Leaves and stems grey-hairy; ray-florets narrow; achenes crowned with a hairy pappus   **Pulicaria** p. 223

                Leaves and stems glabrous; ray-florets broad; achenes without a pappus   **Chrysanthemum** p. 226

          Flowers dull yellow or brownish; ray-florets inconspicuous or absent:
            Leaves grey-woolly or grey-hairy:
              Flowers in small, rounded clusters; margin of the receptacle scaly   **Filago** p. 221

              Flowers not in rounded clusters, usually in spikes or irregular clusters; margin of receptacle not scaly   **Gnaphalium** p. 222

            Leaves green, not grey-woolly or hairy:
              A tall perennial; flowers more than $\frac{1}{4}$ inch diam.   **Inula** p. 223

              A short annual; flowers less than $\frac{1}{4}$ inch diam.   **Senecio** p. 233

          Flowers all white or pink, or with white ray-florets:
            Leaves whitish-felted below; flowers dry, chaffy   **Antennaria** p. 222

            Leaves not whitish-felted below; flowers not chaffy:
              Flower-heads numerous, forming corymbs or flattish clusters; individual flower-heads about $\frac{1}{4}$ inch diam.   **Achillea** p. 223

              Flower-heads solitary or few, not forming clusters; individual flower-heads 1 inch or more diam.   **Chrysanthemum** p. 226

Florets all ligulate (all 'ray'-florets), yellow or yellowish:
  Achenes without a hairy pappus   **Lapsana** p. 242

  Achenes with a hairy pappus:
    Leaves sessile, narrowly lanceolate, tapering upwards from base; stems and leaves glabrous **Tragopogon** p. 246

    Leaves not as above:
      Stems hollow; leaves glabrous or with bristly margins and veins   **Sonchus** p. 248

First Key

For meaning of terms see pages 6 to 12.
For abbreviations see page 13.

Part/page

Non-flowering plants

A/17

which reproduce by spores
(minute non-sexual bodies)

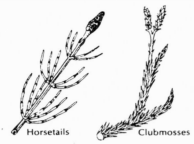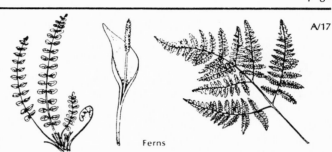

Horsetails　　Clubmosses　　Ferns

Flowering plants and conifers　herbs, shrubs, trees

Plants w. woody stems
(trees, shrubs and undershrubs)

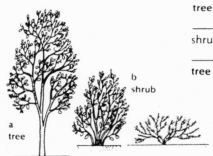

a
tree

b
shrub

c
undershrub

	Part/page
tree w. a trunk [a], in leaf	B/18
shrub, undershrub, or woody climber, [b, c], in leaf	C/21
tree or shrub [a, b, c] with fls. appearing before lvs.	D/26

▼

30
A New Key to Wild Flowers
John Hayward
Cambridge University Press
1987, revised edition 1995
218mm (longest dimension)

30
Very different in approach from the previous example, this programmatic arrangement is intended for 'all who like to know the names of flowers but who are discouraged by more sophisticated, wordy floras'. The logical, step-by-step sequence needs some dedication to digest, and involves searching the *First Key* for the relevant page number of the *Key to Families*, a search of which gives the correct page number of the *Key to Species*. This austere book (no colour illustrations, and moreover set in clear but typographically colourless Optima) seems a little daunting at first, but claims to be reader-friendly. Regular use might show it to be so. Prior to publication it was thoroughly tested in the field by a wide range of users, through the Aidgap organisation (Aids to Identification in Difficult Groups of Animals and Plants).

Amongst the usual apparatus of abbreviations, glossaries, parts of a plant and so on, a *How to Use* section requires fairly intense study. There is a certain ruthlessness in its demands. '(2) The statements in each column *must be read in strict order from the top*. The key will not work otherwise. (3) Some large families have been split into sections. The key to sections *must also be taken in order*.'

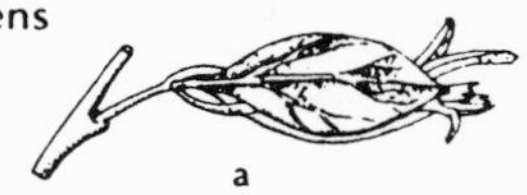 8 stamens	usu. over 50 cm high; petals 4	fls. 2–3 cm, only slightly zygomorphic	ONAGRACEAE	120
a	small, dainty plant w. simple lvs.	fls. under 1 cm [a]	POLYGALACEAE	85
Stamens more than 12, easily seen	petals small, lobed, white or yellow		RESEDACEAE	83
	petals few and large		RANUNCULACEAE	68
Stamens 10, lying within keel of lower petal	calyx w. 5 teeth; fl. of Pea type		FABACEAE	103

Part M Land plants with actinomorphic (radially symmetrical) flowers and a single perianth, i.e. either sepals or petals but not both

Fls. in umbels	petals & stamens 5		APIACEAE	125
	petals & stamens 6	plant smells of onion	LILACEAE	202
Stamens 3 or 0	corolla 5-lobed	tiny compact Scottish plant; fls. green	CARYOPHYLLACEAE	87
		style long, 3-lobed, fls. pink to lilac	VALERIANACEAE	177
	stem twining w. cordate lvs. 	fls. greenish yellow	DIOSCOREACEAE	210
	lvs. linear, over 10 cm 	fls. yellow, orange, blue, or purple	IRIDACEAE	210
Stamens 6	sepals 4; petals 0		BRASSICACEAE	75

▼

45

30 *A New Key to Wild Flowers*

This book shows that publishers today can sometimes be quite open-minded in their approach to bookmaking. This one even has a spiral (Wire-O) binding to facilitate use in the field – a device, no matter how practical, which is usually anathema to publishers.

RANUNCULACEAE Buttercup family

Plants with a variety of form and colour. The flowers have more than 12 stamens (except *Myosurus*) and the fruit is often composed of a number of distinct parts.
Sepals and/or petals are often in 5's.

Leaves are alternate (except *Clematis*), often lobed, and do not bear stipules.
Similar-looking flowers (i.e. with many stamens) may belong to the
Rose family – on p. 110
St John's Wort family – on p. 85.

Woody climber w. creamy flowers	only 4 sepals (which look like petals)	lvs. opposite, pinnate, lflets. well spaced	*Clematis vitalba* Traveller's-joy
Ea. fl. w. 5 tubular petals & 5 spurs			*Aquilegia vulgaris* Columbine
Fls. scarlet; lvs. finely dissected	calcareous soil		*Adonis annua** Pheasant's-eye
Fls. blue/violet/purple	fls. zygomorphic w. large hood	S.W. (except for introductions)	*Aconitum napellus** Monk's-hood
	perianth w. 6 segments	in calcareous turf	*Pulsatilla vulgaris** Pasqueflower
Lvs. linear in a rosette	petals up to 5 mm, greenish yellow; fr. spike up to 7 cm	up to 12 cm tall; may look like a Plantain	*Myosurus minimus* Mousetail
Stamens longer than the 4 sepals; lvs. twice or more pinnate	up to 15 cm tall; fls. in simple loose spike	mts. in N.	*Thalictrum alpinum* Alpine Meadow-rue
	stamens mostly erect		*Thalictrum flavum* Common Meadow-rue
	stamens drooping		*Thalictrum minus* Lesser Meadow-rue

▼

31

Wild Flowers of the Mediterranean
David Burnie
Dorling Kindersley 1995
(Eyewitness Handbooks)
209mm deep

31

This is certainly a prettier and more appealing handbook than the previous example. Very clear colour photographs (by Derek Hall), augmented by small colour illustrations of the complete plant *in situ*, make an attractive page (see overleaf). The photographs are annotated to indicate key features. Distribution, habitat, related species, growth habit, height and flowering time are clearly set out. The concise text amplifies the description.

The mainly visual preliminary identification key is self-explanatory and immediately comprehensible. The explanation of how to use the book is followed by equally accessible sections on life cycles, plant structures, growth habits, leaf and flower types, flower forms, fruits and seeds, and habitats. Although designed for the popular market, its comprehensiveness as a pocket guide would seem difficult to fault at any level. Only the slightly fussy headings, characteristic of this publisher, seem, to my mind, at odds with the clear-minded analysis seen elsewhere. The 1958 guide [29], typically for its period, uses straightforward bold, roman and italic upper and lower case, and slightly letterspaced small caps. Such headings are clearer, more attractive and more co-ordinated with the text than the jumpy capitalised headings with larger initials used here. These add no typographic colour, and merely detract from the images.

Developments in printing technology, as well as photographic materials, have made a decisive contribution to books of this kind. Without refined definition of photographic images, the use of a computer screen for design and page make-up, offset printing and international publishing, a production of this kind would have been well-nigh impossible – certainly at a popular price – forty years ago.

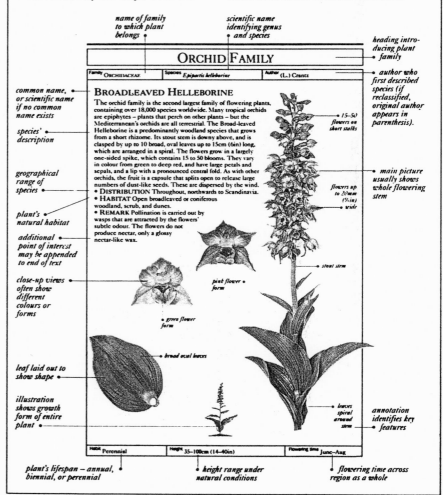

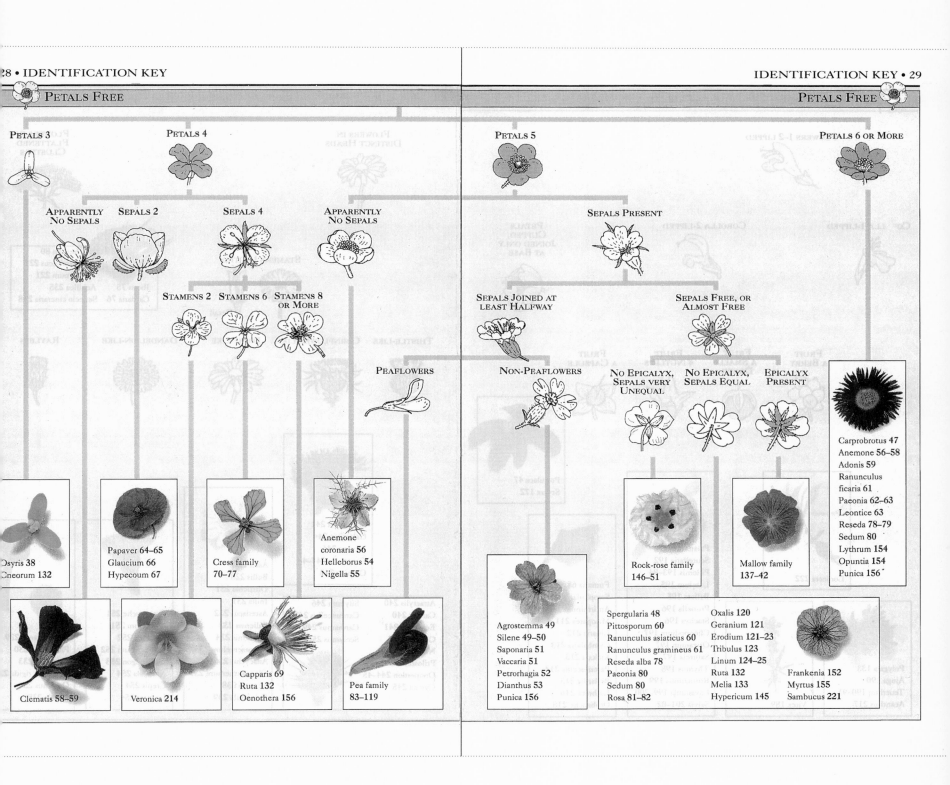

PETALS FREE

PETALS FREE

PETALS 3

PETALS 4

PETALS 5

PETALS 6 OR MORE

APPARENTLY NO SEPALS

SEPALS 2

SEPALS 4

APPARENTLY NO SEPALS

SEPALS PRESENT

STAMENS 2 STAMENS 6 STAMENS 8 OR MORE

SEPALS JOINED AT LEAST HALFWAY

SEPALS FREE, OR ALMOST FREE

PEAFLOWERS

NON-PEAFLOWERS

NO EPICALYX, SEPALS VERY UNEQUAL

NO EPICALYX, SEPALS EQUAL

EPICALYX PRESENT

Carprobrotus 47
Anemone 56–58
Adonis 59
Ranunculus ficaria 61
Paeonia 62–63
Leontice 63
Reseda 78–79
Sedum 80
Lythrum 154
Opuntia 154
Punica 156

Osyris 38
Cneorum 132

Papaver 64–65
Glaucium 66
Hypecoum 67

Cress family 70–77

Anemone coronaria 56
Helleborus 54
Nigella 55

Rock-rose family 146–51

Mallow family 137–42

Clematis 58–59

Veronica 214

Capparis 69
Ruta 132
Oenothera 156

Pea family 83–119

Agrostemma 49
Silene 49–50
Saponaria 51
Vaccaria 51
Petrorhagia 52
Dianthus 53
Punica 156

Spergularia 48
Pittosporum 60
Ranunculus asiaticus 60
Ranunculus gramineus 61
Reseda alba 78
Paeonia 80
Sedum 80
Rosa 81–82

Oxalis 120
Geranium 121
Erodium 121–23
Tribulus 123
Linum 124–25
Ruta 132
Melia 133
Hypericum 145

Frankenia 152
Myrtus 155
Sambucus 221

PEONY FAMILY

Family PAEONIACEAE	Species *Paeonia mascula*	Author (L.) Miller

PAEONIA MASCULA

Peonies are mound-forming herbaceous perennials, with large leaves and flamboyant flowers. Of the dozen or so species found in the Mediterranean, *Paeonia mascula* is one of the more widespread. It grows from swollen underground stems, and its leaves are twice divided into 9 to 16 broad leaflets. The leaves are dark green and hairless above, and hairless or hairy beneath. The flowers are up to 14cm (5½in) across, with spreading red petals, yellow anthers, and 5 sepals. The numerous stamens surround a cluster of 3 to 5 downy follicles, which split open when ripe to release large blackish seeds.
• **DISTRIBUTION** C. Mediterranean, including Algeria; also in parts of C. Europe, and naturalized on Steepholm, an island in the Bristol Channel.
• **HABITAT** Grassy and bushy places, meadows; frequently cultivated.
• **REMARK** Peonies have a long history of medicinal use, although in Europe they are now grown only for ornament. Many species have suffered from over-collection.

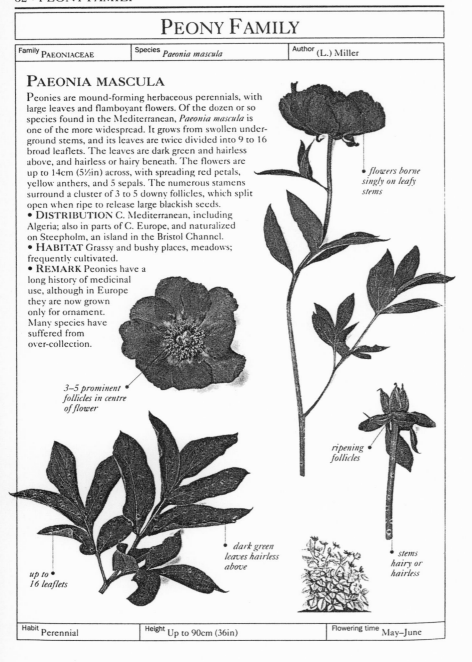

flowers borne singly on leafy stems

3–5 prominent follicles in centre of flower

ripening follicles

dark green leaves hairless above

up to 16 leaflets

stems hairy or hairless

Habit Perennial	Height Up to 90cm (36in)	Flowering time May–June

Family PAEONIACEAE	Species *Paeonia officinalis*	Author L.

COMMON PEONY

Often shorter than *Paeonia mascula* (opposite), this species has 17 to 30 narrower leaflets, which are themselves sometimes partly divided. The leaves are green and hairless above, and hairy beneath. The red flowers, up to 12cm (4¾in) across, have spreading rather than cupped petals. Each flower has a cluster of red-stalked stamens surrounding 2 or 3 hairy follicles. The follicles contain several large seeds, and split when ripe.
• **DISTRIBUTION** W. and C. Mediterranean.
• **HABITAT** Grassy scrub, meadows; frequently cultivated as a single- and double-flowered form.
• **RELATED SPECIES** Most Mediterranean peonies have reddish flowers, but in 2 eastern species the flowers are white. These are *P. rhodia*, found only on Rhodes, and *P. clusii*, found only on Crete and Karpathos.

ring of stamens surrounding central carpels

up to 30 leaflets

stems bear single flowers

Habit Perennial	Height Up to 50cm (20in)	Flowering time May–June

BARBERRY FAMILY

Family BERBERIDACEAE	Species *Leontice leontopetalum*	Author L.

LEONTICE

This curious-looking plant, with its pyramid-shaped flower-heads, grows from a tuber and has hairless, bluish green stems and leaves. The leaves, up to about 15cm (6in) across, are divided into threes, either 2 or 3 times. The flowers, up to 15mm (⅗in) across, produce oval, bladder-like fruit.
• **DISTRIBUTION** N. Africa, Greece, Turkey.
• **HABITAT** Olive groves, fields, particularly those that are regularly ploughed.
• **RELATED SPECIES** *Bongardia chrysopogon* has open clusters of fewer flowers.

6–8 bright yellow petal.

flowers clustered in pyramid

broad-lobed leaves

bluish green leaves

leaves divided 2 or 3 times

waxy, hairless stems

Habit Perennial	Height 30–50cm (12–20in)	Flowering time Feb–Apr

the result that the dome is felt as slightly oppressive and some of the other parts (e.g. the diagonal corner chapels) as somewhat dwarfed.

Altomünster, 1763–6 (15 m. E. of Augsburg, 12 m. N.W. of Dachau; from both, as also from Munich, rail and bus connections). Abbey church (Benedictine foundation eighth century for monks and nuns: since 1485 Brigittine). The last of Fischer's churches, he died before its completion. A type of wall-pillar church of complicated design; to a large octagonal nave are added three eastward sections—a 2-storey section quadrilateral on plan, an apsidal choir and (above and behind) a second choir. The Brigittines being a double Order of monks and nuns, the problem was to construct a church in which three groups (monks, nuns, and lay brothers) could take part in the services unseen, and so undisturbed, by one another; to which had to be added and accommodated the lay folk. Fischer's solution produced, not an oddity as might be thought, but an interior which combines certain well-known features of his churches with other surprising and beautiful vistas.

Noteworthy features. Exterior: The tower and its helm are very shapely. The greatly extended E. limb should be noted. *Interior:* (1) The arrangement to meet the accommodation needs can be clearly made out. We enter the main octagon (with two tiers of galleries), immediately E. of which is the 2-storey section with lay-brothers' choir below and nuns' choir above, then the apsidal sanctuary, then (above and behind the high altar, now used as the parish altar) the monks' choir with stalls and altar. The whole lay-out of the greatest interest as an attempt to meet unusual monastic requirements in a way satisfactory both practically and aesthetically. (2) The decoration is of varying quality. The delicate and restrained stucco work by *Jakob Rauch* (1773), the frescoes by *Josef Mages* (1768), especially fine in the drawing and colouring, that in the nave saucer dome depicting scenes, actual and legendary, from the history of the Order; the two chief altars by *J. B. Straub*, late and fanciful but good.

Other churches of J. M. Fischer

Altomünster was Fischer's last great work; he died, as we have seen, while it was being completed. Of his other, lesser but always interesting and beautiful churches, attention is directed to the following. The first four all show variations of the central octagon theme of which we have spoken and which found its perfect expression at *Rott-am-Inn*.

Rinchnach, 1727–9 (12 m. N.E. Deggendorf, on the Regen-Passau road). The nave is a new construction; choir and tower were taken over from the fifteenth-century church and baroquized. Fine stucco work (artist unknown) and frescoes by *Andreas Heindl*.

Unering, 1731 (4 m. N.W. Starnberg on isolated hill) with interior of great charm; good harmonious contemporary furnishings and nave fresco.

Aufhausen, 1736–51 (12 m. S.E. Regensburg, 16 m. S.W. Straubing). One of Fischer's strongest interiors, its appeal predominantly architectural. Here (as at the contemporary *Ingolstadt Franziskanerkirche* before its total destruction by bombs) the narrow sides of the octagon are pierced by arches at ground and at gallery level so that the diagonal axes thrust through to the outer walls, as later at *Rott*.

Bichl, 1751–3 (just N. *Benediktbeuern*) with frescoes by *J. J. Zeiller*, and high altar with a notable group of St George and the Dragon by *J. B. Straub*. Side altars 1709. No stucco.

Dominikus Zimmermann

In *Dominikus Zimmermann* we have a figure who differs in certain important ways from *J. M. Fischer*. Fischer was an architect pure and simple and his churches were decorated by a variety of artists. Zimmermann, having been trained and achieved distinction as stucco artist and designer of altars as well as architect, united in his own person the practice of several arts. Again, he worked in frequent co-operation with his brother, the painter *Johann Baptist Zimmermann*, who contributed the frescoes to all

32

Baroque Churches of Central Europe
John Bourke
Faber and Faber 1962 (2nd edition)
198mm deep

32

The aim of guides to plants is 'how to identify'. Guides to architecture or places usually describe 'what to look for'. Both types of guides, however, can be regarded as aids to enjoyment.

Charles Jencks once described a deeply academic book on baroque churches as telling you all you want to know about them except how marvellous they are. *This book tells you all you need to know, and* how marvellous they are. Less exhausting than Pevsner, clear and orderly thinking by the author has resulted in the information being presented in a concise and easily-absorbed manner for on-the-spot use. Good writing has been matched with sympathetic design. Set in appropriate airy Walbaum, its appearance is in perfect harmony with these amazing buildings. The designer – presumably Berthold Wolpe – has set out the various levels of headings clearly, and the beautiful lining figures of Walbaum, set within brackets, are just strong enough to allow the author's points to be picked out at a glance without resorting to a jumpy bold.

33 and 34

Guide books present one of the major challenges in information typography. The mother and father of today's guides is Baedeker, seen here in the 1890 edition of Great Britain. Its closest relation today is the Blue Guide, which sometimes follows it astonishingly closely, even in wording (a minor instance can be seen in the opening phrases of the Scarborough descriptions). It is also revealing to compare the degree of detail given in descriptions of the same site, here, for instance, Castle Howard, which shows how tastes have altered in the intervening hundred years.

Allowing for the change of assumption from railway to road travel, the general arrangement of the two guides is remarkably similar. Baedeker mentions hotels ('well spoken of'), boarding houses and lodgings, while Blue Guide, in this faster-changing world, sends you off to the Tourist Information Centre. But both pick out practical information (car parks, railway stations) in bold at the beginning of the descriptions. Both give the population of larger towns. Both set historical notes and sites of lesser importance in a smaller type, use bold or italic freely to

---

418

51. From Carlisle to Newcastle.

66 M. RAILWAY in 2¼-2¾ hrs. (fares 8s. 1d., 6s. 9d., 5s.).

Carlisle, see p. 375. — 5 M. *Wetheral*, in the valley of the *Eden*, with a ruined priory. Opposite (bridge ½d.; ferry 1d.) is *Corby Hall*, a modernized baronial mansion, containing a fine art-collection. The beautiful walks in *Corby Woods*, praised by David Hume, are open to visitors on Wed. — 15½ M. *Naworth* (Inn).

°*Naworth Castle*, the fine baronial residence of the Howards, about ½ M. to the N., most intimately associated with the name of 'Belted Will Howard', Lord Warden of the Marches in the first half of the 17th cent., who is described in Scott's 'Lay of the Last Minstrel'. The castle contains ancient armour, tapestry, and portraits (visitors usually admitted, 10-1 or 2-5). — About 1 M. to the N. of Naworth Castle are the picturesque ruins of *Lanercost Priory*, an Augustine foundation of the 12th century. The nave of the priory-church has been restored, and is used as the parish-church.

20½ M. *Gilsland* (Station Inn, plain), or *Rosehill*, is the station for **Gilsland Spa** (*Shaws Hotel*, 'pens'. 4s.-8s. 6d.; *Orchard House*, between the village and the Spa), pleasantly situated 1¼ M. to the N. (omn. 6d.). Its sulphur-springs and the pretty scenery attract visitors in search of a quiet watering-place. It was at Gilsland Spa that Sir Walter Scott met his future wife, Mlle. Charpentier, and he has immortalized the district in 'Guy Mannering'.

A cottage in the village is said to occupy the spot of the *Mumps Ha'*, in which Dandie Dinmont met Meg Merrilies. — In the wooded °*Valley of the Irthing*, in which the sulphur-well lies, are pointed out the 'Popping Stone', where Sir Walter Scott is said to have proposed to Miss Charpentier, and the 'Kissing Bush', where he sealed the compact!

At *Birdoswald*, 2 M. to the S.W. of the Spa, are abundant remains of a station on the *Roman Wall*, which ran across the N. of England (see p. 376). The walk may be extended to (2 M.) *Coombe Crags*. The archæologist will also find much to interest him in following the line of the Roman wall from this point eastwards to (17 M.) *Chollerford* (°George). — A four-horse coach plies frequently from the Shaws Hotel to *Lanercost Priory* (6½ M.; see above; 7½ M.), the *Northumberland Lakes* (12 M.), the Roman station at *Housesteads* (13 M.), and various other points in this interesting but comparatively unfrequented district.

26 M. *Haltwhistle* (Crown), a small town with 1500 inhab., is the junction of a line to (13 M.) *Alston* (960 ft.), on the slopes of the Pennine Hills, said to be the highest market-town in England. It lies in an extensive lead-mining district.

Featherstonehaugh, *Blenkinsop Tower*, and *Thirlwall Castle* may be visited from Haltwhistle.

31 M. *Bardon Mill* is the nearest station to the pretty little *Northumberland Lakes*, 3½ M. to the N.

35 M. *Haydon Bridge* lies 6 M. to the S. of *Housesteads*, with the most complete remains of the Roman Wall (comp. above & p. 376).

42 M. **Hexham** (*Royal; Grey Bull; Tynedale Hydropathic*), an ancient town with 6000 inhab. and see of a R. C. bishop, on the S. bank of the *Tyne*, is chiefly of interest for its fine *Abbey Church, an excellent example of E.E., dating from the 12th century.

The first church on this site was built by *St. Wilfrid* in 676, and from 680 to 821 Hexham was the seat of a bishopric, afterwards united with Lindisfarne, and now included in the see of Durham (comp. p. 411).

The nave of the present church was destroyed at the end of the 13th cent., and the Saxon *Crypt of St. Wilfrid has been discovered below its site. The *Choir is separated from the *Transept* by a carved *Rood Screen* of about 1500. The *Shrine of Prior Richard* and other monuments deserve attention. — The *Refectory* and a *Norman Gateway* are also preserved.

In 1464 the Yorkists defeated the Lancastrians in an important battle at Hexham. — Branch-lines run from Hexham to *Allendale* on the S. and to *Chollerford* (see p. 418) and *Reedsmouth* (Riccarton, Rothbury, Morpeth) on the N.

Near (45 M.) *Corbridge* are the ruins of *Dilston Castle*. The train now follows closely the course of the *Tyne*. To the left, at (52½ M.) *Prudhoe*, are the ivy-clad ruins of its castle. At (55 M.) *Wylam* George Stephenson was born in 1781, and here the first working locomotive was constructed by William Hedley in 1812. As we near Newcastle the signs of industry increase. 63 M. *Scotswood*, so named from the camp of the Scottish army in the Civil War.

66 M. *Newcastle*, see p. 415.

52. From York to Scarborough and Whitby.

NORTH EASTERN RAILWAY to (42 M.) *Scarborough* in 1-1½ hr. (fares 5s. 7d., 4s. 8d., 3s. 6d.); to (56 M.) *Whitby* in 2-2¾ hrs. (7s. 6d., 6s. 3d., 4s. 8d.).

York, see p. 406. The first stations are unimportant. Near (15 M.) *Kirkham Abbey*, with its ivy-clad ruins, we reach the *Derwent*, the pretty, well-wooded valley of which we follow nearly all the way to Scarborough. — About 3 M. to the N.W. of (16 M.) *Castle Howard* (Hotel, ¾ M. from the park) is **Castle Howard**, the palatial seat of the Earl of Carlisle, containing a beautiful chapel and a fine collection of paintings (Velazquez, Titian, Rubens, Mabuse, Carracci, Reynolds, Clouet), sculptures, bronzes, tapestry, and old glass and china. The house and the *Park are open daily.

21 M. **Malton** (*Talbot; Sun; Rail. Rfmt. Rooms*), an ancient town of 9000 inhab., with large racing-stables and an old priory, is the junction of the direct line to *Whitby* (p. 420), which runs viâ *Pickering*. Another line runs S. to *Driffield* (p. 425).

42 M. **Scarborough.** — **Hotels.** On the South Cliff: GRAND, with 300 beds; CROWN, Esplanade, above the Spa Grounds; PRINCE OF WALES; CAMBRIDGE, near the Valley Bridge, at some distance from the sea, 'pens'. 9s. — On the North Cliff (less expensive): QUEEN; ALEXANDRA, 'pens'. 10s.; ALBION, near the Castle. — In the Town: PAVILION, adjoining the station, R. & A. 3s. 6d., 'pens'. 10s. 6d.-12s.; ROYAL, corner of St. Nicholas St.; VICTORIA, 'pens'. 7s. 6d.; STATION, small. — Several of the hotels are closed in winter, and the rates of the others are lowered. — *Private Hotels* (7-10s. a day), *Boarding Houses*, and *Lodgings* abound.

Cab for 1-3 pers. 1s. per mile, 2s. 6d. per hr.; with two horses 1s. 6d. and 3s. 9d.; double fares between 11.30 p.m. and 6 a. m.; for each package carried outside 2d. — **Steamers** ply during summer to *Filey*, *Bridlington*, *Whitby*, etc. — **Boats** for 1-3 pers. 1s. 6d. per hr., each addit. pers. 6d.

Scarborough, the most popular marine resort in the N. of England, with a resident population of about 40,000, is finely situated, in the form of an amphitheatre, on slopes rising from the sea and terminated on the N. and S. by abrupt cliffs. The air is bracing and the beaches are good for bathing, but the older streets are narrow

27*

33

Baedeker's Great Britain
K Baedeker
Karl Baedeker 1890
160mm deep

34

Blue Guide: England
Ian Ousby
A & C Black/W W Norton 1989
194mm deep

highlight place names or sites, use asterisks to denote places of particular importance, give distances on the assumed route, alternative routes, and cross-refer to fuller descriptions. While the well-honed Michelin Guides, with their fine maps, are for sightseers, Baedeker and Blue Guide are for the serious tourist.

Typographically, the Blue Guides are considerably clearer than Baedeker, even in the format shown here. I find this narrow chunky volume very pleasant to handle and carry around, but the type *is a little small*; later volumes, recognising this, are of slightly wider format and have slightly larger type. The use of an egyptian is unexpected, but successful. Baedekers were set in an economical modern, which though a pleasant type is perhaps not the most readable; clarendon was used for the bold. The Blue Guides use a little linear space between certain groups of information, secondary places of interest, diversions from the main route and so on, which is more reader-friendly than the fairly solidly-set text of Baedeker.

Each Blue Guide is written by a single author, and each thus has a personal character. Although the great Karl's name is on the title page of all his guides, a Preface states that *Great Britain* is by Mr J F Muirhead MA. Other volumes merely mention The Editor. Karl himself died in 1859. If one has ever used his guides in foreign travels, re-reading their characteristic prose is very evocative.

---

83 York to Scarborough

Total distance 41m. **York**, see Rte 81. We follow A64 throughout.
—To (17^1/$_2$m) Malton (bypassed).—To (41m) **Scarborough**.

Maps: OS Landranger 105, 100, 101.

York, see Rte 81. We leave the city by Monkgate and follow A64 across the York plain.—10^1/$_2$m. *Barton Hill* lies 1m SE of *Foston*, where Sydney Smith was rector in 1809–29.

The unclassified road going N from Barton Hill is continued by the five-mile avenue of *Castle Howard (open), the vast baroque mansion which Sir John Vanbrugh, helped by Nicholas Hawksmoor, built for Charles Howard, 3rd Earl of Carlisle.

Vanbrugh produced his first designs in 1699 and finished the main body of the house by 1712, though he was still at work on the grounds and garden buildings when he died in 1726. The fact that he came to the project apparently without architectural experience has provoked speculation about the extent of Hawksmoor's contribution. The N and S fronts and the striking central dome show the same combination of monumentality and exuberance as Blenheim Palace, the other great fruit of Vanbrugh and Hawksmoor's collaboration. The W wing, through which visitors now enter, was completed in a much more restrained Palladian style by Sir Thomas Robinson of Rokeby Park (Rte 86G) in 1753–59.

Inside, the magnificent Great Hall has an elaborate chimneypiece and a painting by Giovanni Pellegrini in the dome. The room was restored after the fire which badly damaged the S front in 1940, though the Music Room and the Tapestry Room also keep some of their original decoration. The impressive collection of pictures and furniture is shown to its best advantage in the Orleans Room, with paintings by Rubens and Domenico Feti, and the Long Gallery, added in 1800, with portraits by Holbein (Henry VIII; the 3rd Duke of Norfolk), Van Dyck, Lely and Kneller. The Chapel, altered in 1870–75, has a bas-relief by Sansovino and stained glass by Morris and Burne-Jones.

The stable block (1781–84; John Carr) to the W of the house contains the largest private collection of historic costume in Britain, with original specimens mainly from the early 18C to the present day; also costumes from the Diaghilev Russian ballet.

With its magnificent avenue, obelisks, gatehouses and lakes, the park creates a formal landscape on the grandest scale. The garden buildings include, both SE of the house, Vanbrugh's Temple of the Four Winds and Hawksmoor's *Mausoleum.

Sheriff Hutton, 4m W of Foston, has the ruins of its 14C castle. The church contains 14–15C effigies, one of them probably of Richard III's son Edward (1471–84), and the brass of two babies (1491).

11^1/$_2$m. *Whitwell-on-the-Hill* is to the left. To the right, in an attractive setting on the opposite bank of the Derwent, are the scanty but beautiful ruins of *Kirkham Priory*, an Augustinian foundation of 1122 (English Heritage, standard opening). They include the sculptured gatehouse and the exquisite *lavatorium in the cloister, both late 13C, and the Romanesque refectory doorway.—To the left of A64 further on is another turning for (3m) Castle Howard, via *Welburn*.

17^1/$_2$m. **Malton** (4100 inhab.; seasonal Tourist Information), bypassed by A64, is a market town on the Derwent, with two partly 12C churches. It stands on the site of the Roman station of *Derventio*, and the *Museum* occupying the 18C former Town Hall in the market place has a good Roman collection. Across the river is *Norton* (5900 inhab.). At *Old Malton*, 1m NE, the late Norman and EE parish church with a beautiful W front and aisleless nave is a relic of the Gilbertine priory founded c 1150.

Castle Howard, 6m SW, is reached by the sideroad which passes (3m) *Easthorpe Hall* (not open), the home of Dickens's friend Charles Smithson (d. 1844), who entertained the novelist here while he was writing 'Martin Chuzzlewit'.

A169 heads N to (7m) Pickering (Rte 84), past (4^1/$_2$m) the turning for *Flamingo Land*, a zoo and amusement park at *Kirby Misperton*, 1^1/$_2$m W.

FROM MALTON TO HELMSLEY, 15m by B1257.—4^1/$_2$m. *Barton-le-Street* has a rebuilt church with good Norman carving and (6m) *Slingsby* the ruins of a fine early 17C country house.—8m. *Hovingham*, a pleasant village, has a church with a Saxon tower, cross and sculptured stone panel which may have been part of an altar or tomb. *Hovingham Hall* (open to parties only, by appointment) is a Palladian house designed c 1750 by its owner, Sir Thomas Worsley. *Nunnington Hall* (NT), by the Rye 2^1/$_2$m N, is a 16C and late 17C manor house with a fine staircase, panelling and chimneypieces. It contains a collection of miniature rooms furnished in the style of different periods.—At (12m) *Oswaldkirk* we join Rte 84 for (15m) *Helmsley*.

From Malton to *Sledmere* and *Great Driffield*, see Rte 82B.

A64 skirts the northern escarpment of the Wolds, with the flat Vale of Pickering on our left.—Beyond (22^1/$_2$m) the attractive spire of *Rillington* church we pass, on the left, the park of *Scampston Hall* (1803; Thomas Leverton).—27^1/$_2$m. *East Heslerton* church was built in 1877 by G.E. Street for Sir Tatton Sykes of Sledmere (Rte 82B). The spire has statues of the Four Latin Fathers designed for Bristol Cathedral but rejected as un-Protestant.—There is a fine view from the Wolds escarpment above (33^1/$_2$m) *Staxton*. Shortly beyond, A1039 branches right for Filey (Rte 82B). We head N on A64 via (36^1/$_2$m) *Seamer*.

41m. **SCARBOROUGH** (41,800 inhab.), the most popular seaside resort in the North-East, is splendidly situated on two sandy bays separated by a rocky headland crowned with the ruined castle. The seafront is laid out with pleasant irregularity, and the cliffs of both bays are covered with delightful gardens.

Tourist Information Centre: St Nicholas Cliff.

Car Parks: Brook Square, Castle Rd, Eastborough, Falconers Rd, Vernon Rd. Westwood, Marine Drive and Royal Albert Drive; also Albion Rd, Esplanade and Weaponess Valley Rd in South Bay, and Burniston Rd, Friarsway and Upper and Lower Northstead in North Bay.

Coach Stations: Westwood and William St.

Bus Station: Junction of Valley Bridge Parade and Somerset Terrace.

Railway Station: Junction of Valley Bridge Rd and Westborough.

Theatres: The Spa (see below); Royal Opera House (repertory drama), St Thomas St.; Open Air Theatre, Northstead Manor; Futurist Theatre, South Bay; Library Theatre, Vernon Rd; and Theatre in the Round, Valley Bridge Parade, known for its premieres of plays by Alan Ayckbourn.

History. The headland has been the site of an Iron Age settlement, a Roman beacon, Saxon and Norman chapels, and the castle, built in a seemingly impregnable position 300ft above the sea. The fishing village developed as a spa town after the discovery of mineral springs in 1620 and as a seaside resort in the second half of the 18C—probably the first place in England where sea bathing became fashionable. Smollett's 'Humphry Clinker' (1771) and Sheridan's 'A Trip to Scarborough' (1777) testify to its early popularity.

Famous natives etc. The painter Lord Leighton (1830–96) and Dame Edith Sitwell (1887–1964) were born here and the painter Atkinson Grimshaw lived here after 1876. Anne Brontë (1820–49) died at a house on the site of the Grand Hotel and is buried in the detached churchyard of St Mary.

The main street, known as Westborough, Newborough and Eastborough, descends NE from the *Railway Station* to the old fishing harbour on **South Bay**. Nearby are the house (c 1350), now a café, where Richard III is said to have stayed and the 17C *Three Mariners Inn* (open).

To the N the broad Marine Drive sweeps round the base of the headland and continues as Royal Albert Drive to (1^1/$_2$m) the quieter **North Bay**, with

1,800 years the local people have maintained this figure against all those who, for their various reasons, would have gladly seen it fade into oblivion.

Map reference:
ST 666017 (metric map 194, 1-inch map 178)
Nearest town: Dorchester
Nearest village: Cerne Abbas
Location: Cerne Abbas village is 5½ miles (9 kilometres) north of Dorchester on the A352 road. Turn right off the main road into the village and find a convenient parking place. Walk down Abbey Street past the church, and at the end of this street take a path through the graveyard and past the ruined abbey (which will be on your left). Follow the path across a field, bearing left towards the base of the hill; then there is a steep climb uphill. The giant is on National Trust property. A good view of the whole figure can be had from the main A352 road just north of Cerne Abbas.

21

Hambledon Hill and Hod Hill hillforts, Dorset

Undoubtedly the most impressive hillfort in Dorset after Maiden Castle, **Hambledon Hill** is encircled by two sinuous ramparts which enclose an area of nearly 24½ acres (10 hectares). It is thought that the present defences were developed over a period of time, but until the site is excavated its history remains conjectural. It was certainly constructed during the Iron Age, however; and there are also the excavated remains of a Neolithic causewayed camp with two banks and ditches to the south-east of the fort. A Neolithic long barrow survived the Iron Age development of the hilltop, and can still be seen, 230 feet (70 metres) long and 6 feet (1.8 metres) high, within the fort about halfway along its length. A walk along the highest rampart round the perimeter of the defences will reveal entrances on the northern, south-western and south-eastern sides. Around 200 hollows within the fort are probably hut platforms.

A short distance to the south of Hambledon Hill is another, smaller, hillfort on **Hod Hill**. This was conquered by the Romans, who built their own fort in the north-west corner. They occupied this during the years AD 43–51.

Left *The hillfort on Hambledon Hill. The long barrow can be seen in the narrowest part of the fort.*

Map references:
Hambledon Hill
ST 845126 (metric map 194, 1-inch map 178)
Hod Hill
ST 857108 (metric map 194, 1-inch map 178)
Nearest town: Blandford Forum
Nearest villages: Child Okeford and Shroton
Location: Hambledon Hill lies to the west of the A350 road, around 5 miles (8 kilometres) to the north-west of Blandford Forum, and between the villages of Child Okeford and Shroton. There are several footpaths into the fort: 1. From Shroton Lines (where you can park on the grass verge by the gate into a field); 2. From a lane north-east of Child Okeford, which joins path 1 (see sketch map); 3. From a lane south-east of Child Okeford (with parking in a nearby layby – not at the lane end, else you risk having your vehicle towed away by tractor); 4. From Shroton village.

Hod Hill is approached by footpaths:
1. From the A350 road near Stepleton House;
2. From Stourpaine village.

35

A Guide to Ancient Sites in Britain
Janet and Colin Bord
Latimer 1978
196mm deep

35

This is a practical guide book for in-the-field use, while also providing information and entertainment for the armchair traveller. Here, contained within a strong grid, are site descriptions, with plans where helpful, maps, map references, and directions for finding these often remotely-situated places. This subject is too often spoilt by poor illustrations of these difficult-to-photograph subjects, and crude maps. These photographs are unusually successful in being both informative and appealing, and the maps are clear and attractively drawn. The orderly design (by Gerald Cinamon) is a considerable bonus.

96

Temple Wood stone circle, Argyll (Strathclyde Region)

Thirteen stones remain out of an original twenty in this circle of 40-foot (12 metres) diameter, and spiral carvings can be seen at the base of one of the northern stones. Inside the circle is a stone burial cist, and this indicates that the stone circle was probably a kerb surrounding a large cairn.

Right The cist inside the circle.
Below The stone with spiral carvings at its base.
Bottom right An overall view of the circle.

Map reference:
NR 827978 (metric map 55, 1-inch map 52)
Nearest town: Lochgilphead
Nearest village: Kilmartin
Location: The circle, which is in the care of the Department of the Environment and is signposted, is beside a minor road about 200 yards (180 metres) south-west of Nether Largie south cairn. (See sketch map on page 138.)

97

Dunchraigaig cairn, Argyll (Strathclyde Region)

Three stone cists were found in this Early Bronze Age cairn, and they contained burnt and unburnt bodies, food vessels, a stone axe and a flint knife. The south cist is covered by a large capstone.

Map reference:
NR 833968 (metric map 55, 1-inch map 52)
Nearest town: Lochgilphead
Nearest village: Kilmartin
Location: A short distance to the south-east of the linear cairn cemetery at Kilmartin, Dunchraigaig is close beside the A816 road and in a grove of trees. (See sketch map on page 138.) It is signposted, and is in the care of the Department of the Environment.

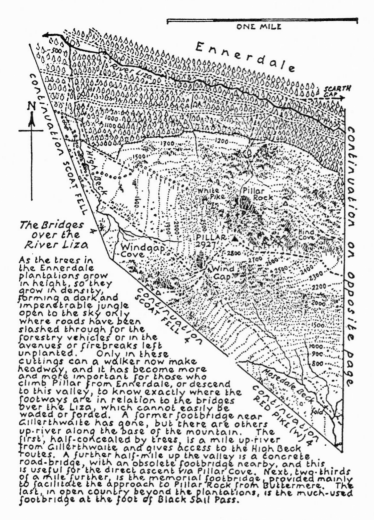

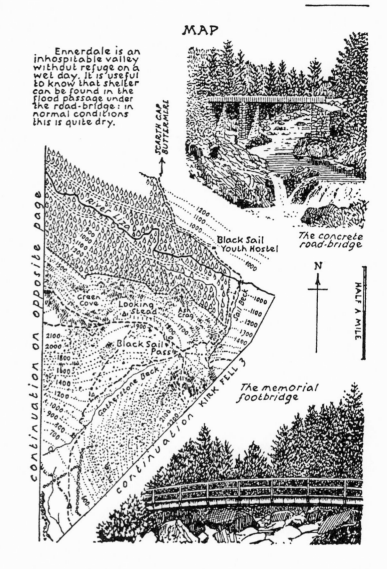

36

A Pictorial Guide to the Lakeland Fells
Book 7 The Western Fells
A Wainwright
Westmorland Gazette 1966
172mm deep

36

Every serious walker in the Lake District knows *Wainwright*, the guides which are entirely hand-drawn, including lettering, from beginning to end. Wainwright, who was Borough Treasurer of Kendal, did all the artwork for all seven volumes same size, initially unaware that it could have been photographically reduced. All practical routes up every fell were surveyed and drawn by him over a period of thirteen years. Each fell is given an introduction, a general map, pages showing the routes, descriptions of summit and view, and ridge walks from it.

The volumes were originally ostensibly published by the then Kendal librarian Henry Marshall. Two thousand copies of Book 1 were published in late May 1955. This was a very odd book by an unknown author. Yet printer and platemaker both agreed not to be paid until the books started selling – if they did. It is not easy to imagine this happening today. In fact,

their bills were paid off by the following February.

The volumes now sell about 25,000 copies a year. In 1985, the one millionth copy was sold. Somewhere around the hundredth edition of each volume the edition number was omitted.

Wainwright did not like word breaks, so none appeared in his books. Most lettering was either justified, or formed a regular shape to fit around maps. Although all the lettering was inimitably his, he had several variations on the basic form. Caps for headings, large roman for basic information, smaller roman for secondary comments, large italic for heights and distances, small italic for tertiary comments, captions, side swipes and peevish remarks; and so on. He invented his own form of 'aerial view/map' to show the routes. Distinctive features helpful to walkers: sheepfold, big rock, four trees, bracken, small tarn, were all shown. His personal, curmudgeonly and misanthropic remarks embedded in the text are famous.

The author may have been a difficult man, and his remarks on womenfolk would get him into deep trouble today; but these seven volumes, the outcome of much thought, hard walking, and love of the fells, are a wonderful achievement.

Exhibition catalogues are a form of guide book. But while the Baedeker concept is still valid, catalogues have been transformed over the last fifty years. *Art for All* is the catalogue for an exhibition of London Transport posters at the Victoria & Albert Museum. Unusually, it was well-illustrated (sixty-eight plates including eighteen in colour), and was conceived more as a permanent record than a true catalogue; only in the Foreword is there any mention of an exhibition.

It was introduced by three short essays. The typographic treatment was generous, but not, one feels, in order to pad it out. It conformed to the overall treatment of other books in this Art and Technics series. A distinct echo of pre-war typography is re-inforced by the inclusion of illustrations by Edward Bawden, Eric Ravilious (seen here) and others.

The general concept anticipates catalogues of thirty years later. Essays, lavish illustrations, large format; these reappear today in enhanced form. Extension of shelf life is the aim in both cases. Only exhaustive academic apparatus is missing here. The examples are not even listed except as plates.

and others by cutting out shapes in different tints of brown paper and mounting them in a series of simple but immensely effective designs. Some excellent examples of their work in this technique are now preserved in the Victoria and Albert Museum. The French use of colour lithography was taken up in England by Dudley Hardy, whose theatrical posters of the 'nineties could hardly be bettered. The melodrama poster of the same period has no claim to any kind of aesthetic value, interesting as some of its products may be to the student of manners. The early years of the twentieth century, however, saw many excellent artists at work on the poster: Frank Brangwyn, John Hassall, Maurice Greiffenhagen, Phil May and others.

As for the subsequent history of the poster in England, it is bound up with the history of London Transport. That is not to make any absurd claim that no good posters have been produced except those advertising the 'Underground'. But the plates in this volume are sufficient to demonstrate that those in charge of the publicity for this organization (in particular, of course, Frank Pick) have had during forty years a very lively flair for discovering the best poster artists in England. *Si monumentum requiris, circumspice.*

37
Art for All
Art and Technics 1949
247mm deep

A POSTER TRADITION

BY HAROLD F. HUTCHISON
Publicity Officer, London Transport Executive

IT was not until 1933 that the name London Transport became the collective title of the whole of London's (and Greater London's) road and rail transport with the exception of the main-line railways. But long before the formation of the London Passenger Transport Board, Londoners had been aware of the unification going on. They had seen the Underground absorb most of its rivals, they had enjoyed the sport of playing at 'pirates', they were quite content when 'General' was finally married to 'Underground'. And throughout this period, though they at all times rightly exercised their privilege of grumbling, Londoners had found a growing pride in a transport service which they felt was already their own. The final integration into a nationalized transport system recognized this feeling, and leaves London's transport

19

38

Much more typical of the period are the next four catalogues. They can hardly be called books, nor are they very well designed. The Ravilious catalogue (sixteen pages, four black-and-white illustrations) was designed by Schmoller in his pre-Penguin days at Curwen Press. Like the following example it contains a brief introduction plus a simple listing of works, here lacking even sizes. The elegant title page is followed by quite unexceptional text and catalogue pages, enlivened only by the Ravilious illustrations.

38
Eric Ravilious
The Arts Council of Great Britain 1948
228mm deep

ERIC RAVILIOUS

1903   1942

*A Memorial Exhibition of
Water-Colours
Wood-Engravings
Illustrations
Designs
&c.*

THE ARTS COUNCIL OF
GREAT BRITAIN
1948–49

the Sussex in which he was brought up and to which he often returned. He also painted in Chiswick where he lived for a time after his marriage in 1930 to Tirzah Garwood, a fellow-engraver, and in Essex where he lived afterwards. He and his wife first went to Essex when they shared a house at Great Bardfield with Edward Bawden, who had been his contemporary at College and with whose development as an artist his own was closely linked. Afterwards they moved to Castle Hedingham and had their home there till just before he died.

Ravilious rarely painted abroad. Figures never played an important part in his pictures, but he liked painting the interiors of ordinary people's houses and the views through windows; also the bareness of winter landscapes and old machinery and outdoor still lifes in the shape of those casual assemblies of objects found in farm and junk yards. He had an affectionate eye for the oddity of such things; not in a whimsical way but simply because he respected clearly marked individuality wherever he found it. He liked things when they were most themselves; for example, when he became a war-artist the Walrus type of aircraft attracted him especially because it had not had the elementary charm of early flying-machines streamlined out of it.

More than with most artists, the subjects Eric Ravilious chose to paint were simply the things he liked, and they were therefore the things that reflect his personality, which was a rare and enchanting one with many facets, impossible to describe to those who did not know him. But at least his intense enjoyment of all the things he liked, whether strange or ordinary, shines out in his work.

J. M. RICHARDS

Catalogue

———

WATER-COLOURS

1. Wannock Dewpond. 1923. *Lent by Martin Hardie, Esq.*

2. Barns at Birling Manor. About 1925. *Lent by Mrs. Garwood.*

3. Pond, Half-past Seven. 1929. *Lent by Lady Sempill.*

4. Portrait of Edward Bawden. Winter 1929–30. *Lent by Edward Bawden, Esq., C.B.E., A.R.A.*

> One of the artist's few oil paintings. The rolls of paper are the cartoons for the murals at Morley College (since destroyed) carried out by Bawden and Ravilious.

7

CONTEMPORARY BRITISH ART

from the collections of the Arts Council and the British Council

New Burlington Galleries, November – December 1949

─────────────────

FOREWORD

ATTENTION HAS recently been called in the Press to the acute shortage of exhibition galleries in London which has been so keenly felt since the war. In particular there is need for a new gallery in which temporary exhibitions both large and small can be shown without causing disturbance to the national collections whose generous hospitality in recent years has slowed down their own programmes of rearrangement and repair. Without this co-operation the Arts Council's exhibitions of *French Tapestries*, *Drawings from the Albertina*, the paintings and drawings of *Van Gogh*, and more recently the *Masterpieces from Munich* and the *Art Treasures from Vienna* could never have been shown. These exhibitions have attracted a total of just under one million visitors.

There have also been a number of other exhibitions of importance and interest, which in almost any other European capital would have been shown in a building centrally placed and specially designed and equipped for visiting exhibitions.

The Arts Council, therefore, has not hesitated, as a temporary expedient, and one which is in no way a permanent solution of the difficulty, to seize the opportunity of restoring the New Burlington Galleries to their original function. With the consent of the former occupiers the original name is perpetuated. Before the war the Galleries were the scene of many memorable exhibitions, and we hope that a not less interesting chapter in their history is now opening. It is also the Council's intention to put these Galleries at the disposal of Art Societies and other bodies connected with the Arts, who today find it increasingly difficult to secure premises for their activities.

It is now nearly ten years since this Gallery was last used for its appointed purpose, and a complete scheme of redecoration and relighting has been undertaken by H.M.'s Ministry of Works, and to all those concerned we express our thanks for their sympathetic understanding of the many problems involved.

ERNEST POOLEY

1

39
Contemporary British Art
The Arts Council/The British Council 1949
241mm deep

CATALOGUE

(Note: The measurements given are of the sight sizes, height preceding width)

OIL PAINTINGS

LEONARD APPELBEE, b. 1914

1. *Barns in a Field*
Oil on canvas, $19\frac{3}{4} \times 23\frac{3}{4}$ in
Signed: *Leonard Appelbee* 1940
Arts Council Collection

MICHAEL AYRTON, b. 1921

2. *Full Moon*
Oil on canvas, $32\frac{1}{4} \times 48\frac{1}{2}$ in
Signed: *Michael Ayrton* 1948-49
British Council Collection

KEITH BAYNES, b. 1887

3. *Château Loches*
Oil on canvas, $27\frac{1}{2} \times 35\frac{1}{2}$ in
Signed: *Keith Baynes* 1948
Arts Council Collection

WILLIAM COLDSTREAM, b. 1908

4. *St. Nicholas Cole Abbey, London* (1946)
Oil on canvas, $19\frac{1}{2} \times 24$ in
British Council Collection
PLATE VIII

5. *Cripplegate* (1949)
Oil on canvas, 30×36 in
Arts Council Collection

ROBERT COLQUHOUN, b. 1914

6. *Seated Woman with a Cat*
Oil on canvas, $37\frac{1}{2} \times 29$ in
Signed: *Colquhoun* '46
Arts Council Collection
PLATE I

7. *The Students* (1947)
Oil on canvas, 30×24 in
Signed: *Colquhoun*
British Council Collection

ROGER DE GREY, b. 1918

8. *Allotments* (1948)
Oil on canvas, 19×29 in
Signed: *de G*
Arts Council Collection

H. E. DU PLESSIS, b. 1894

9. *The Bookcase* (1948)
Oil on canvas, $19\frac{1}{4} \times 23\frac{1}{2}$ in
Signed: *du Plessis*
Arts Council Collection

LUCIEN FREUD, b. 1922

10. *Girl With Roses* (1947-48)
Oil on canvas, $41 \times 29\frac{5}{8}$ in
British Council Collection

CHARLES GINNER, A.R.A., b. 1878

11. *The Rib, Standon* (1939)
Oil on canvas, $17\frac{1}{4} \times 21$ in
Arts Council Collection

SPENCER GORE, 1878-1914

12. *Mornington Crescent*
Oil on canvas, $20 \times 24\frac{1}{4}$ in
British Council Collection

3

39

Contemporary British Art has even more minimal text, only slightly enhanced by the outline headings and decorative rule. There is no relationship between one page and the next. Nor is the catalogue listing well handled. The inclusion of basic information such as size, medium, and collection seems to have been a problem for the designer. Artists' names stray from their works, and loose spacing with oddly-related type sizes make for a disintegrating page. This sixteen-page catalogue is illustrated with eight black-and-white plates, and is mainly remarkable for its parade of all the most eminent British artists of the time.

40

Still in 1949, the *Gilbert Davis* catalogue section (preceded by a short introduction) includes basic data and a brief biography of each artist. The design is a little more confident than the previous example: a pleasing title page has decorative ovals and double rules which reappear in the listing heading. But the listing is confusingly set out. The relationship and relative importance of artist, exhibit number, title and plate number has not been given much attention; and, because of poor use of space, exhibits relate more closely to the following artist. Plate numbers are given undue prominence (are they really as important as the artist's name?) and are oddly positioned.

This twenty-eight-page catalogue has eight black-and-white plates.

BRITISH

WATER COLOURS

AND

DRAWINGS

FROM THE

GILBERT DAVIS

COLLECTION

1949

40
The Gilbert Davis Collection
The Arts Council 1949
219mm deep

Catalogue

LAROON, Marcellus
Second son of Marcellus Laroon the elder ('Old Laroon'), a subject painter, was born in London, 2nd April, 1679. Studied both painting and music and, quarrelling with his father, became an actor. Joined the foot-guards under Marlborough in 1707, fought in Flanders and Spain and retired as a Captain in 1732. Returned to painting and died in Oxford in 1772.

1 THE MORNING RIDE
Pen and wash. 14 x 11 ins.
Signed and dated: *1770*
Probably this drawing was made before 1770 as Laroon dated and signed his drawings in batches some time after they were done.
PLATE 1

TAVERNER, William
An amateur, born in 1703 ; was a son of a procurator-general of the Court of Arches of Canterbury, whose profession he followed. His drawings chiefly in imitation of Italian masters are painted in water colour and in body colour; they usually represent woodland scenes. It has been said that he might 'justly challenge Sandby's claims to the title of father of the English water colour painting in the production of faithful landscape'. The Painters' Hall in the City contains an oil painting by Taverner. He died on 20th October 1772.

2 LANDSCAPE WITH HORSEMEN
Water-colour. 11¾ x 18 ins.
There are faint pencil notes on part of the drawing.

3 LANDSCAPE WITH FIGURES
Water-colour. 12¾ x 15¾ ins.

WILSON, Richard, R.A.
Born at Penegoes, Montgomeryshire, on 1st August 1714 ; was the son of a clergy-man ; was sent to London in 1729 and placed under Thomas Wright, a portrait painter. He lived by portrait painting until the age of thirty-five, when he went to Italy for six years ; during his stay there he almost abandoned portraiture for landscape painting. He returned to London in 1755. His works did not sell well during his lifetime, and he was often in poverty until, towards the end of his career, he inherited some property in Wales, near Llanberis. He died in Denbighshire in May 1782, and was buried at Mold.

4 LARICCIA
Crayon on tinted paper. 10½ x 16¼ ins.
Coll. : *Paul Sandby*. (Bears his mark).
PLATE 3

COZENS, Alexander
Alexander Cozens was born in Russia ; the date of his birth is unknown. He was at St. Petersburg in 1730, and in England by 1742. He studied in Italy perhaps before, certainly after, that date, and may have been in Italy in 1763 and the Tirol in 1764. He taught drawing at Bath and at Eton College, and gave lessons to the Prince of Wales, afterwards George IV. He died in London on 23rd April 1786. He was the father of J. R. Cozens.

5 LAKE SCENE
Sepia. 6 x 7½ ins.
PLATE 2

SANDBY, Paul, R.A.
Born at Nottingham in 1725 ; was descended from an old county family. Through the influence of a borough member, he and his elder brother Thomas obtained employment in the Military Drawing Office of the Tower of London. In 1764 he was engaged as draughtsman on the survey of the roads of the Highlands of Scotland, and made many sketches of the

7

41

The fifty-six-page *Gauguin* catalogue for a prestigious Edinburgh Festival exhibition is more ambitious. Six years later than the previous examples, a simple two-colour cover, unlaminated, was still deemed adequate. But it includes a rather more extended introduction, prefigures today's commentaries on each exhibit, has sixteen plates plus a tipped-in colour frontispiece. There is a biography and a select bibliography. The information in the catalogue has been thoroughly digested and clearly and logically laid out. Exhibit numbers and titles are given priority, plate references are clear but subsidiary. The data even includes metric measurements. Subtle adjustment of linear spacing clarifies the display. This is a miniature forerunner of the heavyweight catalogues of today.

1884–85   PLATE I

10   Self-Portrait in Front of an Easel

Oil on canvas 25⅝ by 21⅜ in. (65 by 54·3 cm.)
Signed upper right (on beam): *P Gauguin*
Lent by Dr Jacques Körfer, Berne

The date of this self-portrait, apparently the first which Gauguin attempted, cannot be established with certainty. But, judging by the style in which it is painted and the assurance of the handling, it was probably executed in the second half of 1884 or early in 1885. It is related both to *Portrait d'Homme* (repr. Malingue, II, p. 88) which is dated *Rouen 1884*, and to the *Portrait of the Painter, Granchi-Taylor* (Kunstmuseum, Basel), which is dated 1885 and was painted after Gauguin's return to Paris. The fact that this picture was obviously painted in an attic (the only accommodation allotted to him by the Gads for painting) and that Gauguin still has a carefree look, suggests that it was executed in Copenhagen. Note the similarity with Renoir's *Portrait of Monet*, 1875 (Louvre).

Early 1885

11   Winter Landscape

Oil on canvas 18 by 12½ in. (45·7 by 31·7 cm.)
Signed and dated bottom left: *P Gauguin 85*
Lent by Mr R. A. Peto, Isle of Wight

Unquestionably a view of Copenhagen, where Gauguin and his family lived with the Gads at 105 Gamle Kongevej. The style of building is not French.

Spring 1885   PLATE III

12   Still-Life in an Interior

Oil on canvas 23½ by 29¼ in. (59·7 by 74·3 cm.)
Signed and dated top right: *P. Gauguin 85*
Private collection, U.S.A.

This picture was almost certainly painted in Denmark before Gauguin returned to Paris and probably represents various members of the Gad family in the salon. In later years, Gauguin was to write: ' I too, am familiar with the north of Europe, but the best thing I found there was most certainly not my mother-in-law, but the game that she cooked so admirably'. The two quail(?) in the foreground still-life are perhaps a symbol of his only pleasurable experience in Copenhagen. Before leaving France, Gauguin

had secured his nomination as agent in Denmark for a firm of Parisian awning-makers (MM. Dillies & Co). He hoped by this means to earn sufficient money to keep his family and be free to continue painting. But things worked out differently since he could not get enough orders, detested the Danes and was resented as a penniless hanger-on by the Gad family. Accordingly he and Mette decided to separate temporarily in June 1885, Gauguin returning to Paris with his son Clovis (aged 6). Though they met on two subsequent occasions, this separation was to prove final.

Some of the pictures in the present exhibition were probably included in the exhibition which Gauguin held in Copenhagen in April 1885. 'One day I will tell you how my exhibition was closed, on official orders from the Academy, after five days, how serious and favourable articles were suppressed in the newspapers', he wrote to Schuffenecker (Letter of 24th May 1885). During the nine months which he spent in Copenhagen, Gauguin drew and painted in every spare moment: he also thought a great deal about artistic theories and began to evolve his own aesthetic.

In this picture Gauguin can already be seen developing his individuality of vision. A daring and original composition with a still-life seen close up from above in the immediate foreground and, seen in another perspective, a spatial opening through to a subsidiary subject behind. Direct light in the foreground, counter-light in the background; not at all an Impressionist conception.

Spring 1885 (?)

13   A Girl by a Duck Pond

Oil on canvas 12½ by 19⅜ in. (31·8 by 49·2 cm.)
Signed and dated bottom right: *P. Gauguin 188(?)*
Lent by Madame I. Moeller de Laddersous, Brussels

The last figure of the date is unclear. The handling of the paint and the subject suggest a date *c.* 1885, cf. *Pola et Aline* (Private coll. Riehen), which is very similar and dated 1885. The figure is perhaps Aline the artist's daughter.

Summer 1886

14   Still-Life with Decanter and Cherries (*La Nappe Blanche*)

Oil on panel 21¾ by 23 in. (55 by 58.5 cm.)

18

42

Sculpture
London County Council/The Arts Council
1951
246mm deep

42

Very different from the previous four
catalogues is this one for the Festival
of Britain, 1951. Unlike the *Gauguin*
catalogue [41] of four years later, it has
only minimal information on the exhibits:
artist's name; place and date of birth;
where living; title and date of sculpture.
There could hardly be less. There is a brief
introduction. But it does illustrate all forty-
four works, usually in two or three photographs. There are eighty-five illustrations
altogether. (See overleaf and page 106.)

The catalogue is notable for the
complete break it makes with the genteel
classicism generally seen prior to this
date. The designer, Harold Bartram, was
studying at the Central School of Arts and
Crafts at the time when Anthony Froshaug
and Herbert Spencer were teaching there,
establishing post-war British typography.
Turning away from the tasteful English
tradition, looking to Continental design –
early Tschichold and Bauhaus typography,
for instance – the new approach had
much in common with the 'international
style' architecture of the period. Space,
function, order and logic dominated the
design process in both fields. A consistent
structure throughout the book (although,
within the grid, there is considerable
freedom in the arrangement of the
illustrations), unclassical margins, the use
of Gill Sans for text; all this is redolent of
the new feeling in British typography. It
had already been seen in work by both
Froshaug and Spencer. It brought a new
discipline into British publishing design at
its best, whether the preferred approach
was symmetrical or asymmetrical,
'traditional' or 'modern' (so-called).

SCULPTURE

an open air exhibition at Battersea Park May to September 1951

Presented by the London County Council
in association with
the Arts Council of Great Britain

Exhibition Advisory Panel

Mrs Hugh Dalton *(Chairman)*
Chairman of the Parks Committee, LCC
Member of the Arts Council of Great Britain

Mrs Unity Lister
Mrs Patricia Strauss
Members of the Parks Committee, LCC

Siegfried Charoux, ARA

Jacob Epstein

Eric C. Gregory

Barbara Hepworth

Philip James, CBE
Director of Art, Arts Council of Great Britain

Sir Eric Maclagan, KCVO
Chairman of the Fine Arts Committee, British Council

F. E. McWilliam

H. D. Molesworth
Keeper of Sculpture, Victoria and Albert Museum

John Rothenstein, CBE, PhD
Director and Keeper of the Tate Gallery

assisted by
the late A. R. Mawson, and L. A. Huddart
Chief Officers of the Parks Department
R. R. Tomlinson
formerly Senior Inspector of Art
and other officers of the London County Council

Howard Roberts
Clerk of the Council
The County Hall
Westminster Bridge
London SE1

Catalogue

1 MARI ANDRIESSEN Born Amsterdam 1907
Lives Haarlem, Netherlands
Concentration Camp *Bronze 1948*
Lent by the War Memorial Committee, Enschede

2 LOUIS ARCHAMBAULT Born Canada 1915 Lives Montreal
Iron Bird *Welded steel plates 1951*
Lent by Museum of the Province of Quebec

3 JEAN ARP Born Strasbourg 1889 Lives France
Hybrid Fruit called Pagoda *Bronze*

4 ERNST BARLACH Born Holstein 1870 Died Germany 1938
Woman in the Wind *Glazed ceramic 1932* Lent by Mr Hugo Körtzinger

5 MAX BILL Born Winterthur, Switzerland 1908 Lives Zurich
Rhythm in Space *Stone 1948–49* Lent by the artist

6 EMILE-ANTOINE BOURDELLE Born Montauban 1861
Died France 1929
Death of the Last Centaur *Bronze 1914* Lent by Petit Palais, Paris

7 REG BUTLER Born Hertfordshire 1913 Lives Hatfield, Herts
Torso 1950 *Iron* Lent by the artist

8 ALEXANDER CALDER Born Philadelphia 1898 Lives Connecticut
Maneater with Pennants (mobile) Lent by Museum of Modern Art, New York
(Not illustrated)

9 LYNN CHADWICK Born London 1914 Lives Cheltenham
Green Finger (mobile) *Copper and brass 1950–51* Lent by the artist
(Not illustrated)

10 SIEGFRIED CHAROUX Born Vienna 1896 Lives London
Evensong *Terracotta 1944* Lent by the artist

11 CHARLES DESPIAU Born France 1874 Died France 1947
Assia *Bronze 1938* Lent by Musée National d'Art Moderne, Paris

12 FRANK DOBSON Born London 1888 Lives London
Woman with Fish *Concrete 1951*
Commissioned and lent by the Arts Council of Great Britain

13 GEORG EHRLICH Born Austria 1897 Lives London
Young Lovers *Bronze 1950* Lent by Mr James H. Lawrie

14 JACOB EPSTEIN Born New York 1880 Lives London
Lazarus *Hoptonwood stone 1949* Lent by the artist

15 ALBERTO GIACOMETTI Born Switzerland 1901 Lives France
Figure *Bronze* *(Not illustrated)*

16 ERIC GILL Born Brighton 1882 Died England 1940
The Deposition *Black Hoptonwood stone 1925*
Lent by the Governors of The King's School, Canterbury

17 ALFRED F. HARDIMAN Born England 1891 Died England 1949
Night *Plaster, coloured bronze* Lent by Mrs Violet Hardiman

18 HEINZ HENGHES Born Hamburg 1906 Lives London
Madonna and Child *Sicilian marble 1950*
Lent by the Church of St Mary-le-Park, Battersea

19 GERHARD HENNING Born Stockholm 1880 Lives Denmark
Standing Girl *Bronze 1928–29* Lent by the artist

20 BARBARA HEPWORTH Born Wakefield 1903 Lives Cornwall
Bicilth *Blue Ancaster stone 1950* Lent by the artist

21 KARIN JONZEN Born London 1914 Lives Suffolk
Bather *Bronze* Lent by the artist

22 GEORG KOLBE Born Germany 1877 Died Germany 1945
Pietà *Bronze 1930* Lent by Georg-Kolbe Museum, Berlin

23 MAURICE LAMBERT Born Paris 1901 Lives London
Pegasus and Bellerophon *Reinforced plaster aggregate 1943*
Lent by the artist

24 GILBERT LEDWARD Born London 1888 Lives London
Caryatid Figures *Roman stone 1929* Lent by the artist

25 WILHELM LEHMBRUCK Born Duisburg 1881 Died Berlin 1919
Kneeling Girl *Bronze 1911* Lent by Mrs Anita Lehmbruck

26 JACQUES LIPCHITZ Born Russia 1891 Lives U.S.A.
Mother and Child *Bronze 1930*
Lent by courtesy of Buckholtz Gallery, New York

27 F. E. McWILLIAM Born Co. Down, Ireland 1909 Lives London
Head in Green and Brown *Hornton stone 1950* Lent by the artist

28 ARISTIDE MAILLOL Born France 1861 Died France 1944
Mediterranean *1901 Bronzed plaster, specially cast for the exhibition*

to abandon representation is legitimate. The sculptor gains in concentration on the real problems of his art what he loses in human appeal. His loss is apparent to everybody, his gain less so. It is obviously easier for us to follow the sculptor, that is to tune our feelings to those intended by him, if he calls his figure *Pomona* than if he calls it *Mobile* or *Column of Victory capable of development*. Yet such works of complete abstraction as these are perhaps more easily comprehended than those which appear equally inhuman and yet are called *Standing Figure* (Henry Moore), *Mother and Child* (Lipchitz) or *Biolith* (Barbara Hepworth). What makes a sculptor choose this ambiguity which, he knows, irritates and confuses his public? A very provisional answer is this, and the name *Biolith*, that is, Stone Alive, points to it. Pure abstraction deprives the sculptor of life, imitation of actual live organisms endangers the effects of æsthetic endeavours by conjuring up non-æsthetic associations. Let there be a modicum of organic life therefore, the sculptor says, just enough to allow growth to be sympathetically felt, or, a little more narrowly and precisely, to allow a sense of bone, of joint, of animal tissue, of root, or of the long-continued effects of wind and water on rock to be conveyed by the sculptor's creations. Such instinctive, irrational feelings may be inhuman but they are profound.

The term 'concentration on the real problems' of sculpture has been used a moment ago. But what are the real problems of sculpture, if they are not a rendering of the human form? If the public is so much less conscious of them than it is of those of painting, this is due to the fact that the nineteenth century was a century of painting. Hence we tend to look at sculpture in two dimensions. Some works, it is true, can be appreciated in the way a painting or a drawing is, that is in the flat, e.g., Eric Gill's *Deposition* which is essentially an exquisite silhouette (see the arm cut off above the head). But the rule is that one can only do justice to sculpture if one sees it in depth as well as in height and breadth. The three-dimensional effect may be primarily one of solid volume in opposition to the space, our space, surrounding it; this is, for instance, the case in McWilliam's harassing *Head* in two monoliths (in which the seemingly arbitrary cutting out of parts and erecting them in front of us tends to let us see these parts overwhelmingly intensified, because over-focused. It is an effect which photography can obtain more easily than sculpture.) On the other hand sculpture can be entirely spatial, with volume reduced to a minimum, as in Reg Butler's configurations which are no more than outlines and lines of section to guide the eye into relations of pure space not before our time accessible to the sculptor. The union of weightlessness with violence is unforgettable. In Lipchitz's *Mother and Child*, on the other hand, massive material and perforations keep in balance. Volume and outline speak as audibly as the inner spaces.

The McWilliam head is of Hornton stone, the Lipchitz of bronze, the Butler chiefly of forged iron bars. Materials obviously have a bearing on form, or rather the sculptors choose their materials to help the forms which they visualise. The basic difference is between stone-carving and modelling for bronze casting. In the first case the sculptor shapes by taking away; it is hard work with a chisel. In the other case the sculptor builds up a clay model by adding bits of soft clay. This lighter work tends to livelier surfaces and a freer play of light and shadow. Reflections on the bronze surface have also to do with that, just as in stone the character of a figure is much influenced by polished (Eric Gill) or matt surfaces (Ledward). Skeaping's *Torso*, of a particularly hard stone, granite, is an example of typical stone carver's art, Despiau's *Assia* or Kolbe's *Pietà* could be nothing but bronze. Stone tends to give this a look of permanence, bronze of movement.

In this lies yet one more basic problem of sculpture which needs comment. The sculptor is—as the painter—confined to representing one moment. Hence his liking through the ages of the standing human figure. Here, he felt, life could be re-created confined into one gesture. If the artist wants, like Maillol, to represent repose, sculpture is his natural means of expression. If on the other hand he sees life as movement, he has to devise special expedients. Kolbe's *Pietà* appears to turn round slowly as we look at it—no one view is sufficient to appreciate the wealth of movement. We have to walk round the figure to understand it fully. The same is true of Lipchitz's *Mother and Child*: these figures have to be studied from all sides to understand the interplay of their antediluvian forms, and 'interplay' implies, of course, that more than one moment is meant to appear before us. Recently a decisive step has been taken to free sculpture from the past limitations to the fixed moment. Calder's Mobiles do not only seem to move before our eyes, they really move, and move in a calculated way, although accident is no doubt left its share, a share welcomed centuries ago by the most resourceful artist there ever was, Leonardo da Vinci.

In the case of Mobiles, exhibition in the open air is a revelation. Indeed all primarily spatial sculpture must benefit from nature around it. Other pieces—even some displayed in the open in this exhibition—are no doubt conceived for an indoor position, Epstein's *Lazarus*, e.g., one would think. But whether meant to be seen outdoors or indoors, display in sunshine and rain proves in nearly all cases an experience worth having and a test of sculptural qualities.

There is nothing aggressively modern about this catalogue, but the school of thought of which it is part made feasible the integrated books to come. The approach allows greater freedom of page layout, yet provides a strong structural grid controlling all elements throughout the book.

As Tschichold (and, later, Schmoller) realised at Penguin, the provision by the designer of specific and detailed instructions for the printer, with comprehensive, carefully marked-up layouts, was a necessary part of post-war typography. This was a new concept in British publishing and printing. The casual reliance on traditional skills was no longer a realistic option.

This catalogue was printed by Lund Humphries, one of the best and most forward-looking printers of the day; yet, in those early years of 'modern' typography, even they had difficulty in overcoming certain ingrained prejudices in layout. Today all printers are used to working with designers; some are flummoxed if such an intermediary has, for one reason or another, for better or worse, not intervened at every stage.

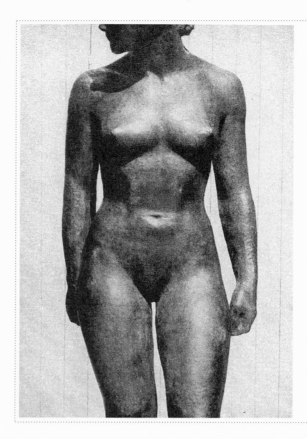

II DESPIAU. *Assia Bronze*
Photos Van Wingerden, Antwerp (above)
Bernes-Marouteau, Paris (left and right)

38 RODIN. *Orpheus Bronze 1892*
Photos Archives Photographiques, Paris

RODIN. *Orpheus (detail)*

Painting & Sculpture of a Decade

54

Painting & Sculpture of a Decade

64

organized by

the Calouste Gulbenkian Foundation

at the Tate Gallery London

22 April - 28 June 1964

43

Painting & Sculpture of a Decade 54-64
Calouste Gulbenkian Foundation 1964
253mm deep

43

The last of the earlier form of catalogue I show, dating from a period before catalogues became a variant of the integrated book, is this deliberately 'modern' conception designed by Edward Wright and Robin Fior. Here the grid is almost ostentatious. An introduction is interspersed with twenty full-page colour illustrations. The catalogue itself includes no commentaries, merely the basic data seen here (overleaf). Although the design is apparently a little mannered, all information is clearly and systematically displayed, including the index, and the concept is entirely in keeping with the period the catalogue covers.

born 1930 in Wendorf, Mecklenburg, Germany. member of Zero group. lives in Dusseldorf

Gunther Uecker

330
Lichtscheibe
1960 nails 59in / 150cm diameter
collection : the artist

born 1931 in Berlin, Germany, but grew up in England. studied at St Martin's School of Art, and Royal College of Art, London. lives in London

Frank Auerbach

331
Half-length of E.O.W. nude
1957 oil 30in x 20in / 76cm x 51cm
collection : Lady Elizabeth Montagu

332
Head of E.O.W. IV
1961 oil 23½in x 22in / 59cm x 56cm
collection : Mr Daniel Farson

333
E.O.W. on her blue eiderdown II
1962 oil 23½in x 30in / 60cm x 76cm
collection : Beaux Arts Gallery

254

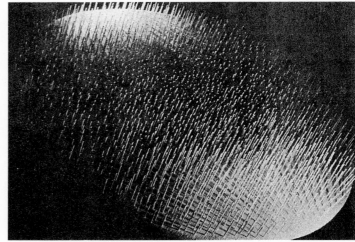

330

331

332

333

born 1917 in Melbourne, Australia.
studied in Melbourne then moved to
Sydney 1948. later moved to London,
but has also worked in New York
and Africa. lives in London

Sidney Nolan

208 Convict and Billabong
1957 plastic paint 48in x 60in / 122cm x 152cm
collection : Sir Kenneth Clark, KCB

209 Landscape
1963 oil 60in x 48in / 152cm x 122cm
collection : the artist

born 1918 in St Ives, Cornwall.
studied at the Penzance and Euston
Road Art Schools. Marzotto prize-
winner 1962. lives in St Ives, Cornwall

Peter Lanyon

210 Offshore
1959 oil 60in x 72in / 152cm x 183cm
collection : Birmingham City Museum and Art Gallery

211 Rosewall
1960 oil 72in x 60in / 183cm x 152cm
collection : Mrs Shiela Lanyon

212 Wreck
1963 oil 48in x 72in / 122cm x 183cm
collection : Gimpel Fils

208

209

210

211

212

174

The catalogues I show later are effectively
integrated books. The development of
these will now be examined.

born 1914 in St Petersburg, Russia.
died in Antibes, France, 1955

Nicolas de Stael

190 Les Martigues reproduced in colour
1954 oil 57½in x 38in / 146cm x 97cm
private collection

191 Palette
1954 oil 35in x 45in / 89cm x 114cm
collection : Mr and Mrs Oscar Weiss and Dr Nigel Weiss

192 Nature morte au bocal
1955 oil 29in x 39½in / 74cm x 100cm
collection : Mr and Mrs Chester Beatty

193 Le Fort d'Antibes
1955 oil 51in x 35in / 130cm x 89cm
collection : Mme Jacques Dubourg

194 Chemin de Fer, du bord de mer, Soleil Couchant
1955 oil 29in x 39in / 74cm x 99cm
collection : Mrs Jocelyn Walker

191

192

193

194

162

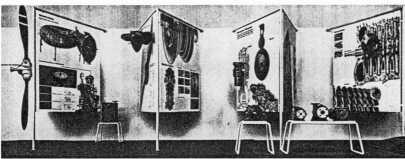

44

With the end of the war, British designers (and publishers) could begin to look beyond the insular tradition. The Swiss had been peacefully working away at refining Bauhaus concepts, incorporating the freedoms of asymmetry, the discipline of strict grids, and the use of 'rational' grotesque typefaces in a very limited range of sizes. They tried to bring to these ideas a more logical and aesthetically-pleasing arrangement than the often aggressive Bauhaus idiom. Their work was to be very influential in British print design, even bookwork. The intellectual and rational basis of the Swiss style seemed appropriate for the new world that, it was hoped, would grow out of the ashes of war. In the end, it became a bit of a formula and thus sterile, but at the time its precision was greatly beneficial, and the effects can still be seen in the best designs today.

A classic example of the Swiss (actually German-Swiss) 'hard-edge' school is seen here. The method results in a more coherent resolution of several hitherto unsatisfactorily-treated problems, particularly the relationship of photographs and awkwardly-shaped plans and elevations to the text. The text here is in three languages. Although the four-column grid is strictly adhered to, holding all the elements together, its use has not obviated the need for aesthetic judgement. As in architecture, space plays a vital part; it is not just holes left over, but a dynamic contribution to the page. It allows headings to be displayed with merely a minimal change in type size. Only the captions seem to me a little unhelpfully treated.

The amazingly narrow margins require Swiss machining and guillotining skills to achieve. But such hard-won cool precision is all of a piece with the apparent simplicity of the design. There is nothing formulaic about this book. Every spread has its own problems, satisfactorily solved by the author/designer allowing the material to dictate the form within the overall grid structure.

Sveriges Paviljong

Exposition Internationale, Paris, 1937

Architekt Sven Ivar Lind
Stockholm

Thema

Zwischen dem britischen und dem tschechoslovakischen Pavillon und direkt unter dem Eiffelturm am Pont d'Iéna gelegen, stand der schwedische Ausstellungskommission im Zentrum der Weltausstellung ein hervorragendes Terrain zur Verfügung, welches sowohl vom Quai d'Orsay als auch vom untern Seine-Quai zugänglich war. Die Ausstellung sollte eine Empfangshalle, eine Sektion für Malerei, Grafik und Kleinplastik, Hallen für eine Sozialabteilung, Kunstgewerbe und kunstgewerbliche Industrie enthalten. Die vorhandenen Freiflächen wurden für Plastiken und Ruheplätze reserviert. Am Seine-Quai wurde ein Restaurant sowie ein Kinoraum, am Quai d'Orsay eine der Touristenwerbung dienende Fotoausstellung angeordnet. Thematisch bedeutsam war die Sozialabteilung, welche durch grundlegendes Material über Sozialfürsorge, Wohnbaupolitik, Familienschutz usw. besonderes Aufsehen erregte.

Form und Konstruktion

Mitbestimmend für die äußere Form war das Raumprogramm sowie der Umstand, daß unter dem oberen Teil des Pavillons ein Tunnel verlief, der nicht belastet werden durfte. Es sollte ferner eine durchgehende Zirkulation des Publikums gewährleistet werden, was bei der mehrstöckigen Anlage gewisse Probleme aufwarf. Vom Eingang am Quai d'Orsay her erreichte man die Kunstabteilung und über eine Treppe die Sektion für Sozialarbeit, welche im obersten Geschoß lag. Von dieser gelangte man ins Entresol, mit den Abteilungen Kunstgewerbe und kunstgewerbliche Industrie. Ohne Kreuzung wurde der Strom der Besucher durch parallel gelegte Doppeltreppen hinauf- und hinabgeleitet. Durch lebendigen Wechsel hoher, halbhoher und niedriger Räume entstand bei aller Beschränkung an Raum ein heiles, offenes und übersichtliches Gesamtmilieu, das die typische Atmosphäre des lichten, im hohen Norden Europas liegenden Landes klar herausstellte. Mit durchgehend natürlich verwendeten Materialien, Stahl und Heraklithplattenverkleidung, wurde ein neutraler Grund für das Ausstellungsgut geschaffen. Leider war dessen formale Präsen-

tation nicht entsprechend dem Niveau der architektonischen Durchbildung und dessen Aufbau teilweise ungeordnet. Der Pavillon gliederte sich in einen einstöckigen Teil, der sich über dem Métrotunnel aufbaute und einen dreistöckigen Bau gegen die Seine. Die Bauvorschriften, besonders im Bereich des Eiffelturms, diktierten weitgehend die Materialauswahl. Der Bau bestand aus einem sichtbaren Stahlskelett auf Eisenbetonfundamenten. Die Dachbinder erhoben sich über den Dachflächen und waren untereinander diagonal versteift. Außer diesen Verstrebungen dienten dem Windverband V-förmige Pfeiler, Kreuzverbände in den Außenwänden und Blechversteifungen in den Außenecken der obersten Decke. Die Treppen bestanden aus fertig gegossenen, armierten Stufen auf Stahlträgern. Als Ausfachung kamen hauptsächlich Heraklithplatten zur Verwendung.

Farben

Die vorherrschende Farbe, die dem Bau seine charakteristische Note gab, war das helle Grau der Heraklithplatten zwischen rot gestrichenen Eisenskeletteilen.

Fassade gegen den britischen Pavillon. Unter dem links liegenden Bauteil verläuft der Métrotunnel. Façade donnant sur le pavillon britannique. Le tunnel du métro passe sous la corps de bâtiment visible à gauche. Front facing the British Pavilion. The Métro tunnel passes under the unit on the left. 1: 500

Grundriß des Hauptgeschoßes auf Höhe des Quai d'Orsay mit Skulpturenterrasse, Empfangshalle, Kunstabteilung und Entresol der Kunstgewerbeabteilung. Plan de l'étage principal, à la hauteur du Quai d'Orsay, avec la terrasse et ses sculptures, halle de réception, section artistique et entresol du département des arts artisanaux / Plan of principal floor at Quai d'Orsay level, with terrace accommodating sculptures, reception hall and art section, and mezzanine with arts and crafts department. 1: 500

1 Eingang Entrée Entrance
2 Halle Hall
3 Terrasse mit Plastiken Terrasse avec les sculptures Terrace with sculptures
4 Kunsthalle Section des Arts Art room
5 Restaurant
6 Kunstgewerbe Arts artisanaux Applied arts
7 Sozialabteilung Département social Social welfare

Schnitt durch den gegen die Seine liegenden mehrstöckigen Bauteil. Coupe transversale à travers le bâtiment à plusieurs étages, au bord de la Seine / Section of the three-storey unit on the Seine bank. 1: 500

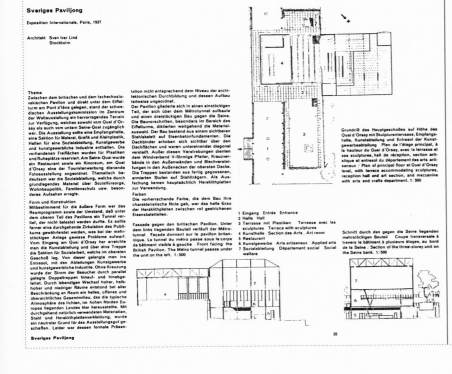

Gesamtansicht. Stahlskelett und frei stehende Dachbinder rot. Putzflächen weiß.
Vue générale. Ossature métallique et fermes de la toiture, peintes en rouge; surfaces crépies, blanches.
General view. Steel framework and visible roof ties in red. Rendered surfaces white.

Konstruktion des Stahlskelettes
Construction du squelette d'acier
Construction of the steel framework

Sala dei Primi voli

Subject

Among the Italian aeronautical pioneers Enrico Forlanini, born in Milan in 1848, assumes a place of great importance. During his military career he constructed the first helicopter model. In 1876 Alessandria saw a second steam-driven helicopter which went through its first trials in Milan during the following year.
As the owner of a foundry Forlanini was later able to concentrate particularly upon specific technical problems, mainly the design of propellers. In the course of his research he gained the conviction that the problem of flying could not be solved by the helicopter system and he therefore attempted to develop other methods of propulsion for the airplane. He finally succeeded in developing a rocket with a powder charge of 200 grams, with which models reached a height of 180 metres and speeds of 12-15 metres second. Later he constructed a small 8 HP steam engine with two cylinders. In 1910 he built a hydroplane whose maximum speed was 82 km hr. In later years Forlanini again reverted to the construction of propeller vanes and achieved pioneer results in this field which for a long time remained unsurpassed.

Form and construction

True to the contents and character of the subject, the exhibition comprised mainly documents of Forlanini's pioneer work. As is the case with all documentary exhibitions, the material was the decisive factor for the effect of the whole. The epic nature of the pioneer work found its effective expression in the photographic documents of the first flying experiments with dirigible airships. These documents revealed the atmosphere of the stupefied curiosity reigning among the spectators, blended with the distrust and disbelief inspired by the first miracles of flying.
The stage of development of the contemporary era was characterized by numerous engines, propeller vanes, gauges and experimental models.
With the absolute effect created by their shapes, two large airships suspended from the ceiling of the exhibition hall dominated the show.
Propeller and controls in a glass case in front of a black wall bearing the name Forlanini interpreted, with their elementary design, the heroic atmosphere of the period.
The simplicity of the technical elements together with the silent witnesses of those pioneer achievements created an appearance of size.

Colours

Black and white.

Esposizione dell'Aeronautica italiana, Milano, 1934

Architekten Studio Architetti BBPR
G. L. Banfi
L. di Belgioioso
E. Peressutti
E. N. Rogers
Milano

In der Abteilung, welche sich unmittelbar an den Saal Forlanini anschloß und zu dessen eine Ergänzung bildete, kam die Geschichte der Entwicklung des Motorfluges in Italien in eindrucksvollen Zeugnissen zur Darstellung. «Delagrange volerà». Dieser Ruf, einem Manifest gleich, in dem sich Hoffnung und Überraschung der beginnenden Epoche des Motorfluges ausdruckte, wurde durch seltene zeitgenössische Fotodokumentation, Briefe, Traktate über die ersten Motoren von Anzani, Savoia und Caproni nochmals lebendig gemacht. Die primitiv wirkenden Traggestelle der Aeroplane, welche Skeletten ähnlich von der Decke des Rundganges herunterhingen, gaben der Abteilung durch ihr phantastisch wirkendes Gestänge, ihre unverhullte Konstruktion, Drahtverspannungen und Überschneidungen einen mythisch wirkenden Charakter und bildeten die Schwerpunkte der Ausstellung. Dem gesamten Stil entsprechend waren die Ständer-, Stützen- und Rahmenelemente, zwischen denen Modelle und Konstruktionsteile montiert waren.

Dans la section prolongeant et complétant la salle Forlanini, était traitée l'histoire du développement du vol à moteur en Italie. «Delagrange volerà», cet appel tel un manifeste, expression de l'espoir et des surprises des débuts du vol à moteur, trouvait son reflet dans l'exposition de photographies, lettres et articles de l'époque relatifs aux premiers vols, et des premiers moteurs de Anzani, Savoia et Caproni. Les châssis primitifs des aéroplanes suspendus au plafond et pareils à des squelettes avec leurs fragiles nervures, leurs tendeurs en filins métalliques, leurs entailles et recoupements, donnaient un caractère saisissant à l'exposition, tout en en constituant le centre de gravité. Les montants, supports et éléments à cadres, entre lesquels de petits modèles et des parties de la construction étaient montés, s'harmonisaient bien avec le style de l'ensemble.

In the department adjacent to and complementing Sala Forlanini, the evolution of flying in Italy was illustrated by impressive specimens. "Dela-

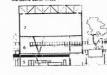

Glasvitrine mit Propeller- und Flügelkonstruktionen, an der Rückwand Foto der Flugversuche Forlaninis.
Vitrine avec constructions d'hélices et d'ailes; paroi du fond, photographies des essais de vol de Forlanini.
Glass show-case with propeller and wing designs; photo of Forlanini's flying attempts on far wall.

grange volerà" – this slogan, almost a manifesto expressing the hopes and amazement prevailing at the outset of the era of flying, was revived by rare contemporary photographic documents, letters, treatises on the first flights as well as by the first engines built by Anzani, Savoia and Caproni. The primitive-looking aeroplane fuselages suspended like skeletons from the ceiling of the circular walk gave the department a mythical character with their fantastic framework, visible construction, wire struts and intersections. The stands, supports and frame elements, between which models and structural parts were mounted, were in accord with the style prevailing in the whole.

Saal «Primi voli» mit dem Zweidecker von Giovanni Caproni, konstruiert 1910. Links und rechts fotografische Dokumente, Briefe und Manifeste.
Salle «Primi voli», avec le biplan de Giovanni Caproni, construit en 1910; à gauche et à droite, parois avec documents photographiques, lettres et manifestes.
Primi voli (First flights) Hall with the biplane constructed by Giovanni Caproni in 1910. Right and left, photographic documents on the walls, letters and manifestos.

Godefroy, Genéve 1893
Plakat für illustrierte Postkarten
poster for illustrated postcards
affiche pour cartes postales illustrées

Jules Chéret, Paris 1895
Plakat für eine Revue
poster for a musical show
affiche pour un spectacle de variétés

Alphonse Mucha, Paris 1895
Theaterplakat
theatre poster
affiche de théâtre

Beggarstaff Brothers, London
Theaterplakat
theatre poster
affiche de théâtre

37 **Auch das Format ist nicht selbstverständlich**

Noch hindern keine Rationalisierungs-
bestrebungen der Aushängegesellschaften, keine
Bemühungen zur Normierung und Reglemen-
tierung der Plakatflächen die Arbeit der Gestalter.
Das Format wird somit im Blick auf den erstrebten
Effekt gewählt, also als Werkzeug der künst-
lerischen Intention eingesetzt. Wird später einmal
das Standardformat geschaffen sein, muss die
Plakatkunst zur Erreichung ähnlicher Wirkungen
andere Wege finden.

Sizes still made to measure

As yet the designer's work was still unhampered
by efforts on the part of the companies to
rationalize advertising and introduce standard
sizes of poster. The size and shape were thus
chosen with an eye to the effect required; they
were in fact regarded as a means of realizing the
artist's intentions. When the standard size was
subsequently introduced, poster art had to devise
other means of achieving similar effects.

Le format non plus ne va pas de soi

Jusqu'à présent les maisons de publicité n'ont
pas encore cherché à réglementer les
dimensions des affiches, et par cela à influencer
les créateurs. Le format est choisi uniquement en
vue de l'effet à produire, il sert d'instrument à
l'artiste. Si, plus tard, on doit adopter un format
standard, il faudra, pour atteindre les mêmes
effets, trouver des moyens différents.

45
The New Graphic Art
Karl Gerstner and Markus Kutter
Arthur Niggli 1959
230mm deep

45
The same basic concepts are used to structure the more simple elements shown here. One type size is used throughout, with a related bold for headings. The three languages are more easily sought out than in the previous example, but space is again a vital ingredient, and the grid copes with the varied shapes and sizes of the illustrations. Following the principle behind all Swiss 'hard-edge' work, a deliberately cool, neutral design allows the examples to call the tune, the text being merely a quiet background voice. Theoretically, the designer is anonymous. In practice, his presence is apparent everywhere. Advantageously so, in my opinion.

CYCLISTS KEEP THEM CLEAN

MAKE SURE YOU ARE SEEN

Tom Eckersley, London 1947
Königliche Gesellschaft für Unfallverhütung
Royal Society for the Prevention of Accidents
Société royale pour la prévention des accidents

196

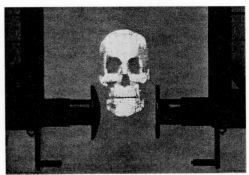

Tom Eckersley, London 1951
Königliche Gesellschaft für Unfallverhütung
Royal Society for the Prevention of Accidents
Société royale pour la prévention des accidents

Waldemar Swierzy, Warschau 1957
Unfallverhütung
prevention of accidents
prévention des accidents

197

Das Plakat als Mahner

In einer – nicht zuletzt dank der Werbung! – auf Genuß und Befriedigung, auf Verharmlosung und Komfort bedachten Gesellschaft von Konsumenten ist das Plakat eines der wenigen Ausdrucksmittel, das in einer ebenso unmißverständlichen Sprache auch anders zu reden versteht. Es kann sich selbst so eindeutig ausdrücken, daß es in der Welt des 20. Jahrhunderts als Nachfolger der spätmittelalterlichen Totentänze auftritt mit der alten Mahnung: Mitten im Leben …

The poster as a warning

In a society whose mind – and advertising is in part responsible – is centred on enjoyment and satisfaction, on comfort and living on tolerable terms with the disagreeable, the poster is one of the few modes of expression capable of talking a very different kind of language. It can tell a plain, unvarnished story to such effect that it becomes the 20th century Dance of Death with its old warning: In the midst of life …

L'affiche comme moyen d'avertissement

Dans une société de consommateurs aspirant – encore grâce à la publicité! – à satisfaire son goût du plaisir, de la facilité et du confort, l'affiche est un des rares moyens d'expression qui saura, et de façon aussi nette, parler un autre langage. Elle a trouvé sa formule propre, si bien qu'elle apparaît au vingtième siècle parfois comme le successeur des danses macabres du lointain moyen-âge avec leur douloureux avertissement.

anonym, Paris ca. 1920
Hauswandreklame
outdoor poster
réclame sur le mur d'une maison

Charles Loupot, Paris 1948
Lichtreklame
advertising by neon light
réclame au néon

quinquina

Atelier Charles Loupot, Paris 1956
Inserat
advertisement
annonce

405, 406, 407

232

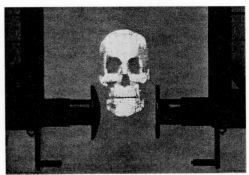

quin quina

Atelier Charles Loupot, Paris 1957
Straßenwerbung
outdoor posters
réclame sur la voie publique

408

233

St. Raphaël Paris

Was für die figürliche Gestaltung der beiden Kellner gilt, gilt auch für die Schrift: die ursprüngliche anonyme Blockschrift wird umgestaltet und in einen Namenszug von so ausgeprägtem Charakter verwandelt, daß er nun gleichfalls in einzelne, den Silben des Namens entsprechende Bestandteile zerlegt werden kann. Das Problem der Lesbarkeit rückt in den zweiten Rang; die Kombination des zerlegten Namenszuges mit den abstrakten Elementen der Bildmarke in den ursprünglichen Farben strahlt den werbenden Appell nicht weniger intensiv aus.

St-Raphaël Paris

Changes similar to those effected in the figures of the waiters have also taken place in the treatment of the lettering. The original undistinctive block lettering has been transformed into a stylized name with such marked characteristics that it can now also be broken down into component parts corresponding to the syllables of the name. The problem of legibility becomes subordinate. The combination of the broken-down name and the abstract elements of the pictorial mark in their original colours are no less effective in putting a message across.

St-Raphaël Paris

Ce qui est valable pour la présentation graphique des deux garçons l'est également pour le commentaire écrit: les gros caractères d'abord anonymes se transforment en une signature si caractéristique qu'elle pourra, à son tour, être séparée en parties isolées correspondant aux syllabes du mot. Qu'il soit lisible devient un problème secondaire; la combinaison de la signature découpée et assemblée avec les éléments abstraits de l'image dans ses couleurs originales, est, elle aussi, d'un effet publicitaire.

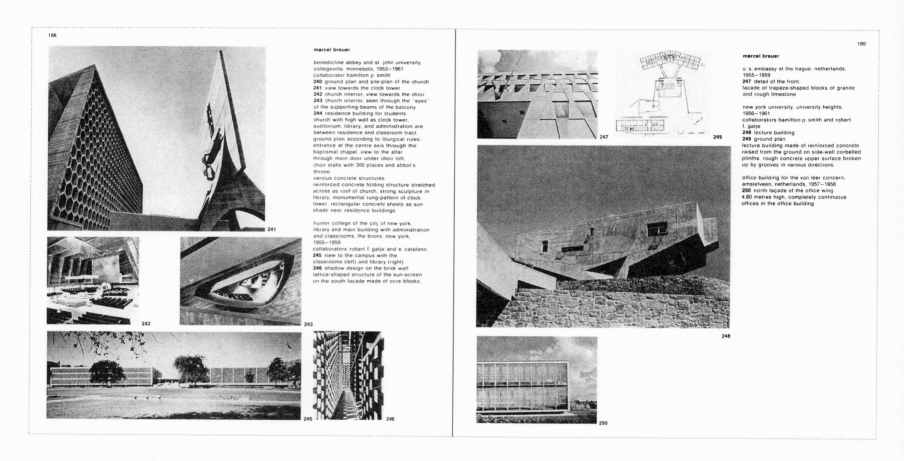

marcel breuer

benedictine abbey and st. john university,
collegeville, minnesota, 1953–1961
collaborator hamilton p. smith
240 ground plan and site-plan of the church
241 view towards the clock tower
242 church interior, view towards the choir
243 church interior, seen through the "eyes"
of the supporting-beams of the balcony
244 residence building for students
church with high wall as clock tower,
auditorium, library, and administration are
between residence and classroom tract.
ground plan according to liturgical rules:
entrance at the centre axis through the
baptismal chapel. view to the altar
through main door under choir loft.
choir stalls with 300 places and abbot's
throne.
various concrete structures:
reinforced concrete folding structure stretched
across as roof of church, strong sculpture in
library, monumental rung-pattern of clock
tower, rectangular concrete sheets as sun
shade near residence buildings.

hunter college of the city of new york,
library and main building with administration
and classrooms, the bronx, new york,
1955–1959
collaborators robert f. gatje and e. catalano
245 view to the campus with the
classrooms (left) and library (right)
246 shadow design on the brick wall.
lattice-shaped structure of the sun-screen
on the south façade made of ocre blocks.

marcel breuer

u. s. embassy at the hague, netherlands,
1955–1959
247 detail of the front.
façade of trapeze-shaped blocks of granite
and rough limestone

new york university, university heights,
1956–1961
collaborators hamilton p. smith and robert
f. gatje
248 lecture building
249 ground plan
lecture building made of reinforced concrete
raised from the ground on side-wall corbelled
plinths. rough concrete upper surface broken
up by grooves in various directions.

office building for the van leer concern,
amstelveen, netherlands, 1957–1958
250 north façade of the office wing
4.80 metres high, completely continuous
offices in the office building

46

50 Years Bauhaus
Royal Academy of Arts 1968
219mm deep

46

A jam-packed catalogue for the big
Bauhaus exhibition of 1968 shows a more
aggressive 'let-it-just-happen' approach.
The differences between the German and
the Swiss schools are revealing. Here in
practice is the Bauhaus stricture against
the use of capitals, which the Swiss
(rightly) disregarded. Spaces on these
pages are just holes where the elements
stop, rather than a dynamic part of the
page. There is a less happy relationship
between the two pages of a spread. It is
sometimes difficult to know to which
illustration the figure number refers. Part
of the reason for these awkwardnesses
may be the wish of the designer, Herbert
Bayer, to make a dogmatic statement, a
reaffirmation of Bauhaus principles. But it
does show how – perhaps surprisingly –
the Swiss brought greater sensitivity to the
modern design idiom. Bauhaus design,
although very influential, could be brutal.
It cleared the air, but development and
refinement were required to make it more
generally acceptable.

196

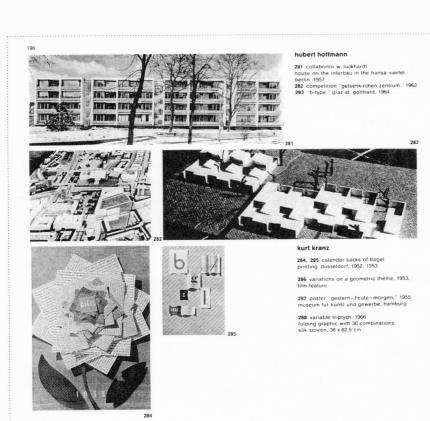

hubert hoffmann

281 collabortor w. luckhardt.
house on the interbau in the hansa viertel.
berlin, 1957
282 competition "gelsenkirchen zentrum," 1962
283 "b-type," graz-st. gotthard, 1964

kurt kranz

284, 285 calender backs of bagel
printing, dusseldorf, 1952, 1953

286 variations on a geometric theme, 1953,
film-feature

287 poster "gestern—heute—morgen," 1955
museum fur kunst und gewerbe, hamburg

288 variable triptych, 1966
folding graphic with 30 combinations,
silk screen, 36 x 62.5 cm

197

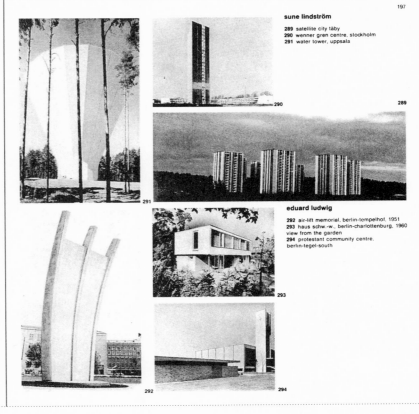

sune lindström

289 satellite city täby
290 wenner gren centre, stockholm
291 water tower, uppsala

eduard ludwig

292 air-lift memorial, berlin-tempelhof, 1951
293 haus schw.-w., berlin-charlottenburg, 1960
view from the garden
294 protestant community centre,
berlin-tegel-south

198

georg a. neidenberger

295 catalogue "22 berliner bauhäusler," 1950
1955
296 poster, advertisement, printed matter for
"interbau," berlin, 1957

ernst neufert

rawmaterials storage hall for eternit, corp.,
heidelberg-leimen, 1965
297 south view

administration building of the dyckerhoff
cement works, corp., wiesbaden-amoneberg
298 southwest corner
299 south view

199

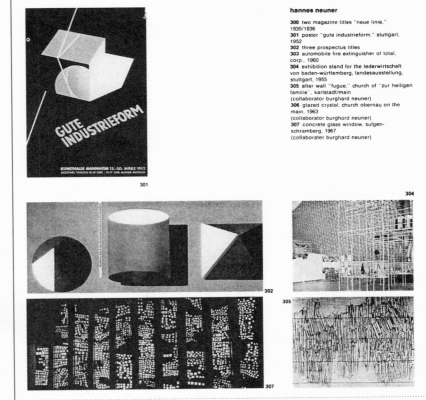

hannes neuner

300 two magazine titles "neue linie,"
1935/1936
301 poster "gute industrieform," stuttgart,
1952
302 three prospectus titles
303 automobile fire extinguisher of total,
corp., 1960
304 exhibition stand for the lederwirtschaft
von baden-württemberg, landesausstellung,
stuttgart, 1955
305 altar wall "fugue," church of "zur heiligen
familie", karlstadt/main
(collaborator burghard neuner)
306 glazed crystal, church obernau on the
main, 1963
(collaborator burghard neuner)
307 concrete glass window, sulgen-
schramberg, 1967
(collaborater burghard neuner)

Amongst the greatest impacts which St Mark's Square delivers can be counted the approach. This epitomizes the 'surprise approach, explosion of space' concept used in so many of the Italian squares; it is carried here to the ultimate. Down a narrow, somewhat tortuous sidewalk lined by high shops on either side, one sees a small arched opening beckoning in the distance (photograph 1). As one draws nearer, this arch form takes precise shape and, drawn on by the magnetically sharp perspective of the Procuratie Nuove on the right, the splash of vivid color on the distant Doge's Palace, the temptation of the Campanile disappearing upward, and the promise of free unconfining space, one is impelled forward with an irresistible urge (photograph 2). And, then, before one, dancing and sparkling in the brilliant sunshine, in a fusion of architecture, space, color and pageantry, lies the greatest square in the world (photograph 3).

Coducci, ma finite solo quindici anni dopo.) Comunque il lato nord della Piazzetta dei Leoni è egoistico, disarmonico e sbagliato.
Uno degli elementi più emozionanti di Piazza San Marco è l'arrivo. Il concetto dell' 'accesso a sorpresa, dell'esplosione dello spazio', adottato in tante piazze italiane, qui è portato al massimo. Da una viuzza stretta e tortuosa fiancheggiata da negozi eleganti, si scorge in lontananza una piccola apertura ad arco che invita (foto 1). Avvicinandosi, questo arco si precisa, e attratti dalla prospettiva magneticamente nitida delle Procuratie nuove a destra, dalla macchia di caldo colore sul lontano Palazzo Ducale, dalla tentazione del campanile che si perde in alto e dalle promessa di uno spazio libero senza confini, si è spinti avanti da un irresistibile impulso (foto 2). E allora, viva e sfavillante nel limpido sole, in una fusione di architettura, spazio, colore e fastosità, ci si apre dinnanzi la più bella piazza del mondo (foto 3).

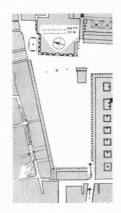

74

1

2

3

47
Italy Builds
G E Kidder Smith
Architectural Press 1955
277mm deep

47
The Architectural Press, particularly in its journal *Architectural Review*, certainly took a more relaxed line. Although entirely modern in concept, both journal and books made frequent use of 'softening' elements such as decorative display typefaces (often Victorian in origin), coloured papers, pages turned on their side (acceptable in a magazine) for drama and surprise, and other very un-Swiss devices. The typefaces especially did not always have a beneficial effect on the work of their architect-readers, but the publications had a liveliness and wit missing from today's computer-generated

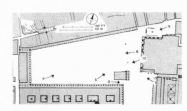

4 5   6

In analysing the piazza, one is highly impressed by the contrasts which produce such an important part of its impact. There is contrast between the confinement of the approaches and the openness of the square; between the horizontality of the buildings which delimit it and the aspiring pivotal campanile which punctuates it; between the comfortable enclosure of the piazza and the exciting 'escape' of the piazzetta; between the sober rhythm of the two Procuratie and the architectural fantasy of the church they flank. These counterpoints are poised in a masterfully defined space, and one which has a 'Pushmi-Pullyu' effect that delights whether one approaches the church or leaves it. And when the whole is bathed with the Venetian light and colors, the result is indescribable. Intimately bound to the effect is the fact that there is total and complete separation of pedestrian and vehicular traffic, or as Le Corbusier says, 'The pedestrian is master of the ground.'

The photographs are divided into groups of approach— looking toward the church, looking away from the church, looking out the piazzetta. Photographs 1, 2 and 3 are, as mentioned, of the main entrance into the square. 4, 5 and 6 continue this direction up to the church and campanile. Note, in 6, the wonderful 'come-on' glimpse of the Doge's Palace behind the campanile, a small spatial hint of what lies beyond.

Photographs 7–10 were taken looking back towards the west end of the square. In 8 and 9 the one 'awkward' corner of the piazza is visible.

Analizzando la piazza colpiscono molto i contrasti che costituiscono un elemento così importante della sua forza. C'è contrasto tra la strettezza delle vie d'accesso e la spaziosità della piazza, tra l'orizzontalità degli edifici che la delimitano e la verticalità del campanile-cardine che le dà l'accento, tra l'accogliente intimità della piazza e l'eccitante 'fuga' della piazzetta, tra il ritmo sobrio delle due Procuratie e la fantasia architettonica della chiesa. Questi contrappunti si equilibrano in uno spazio magistralmente definito che ha un delizioso effetto di 'tira-e-molla' sia avvicinandosi sia allontanandosi dalla chiesa. E quando il tutto è inondato dalla luce e dai colori veneziani, la sensazione è indescrivibile. Contribuisce molto all'effetto la separazione totale e completa tra il traffico pedonale e dei veicoli; qui, come dice Le Corbusier, 'Il pedone è padrone del suolo'.

Le foto sono divise in gruppi secondo i punti di vista: verso la chiesa, dalla chiesa e dalla piazzetta. Le foto 1, 2 e 3 sono, come abbiamo detto, dell'ingresso principale alla piazza. Le foto 4, 5 e 6 seguono questo percorso verso la chiesa e il campanile. Si noti, nella 6, il prodigioso scorcio del Palazzo Ducale che fa l'occhietto dietro il campanile, piccola indiscrezione spaziale di quello che c'è più oltre.

Le foto 7–10 sono prese guardando verso l'estremità occidentale della piazza. Come si vede, tutta la piazza è circondata da portici. Si noti, nella 7 e nella 8, la straordinaria quantità di vetro nella facciata delle Procuratie Vecchie, progettata più di 450 anni fa! Nelle 8 e 9 si vede l'unico angolo mal risolto

7   8   9

76

10

designs. For all their faults, these period pieces were the work of real fully paid-up members of the human race.

This book was designed by its author, an American architect/writer, but it bears all the hallmarks of AP designs: freedom of layout, the use of a clarendon for headings, and (very typically) the use of a series of photographs to demonstrate the progression through a townscape.

An introduction on the land and regional architecture is followed by a section on the urban setting, with analyses (such as the sequence shown here) of examples and features of historic townscape; the book concludes with descriptions of selected modern Italian buildings.

The only constant grid is the text, with Italian text in italic, but there is no sense of disorder. The very varied picture sizes, occasional engraving or plan, dramatic photographs freely arranged; all these give the sequences excitement. The intention of this book is to inform and instruct. The conception and structure achieve this admirably. Its freedom of design derives directly from its content.

11 12   13   14   15   16

Photographs 11–14 attempt, insofar as possible, to recreate for the observer the delightful plastic sensation of the piazzetta, that wonderful transition between enclosed piazza and open sea, between restrained self-sufficiency and ebullient marriage with environment. From the Piazzetta dei Leoncini, the Clock Tower, or the front of the church, we are lured by two compelling 'space interrupters', the two granite columns of ancient vintage which pull the spectator forward and push the distant island Church of San Giorgio back. As we come ever nearer, the piazzetta blossoms out and the columns, and even the Victorian lamp-posts, continue their space modulating. At the left the transparent corner of the Doge's Palace beckons (photograph 15), in the distance sails glide silently by in the lagoon, and San Giorgio and its island vibrate behind the columns carrying the Winged Lion of St Mark and St Theodore with his crocodile.

Having thus pulled us to the edge of the *Molo*, the two columns now relinquish their job to the gondolas whose bobbing forms and rustic tie poles are brandished in the space between the spectator and Palladio's lovely church floating across the blue lagoon, the lagoon whence Venice sprang.

della piazza. Dalla loggia superiore esterna della chiesa si ha una superba vista della piazza, così viva e animata (foto 13).

Nelle foto 11–14 si vorrebbe tentare di ricostruire il delizioso senso plastico della piazzetta, magnifico punto d'incontro tra l'intima piazza e l'aperto mare, tra la contenuta autonomia e l'esuberante accoppiamento con l'ambiente. Dalla Piazzetta dei Leoni, dalla Torre dell'Orologio o dalla facciata della chiesa, si è attratti da due potenti 'rotture di spazio', le due colonne granitiche di antica origine che richiamano l'osservatore e respingono la Chiesa di San Giorgio all'isola. Avvicinandosi ancora, la piazzetta si schiude interamente, le colonne e il lampione vittoriano continuano a modulare lo spazio, l'angolo trasparente del Palazzo Ducale invita, lontano le vele scivolano silenziose sulla laguna e San Giorgio e l'isola vibrano dietro le colonne con il Leone alato di San Marco e San Teodoro e il coccodrillo.

Dopo averci così attratti al Molo, le due colonne cedono il compito alle gondole che si stagliano nell'aria tra l'osservatore e la deliziosa chiesa del Palladio galleggiante sull'azzurra laguna, la laguna da cui sorse un tempo Venezia.

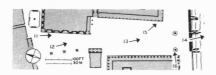

17

78

79

The book was written at a time when Italian design led the world in every sphere: graphic design, furniture, industrial design, architecture, cars, scooters. It couldn't last. Designers came to realise that, instead of creating a better society, they were merely making rich manufacturers richer. Serious designers such as Ettore Sottsass, disillusioned, began creating anti-design products. Although these presumably still made rich industrialists richer, they were, I suppose, a declaration that visions of a saner and fairer society were mere wishful thinking.

top 218, 219; bottom 220, 221

222, 223

Pile-up

A deeper dive into the unofficial topography of the street reveals *objects*, in the sense used in the introduction to this section, taking over their full responsibilities. These have equal claims with the official monuments to acceptance as urban sculpture both in 221, the deliberate, and 218, the accidental form. Or in window-dressing without the window. Display, but in another sense to that already used. The pile-up (genteelism and its ploys apart) is the secret of successful

144

shop décor and Italians are its supreme exponents. Thus the bags at Florence market, 220 (notice how easily they dominate the official sculpture), thus the candles at Loreto, 219. The picture-postcard technique, 222. Bookshops, chemists, wine-merchants, grocers, greengrocers, delicatessens they all practise the pile-up with consequences which make Italian shops, outside or in, the most tempting in the world. The door-to-door salesman, 223, is an unusual mobile in the same tradition.

48
The Italian Townscape
Ivor de Wolfe
Architectural Press 1963
235mm deep

48
But in 1963, architects and designers had yet to be disillusioned. AP publications, while wholly supportive of modernism, had always encouraged the examination of historic exemplars. Mediterranean lands were particularly rich in such life-enhancing material, and this book, lavishly illustrated with details of Italian town-scape, is a fine example of the Press's didactic yet entertaining approach. The almost chaotic layout of the book is entirely in keeping with its theme: that the richness and variation of texture, pattern and accidental effects to be found in the close-knit Italian town – the chaos of real life – has lessons for today's planners.

This book, like the previous example, exhibits characteristic AP devices: a Victorian display type for the headings, the use of tinted paper, the incorporation of simple vivid sketches clarifying points made in the text, the cramming together of photographs with a minimal white space separating them. This is even more of a truly integrated book than *Italy Builds*, with commentary and illustrations running together. The text, in essence a continuous series of captions, demands to be read. The book is the printed equivalent of a good TV documentary. The illustrations are not always identified on the page – the location is irrelevant to the point being made – but a list at the beginning explains all.

An essentially visual subject almost demands this binding together of text and illustrations. The purist will be dismayed by the mise-en-page, but the thesis of the book is effectively made.

76, 77

80, 81

wings 4

as a way of ringing the changes on street width, or, conversely, creating small piazzas—object always the same, *enclosure*—until the moment arrives when the wing

78, 79

wings 2.

wings 5

82
83

the humble stepped narrows, highly congested, with a delightful un-axial use of the tower, 80, to the full blown civic composition, 83, again occupying so much of the available space as to graduate from side-screen to stage-set, including back-cloth, though in fact a large main street gets through. A particularly engaging variation, also hailing from the stage, though next to impossible to photograph, is the inclined wing, which may start as a chamfered corner, 84, but quickly develops a functional meaning in its own

wings 3

itself occupies so much of the stage as practically to stop the show so that we are nearly back with the dead-end. Not quite though, 79. There are endless variations, from

335
336
337

Outrage

When people or markets or cafe tables can't provide it the traditional cure for a dead patch in the town is a monument, sometimes by this race of extremists carried to extremes with the springing of a very canny townscape trick which consists in forcing a quart-size monument into a pint-size Piazza. Museum example, the Trevi fountain, 338, depending for its effect, like a poster, on outrage to the conventional urban scale. More violence. Biggest of all these sculptures, occupying the greatest available space in the smallest possible enclosure, is the Florentine dirigible known as the Duomo, 91. From none of the many approaches to it can this monument be really seen, a fact which fills the artless planner with despair while giving the sophisticate much quiet satisfaction.

Remoteness

Genuine remoteness is for the bloody-minded. Most of us get embarrassed alone on mountain tops faced by what Dostoevsky called the silence of the universe. Moral remoteness, however, is a luxury, a perquisite only a highly integrated society can provide. The victory over promiscuity: the feeling that although you may be within a few yards of others you are sequestered, not trampled into the ground by the herd. Difficult to achieve in a city, yet done with success again and again, notably in university towns. Notably too in Rome, where low-level quays, 334, are gradually replacing the mud along the Tiber. Down on the quays one

has a sense of isolation, of being withdrawn a hundred miles from the city. The traffic pouring over the bridges seems to belong to another dispensation and doesn't destroy the illusion, enhances it. In a way remoteness is at its most pregnant within spitting distance of the hurly-burly. Coventry City Centre is an English example, where the roof car-parks provide a delightful sense of isolation.

334

204

338

18 Western Classicism

Italian Influence *109.* In Italy itself Baroque energy in painting and landscape remained vital through such individuals as the Venetian painters G. B. Tiepolo (1696–1770), G. A. Canaletto (1697–1768), G. F. Guardi (1712–93) and the Roman architects N. Salvi (1699–1751) and F. de Sanctis (1693–1740). The Italian influence abroad continued to widen. Austria was physically and emotionally closer to Italy than to France, and the defeat of the Turks outside Vienna in 1683 created an unprecedented exuberance of spirit that for a brief period flowered in Baroque architecture and the landscapes of palaces and monasteries. Inspiration was both Italian and Austrian. The Belvedere at Vienna is a classical Baroque canvas of gardens, city and sky; in contrast the Monastery of Melk is a romantic Baroque composition, based on medieval relation to site. Elsewhere in Europe, with the possible exceptions of Holland and Portugal (Lisbon replanned 1755), classical landscape was mainly influenced by the French, architecture by the Italians; Wilhelmshöhe is a freak composite of Italy, France and England. In England the new and revolutionary concept of romantic landscape that had taken the place of classicism, turned architecturally as a compensating and stabilizing factor to the strict Italian Palladianism of two centuries earlier. A hybrid Baroque architecture was introduced into China by the Jesuits for Ch'ien Lung (Emperor 1735–96), together with hydraulic experimental fountains and other delights.

French Influence *110.* French landscape energy was now concentrated at the Court of Versailles, and in the extension of the Tuileries in Paris. Landscape was further to merge into town-planning: at Nîmes a fortress engineer inserted a landscape spine to co-ordinate the town plan as a whole (1740), and in the Place Stanislas at Nancy (1760) pleached limes were an integral and permanent part of the architectural structure of town design. The French sense of the organization of space dominated the era, laying the foundations of an autocratic form of town-planning which created Washington and most major new cities until modern times. Emulation of the Grand Monarch led to prodigious projects by the independent German princes, many of whose landscape estates have since become the basis of a modern town. The declining Spanish monarchy followed the French closely, but the landscape architecture of the Tsars of Russia, who founded St Petersburg in 1703, was more independent and cosmopolitan, being influenced by Baroque Italy and their own Oriental traditions as much as by contemporary France.

Comment *111.* Throughout the century French classical influence mingled with Italian to encourage extension of formal space through geometry. The main elements were the closed avenue with open spaces and these turned easily from the green walls of clipped *charmilles* into the streets and squares of city-planning. Germany rather than France established the conditions for landscape expression of all kinds, sometimes to the point of freakishness. Originality and inventiveness appeared in innumerable landscapes and gardens, foreshadowing the German outburst of philosophy and art at the end of the century. The development of the concept of landscape-planning as an extension of parks and even town-planning, may have been due to land claustrophobia. Potsdam, for example, was an expression of the aspirations of a monarch, Frederick the Great, who founded the greatness of the Hohenzollern dynasty; in the plan and its universal elements was the mark of an enlightened autocrat and brilliant administrator whose territorial ambitions extended far beyond his own limited boundaries.

The Monastery of Melk, Austria (345). symbolizes Counter-Reformation confidence, projecting it into the new century. It was begun in 1702, to the designs of Jakob Prandtauer. In its triumphant use of the steep site overlooking the Danube it is a proclamation of the same spirit that created Durham (**237**) five centuries previously.

49
The Landscape of Man
Geoffrey and Susan Jellicoe
Thames and Hudson 1975
284mm deep

49
Another lavishly-illustrated book is this classic on landscape design. The wide-ranging illustrations are tightly packed in, but the arrangement is more orderly than in the previous example. Again, the text is mainly in the form of running captions, within which the title of each illustration is picked out in bold (see overleaf). The various chapters are handled in a systematic way: the authors, pioneering landscape architects, display orderly and analytical minds. A mass of material and information has here been thoroughly worked on and presented in a concise, clear and easily-digested way.

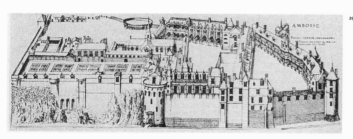

294

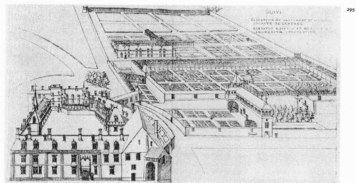

295

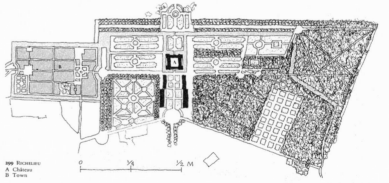

296

THE RENAISSANCE IN FRANCE began with the return of Charles VIII (r. 1483–98) from Italy in 1496, bringing with him architects, sculptors and men of letters to his home and birthplace at Amboise in the Loire Valley. The sixteenth century was a period of transition from medievalism to classicism; the essence of the Touraine landscape was the blend of romanticized indigenous Gothic architecture with the slowly maturing classicism. **Amboise** (294) was remodelled in 1496. The only sign of the new Italian influence is the garden extension, surrounded with lattice and pavilions (Italian designer: Pasello da Mercogliano). The gardens of **Blois** (295), birthplace of Louis XII (c. 1500 by Mercogliano), are still medieval in their compartmentation, but their size and independence from the house reflect the growing love of the Renaissance landscape. At **Chenonceau** (296) on the River Cher the water scenery is essentially French in its poetic combination of medievalism and classicism. The castle itself was begun in 1515; the bridge was added by Philibert de l'Orme in 1557 and the gallery over by Jean Bullant c. 1576.

Marie de Médicis married Henry IV in 1600, giving a superficial impetus to Italian influence upon French culture. A comparison between the form of the Boboli Gardens (267), her home in Florence, and the **Luxembourg Gardens** (297) shows a nostalgic similarity. The detail, however, was original and French. The **compartiments de broderie** (298), for instance, were first introduced here by Boyceau (d. 1638), executed in box, flowers and coloured sands. Cardinal Richelieu (1585–1642), on the other hand, who unified France and laid the foundations of absolute monarchy, ushered in a new and pure French concept of comprehensive planning and space design. The landscape of the **Château de Richelieu** (299) in Touraine was a unified design carved out of woods, with decorative canals arising from drainage, and inclusive of a town as a subsidiary element. The concept, designed 1627–37 by J. Le Mercier, prepared the way for the work of Le Nôtre.

297, 298

299 RICHELIEU
A Château
B Town

0   ¼   ½ M

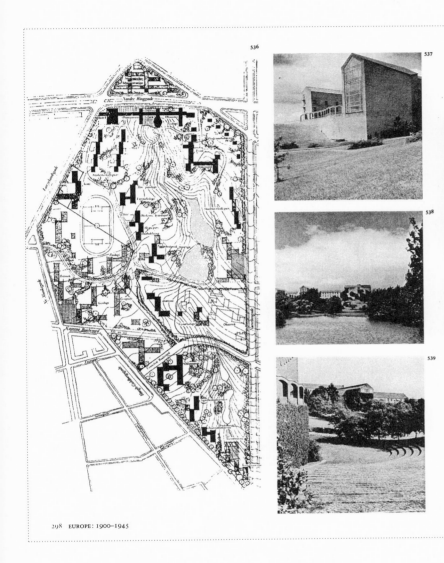

536

537

538

539

540 PARTICIPATION IN ECOLOGY was recognized as an integral part of adult education in the design of **Aarhus University, Denmark**, in 1932. In contradiction to the classical view, the university was conceived as a romantic biological group in relation to site, growth and domesticity. It was designed by Kay Fisker, C.F. Møller and P. Steegmann, architects, and C.Th. Sørensen, landscape architect, who appears to have been the presiding genius. Growth has been continuous, the form adapting itself to circumstances but never departing from original principles. The **plan of 1965 (536)** shows the university as then existing (black) and as envisaged. The buildings are grouped round a glacial ravine and interplanted mainly with oak, thorn, maple and beech. The architectural unity is based on parallelism, simplicity of block form and standard brick facing with low-pitched tile roofs. There is no difference in character between teaching and residential units. The **general view (538)** and the detail of the **open-air theatre and assembly hall (537)** were photographed in 1950, that of the **assembly hall and library (540)** and **theatre (539)** in 1972. The library completes the composition, which is now partly obscured by matured trees. The walls throughout are slowly being transformed from mellowed brick to textured green by Virginia creepers and ivies, as shown in the **Department of Pharmacology (541)** and by comparison of (537) with (540).

541

Dumont. He bridged the gap between the specialists those like Levavasseur and the Voisin brothers who were directly involved in invention and development—and the larger non-specialist public. He *translated* the engineering and aerodynamic achievements into the common language of ordinary people. But although pre-eminent, Santos-Dumont was not alone. In France there were others who tried to do as he was doing, not on the same scale, but in something approaching the same way.

As adulation for Santos-Dumont mounted, recognition of the work of other great pioneers faded. Clément Ader had been partly forgotten. His work as an electrical engineer and inventor of the microphone and therefore, to some extent, of the Bell telephone, was still recognized but not his work as an aviation pioneer.

A new generation of practising airmen appeared contemporary with Santos-Dumont. The Voisins were collaborators with Alberto, for Gabriel helped him with his first aircraft. Moreover Santos-Dumont had watched Voisin's Seine experiments.

His 1907 box-kite, intended to carry the *14 bis* concept forward to a more practical stage, was totally unsuccessful. His *Demoiselle* closely approached the concept of a small aircraft which might be used for touring by private pilots. It failed in many respects, but it proclaimed the kind of ideals Santos-Dumont had in mind for the aircraft of the future.

He thought of aircraft as elegant carriages in which men and women would be able to pay visits, to tour the country, to go to the restaurant and the theatre, to engage in sport and entertainment of all kinds. He saw

aircraft, in fact, as instruments of peaceful amusement. Unlike the Wrights and other great constructors he did not, it seems, think of them as instruments of war.

During the years 1904 and 1905 the Wrights had made a number of attempts to sell their invention to the war departments of different countries, among them the United States, Great Britain and France. They were of the opinion that flying would be used in time of war particularly for reconnaissance and for communications and in the approach the brothers made to Congress early in 1905 they referred specifically to 'scouting and carrying messages in time of war.'

89 The original Santos-Dumont *Demoiselle*, with engine mounted above the wing, 19 November 1907

90 The Wrights' *Flyer III*, September 1905

Government representatives, however, were inclined to call for practical demonstrations before they would consider purchasing patents. The United States Board of Ordnance and Fortification insisted that the stage of practical operation must be demonstrated to their representatives before they would move. They said this at the beginning of 1905 and they repeated it in more detail in October of the same year when they indicated that they had no further interest in the invention 'until a machine is produced which by actual operation is shown to be able to produce horizontal flight.' The British government was also asking for demonstrations.

It was a sign of the success with which the Wrights had maintained their policy of secrecy for they reported, as became known later, that they had made 105 flights during 1904. Moreover towards the end of that year they spoke of flights of five minutes' duration and some in which they encircled the Huffman field on the property of Mr Torrence Huffman, a local banker, they were then using as their base. They had flown distances of three miles and at speeds of 35 miles per hour. They had flown in a straight line, in circles and over S-shaped courses. To cap it all they flew slightly over 24 miles on 5 October 1905.

The Wrights kept detailed information about these flights. They were made at heights of between 10 and 20 ft and in a single week in 1905 seven experiments were made, covering an estimated distance of 15 miles. The 1904 work had been done with a new machine having a total weight of 915 lb. This weight, however, included 70 lb of steel bars which were used as ballast.

68

Wilbur Wright estimated that the aircraft, with water and fuel for one hour's flight and with one man on board, would weigh 850 lb. Rail launching was used and the landing was done on skids.

It was in April of 1905 that Wilbur Wright began discussing the possibility of building a two-seater and of modifying some of the control details. All the signs were that the Wrights were confident that they had solved the major problems of flight. It is therefore the more remarkable, when the events are seen in the perspective of the years, that Wilbur himself, when he made contact with the French ambassador with the object of interesting the French war office as a possible purchaser of their patents, should refer frankly to the widespread incredulity about their achievements. 'It will seem incredible,' he wrote to the French ambassador in November 1905, 'not only that long flights have really been made with motor airplanes, but also that they have been made so quietly as to escape the attention of the newspapers.'

Nevertheless the Wrights had invited a number of witnesses to see their performances and in their copious correspondence with Chanute they had poured out the fullest information about what they were doing and how they were doing it.

It has been said that the early Wright aircraft took off from rails and landed on skids. Their controls showed steady development as they acquired the art of piloting. Thus the project of adding a front rudder for assisting control in yaw was brought forward when the 1905 machine was being designed. And there was the important decision, later, to divorce the lateral control from the directional. At first the Wrights introduced wing warping connected with the tail controls. It was in part this form of interconnected control that led later on to a number of unfortunate disputes, some leading to the courts of law, about priorities in the employment of warping wings.

Warping wings, as we have seen, are a crude means of applying control about the fore and aft axis or lateral control. But warping wings are essentially the *natural* form of control and in theory might well be shown to be the most efficient. For in wing warping the entire wing is deformed to produce an increase in lift on one side and a decrease on the other whereas when conventional ailerons are used only a small rectangular cutout is moved to produce the lift differential.

Wing warping was certainly the first idea for lateral control. It was used by Clément Ader in 1890. Professor R. Marchal, a scientist in the atomic division of the French SNECMA engine company, made a study of Ader's inventions in the 1960s and quoted Ader's claims in his application to the Bureau de la Propriété Industrielle in August 1890. These claims include a clear indication of wing warping 'à gaucher le bout de l'aile' and one can only assume that it was translator trouble that prevented this from being more widely known.

After Ader there was S. F. Cody who used wing warping for the control of his man-lifting kites. This is stated by his biographer G. A. Broomfield but the point has been disputed. In his book *Early Aviation at Farnborough* (1971), however, Dr Percy B. Walker, a leading

Farnborough scientist, states categorically that Cody used wing warping in 1903 for control in pitch and that he may have used it also for control in roll, that is about the fore and aft axis. Walker mentions that although the Wright brothers contested infringements of their lateral control patents in France and America, they attempted no legal action when Cody used wing warping in his powered machines.

The Wrights' policy of working in secret which had done so much to encourage scepticism about their claims

in many parts of the world was abandoned in 1908. They had sent an aircraft to France and in the summer of that year they obtained the co-operation of the automobile pioneer Léon Bollée and were given permission to give demonstrations at a race course close to Le Mans, at Hunaudières. The promise that all the mystery which had surrounded the work of the Wrights was suddenly to be swept away had the well known stimulating effect upon the news media and great excitement prevailed among the French public. Would the claims be justified? How did the Wrights' way of flying differ from the ways that had been developed in France?

91 Wilbur Wright on *Flyer III* at Issy, 1908

92 The 1908 Wright *Flyer III* flown by Wilbur on 21 September 1908 at Auvours near Le Mans

69

50

The Conquest of the Air
Frank Howard and Bill Gunston
Paul Elek 1972
293mm deep

50

Following his earlier adventurous use of illustrators, Paul Elek later produced a series of sumptuous books on architecture, the early ones richly printed by photogravure. A single photographer, Wim Swaan, was commissioned to take almost all the photographs and, in some cases, to write the text too. One person's viewpoint is likely to make for a more interesting, certainly a more unified book; just as these books were the concept of one man, Paul Elek himself.

A very different subject from the same publisher and, like those books, designed by Harold Bartram, this history of flight follows the same format. It inevitably necessitated the use of illustrations from numerous sources, and the historical sequence inevitably creates a changing impression on the page. Yet all is held together by the use of the grid and the illustration pattern. The dogmatic Swiss approach is softened. Captions are grouped and tucked away in the narrow outer column. The strong and usually conflicting diagonals that come with this subject – generally a source of trouble on the printed page – seem here, because the picture pattern dominates, to add excitement rather than confusion.

later, by which time there was a Fokker works in the United States, he produced the classic F.VII ten-seater, with a 360 hp engine and cruising at 84 mph. From this he derived the F.VII/3m, which was possibly the best known and most widely used airliner of the whole 1920s. As the designation suggests, it had three engines instead of one; the most famous F.VII/3m, the 'Southern Cross' of Sir Charles Kingsford-Smith, had 220 hp Wright Whirlwinds, but several other types of engine could be used. This classic design, with a high wing, an engine in

able foundations for the future. This was the US Air Mail, which was first organized by the US Post Office in May 1918 between New York and Washington and was soon extended right across the nation to San Francisco. After six years the central sectors of this great route were equipped in a primitive but effective way for flying by night, with large bonfires at intervals of about 20 to 30 miles and powerful beacon lights at the frequent airfields.

By 1926 the Federal government had taken over

374

377

375

376

378

380

379

the nose, one under each wing, and a big box-like fuselage, was copied by many other constructors including the American car magnate Henry Ford whose Ford Trimotor – which differed from the Fokker transports in having all-metal construction with a corrugated skin – is still to be seen on active service in several places.

American designers did little of note in the early 1920s, apart from Glenn Curtiss whose record-breaking seaplanes have already been described. United States airlines in the early 1920s were non-existent. Cars, buses and trains handled virtually all the passenger traffic, and there was no transcontinental air service of any sort until July 1929 when an air/rail service was opened in which passengers flew by day and travelled in rail Pullman cars by night.

While US airlines remained no more than ideas in their promoters' brains, there was one American development that involved much arduous pioneer flying and laid valu-

responsibility for the US mail routes, and established airfields, radio systems and the other supporting services needed. On the other hand, by the same year the actual operation of flying the mail had passed to private enterprise, and this was the beginning of what is today the biggest and busiest network of air routes in the world. Each route was opened to competitive bidders and awarded on a contract basis at a price of an agreed number of cents per ton of mail flown from end to end of the route. By 1928 there were 33 contracts, covering more than 14,000 route-miles. This mileage climbed to over 30,000 miles in 1930, exceeded 60,000 miles in 1947 and is today well over 100,000. One of the biggest single influences in promoting the 'take-off' of commercial aviation in the United States was the dramatic flight of Charles Lindbergh. Another was the swift improvement in the available aircraft. The first mail services were operated with wartime types, notably the excellent

de Havilland DH.4a. In 1927 Boeing, already a renowned aircraft constructor, put in a bid for the vital mail route from Chicago to San Francisco that staggered everyone. Most observers predicted the company would, in the idiom of the time, 'lose its shirt', because the rate offered was half that of the next lowest bidder. In the event Boeing Air Transport, which was formed as a subsidiary to run the route, made money; it did so because Boeing had designed a new mailplane far more efficient than anything seen previously. A key to its performance was the Pratt & Whitney Wasp engine designed in 1925 by a fine team that broke away from the Wright company. Although intended initially for Navy fighters the Wasp soon opened up broader horizons for the designers of transports.

374 De Havilland 66 Hercules of Imperial Airways flying with port engine stopped, 1926
375 Armstrong Whitworth Argosy of Imperial Airways with supply vans at Croydon Airport, 1929
376 Fokker F.II after first KLM service to Croydon, September 1920

377 Fokker F.VIIA of KLM about to leave Schiphol for Djakarta on first long-distance charter flight, 1927
378 Fokker Trimotor, with Wright J-5 engines, in service with Pan American, about 1928
379 Interior of KLM Fokker F.VIIA
380 First sustained air mail service: Curtiss JN-4 (150 hp Hispano engine) leaving Washington Polo Grounds, 15 May 1918

166

167

The last two examples, and all hereafter, were printed offset. Although printing by letterpress never prevented the integration of text and pictures, photographs usually required glossy art paper if satisfactory reproduction was to be achieved, and, in practice, particularly with art books, the monochrome plates would be banished to a kind of limbo-land at the back. Offset encouraged integration, although for at least two decades the printed results were decidedly grey. Soon, letterpress (and also, sadly, photogravure) lost out to the various practical advantages of offset, including price. And this technical change seemed to go hand-in-hand with what I suppose must be called a more professional approach to publishing. This was the time of the 1973 oil crisis, with its widespread reverberations. The days of the individual publisher were numbered: the John Lehmanns, the Hugh Evelyns, the Paul Eleks, the Alan Ross's (who, amongst other things, was and is the editor of *London Magazine*. 'Everyone you publish is well-known.' AR: 'They weren't when I published them.') Now began the time of long-established firms being gobbled up by conglomerates, who seemed to switch their 'holdings' like schoolboys swapping

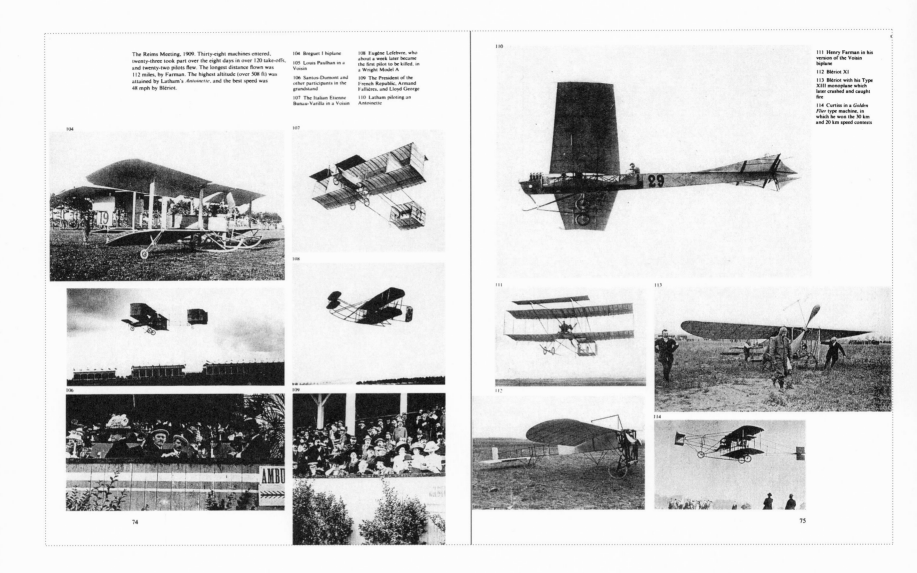

The Reims Meeting, 1909. Thirty-eight machines entered, twenty-three took part over the eight days in over 120 take-offs, and twenty-two pilots flew. The longest distance flown was 112 miles, by Farman. The highest altitude (over 508 ft) was attained by Latham's *Antoinette*, and the best speed was 48 mph by Blériot.

104 Breguet I biplane

105 Louis Paulhan in a Voisin

106 Santos-Dumont and other participants in the grandstand

107 The Italian Etienne Bunau-Varilla in a Voisin

108 Eugéne Lefebvre, who about a week later became the first pilot to be killed, in a Wright Model A

109 The President of the French Republic, Armand Fallières, and Lloyd George

110 Latham piloting an Antoinette

111 Henry Farman in his version of the Voisin biplane

112 Blériot XI

113 Blériot with his Type XIII monoplane which later crashed and caught fire

114 Curtiss in a *Golden Flier* type machine, in which he won the 30 km and 20 km speed contests

marbles. Staff were sacked by the dozen. Ironically, many of the sacked, reluctant to leave the world they knew and loved, set up on their own. Against the odds, even in big, conglomerate publishers, some commissioning editors have continued to seek out and support unknown authors. But the earlier rather risky spirit of adventure was seen more rarely in this tougher-minded world.

It could still be found. Alan Ross, who had no staff to sack, being, at times literally, one man and his dog, kept London Magazine Editions going until 1986. 'Publishing has always been for me an amateur activity in the strictest sense of the word … I have never earned a penny out of it … There is more to be gained by helping writers on the way up – or on the way down for that matter – when

you are acting on our kind of scale, than taking the safer course.' More commonly though, when the country of post-war austerity changed into affluent Britain, money men – the result of prosperity, not the cause – popped up to insist that cash flow governed all things. (Debt management and gearing were to come.) Why, and how, has this happened?

they were known as *di penates publici*. They and Vesta shared an antique place of worship at Rome's alleged mother city, Lavinium. The Romans did not know where the cult of the Penates had come from, but identified them with gods of the Aegean island of Samothrace, and declared that Aeneas, the mythical forerunner of Romulus, had brought them from there on his migration from the ruins of burning Troy.[8]

They were habitually associated with the Lares, who may originally have been powers guarding farms. But then, like the Penates, they were imported to the city in the capacity of national as well as household gods. And they too were given a shrine, at the summit of the Sacred Way.

Each year, the new crop of grain became more and more sacred as harvest-time approached, reaching the climax of its sanctity when the Festival of Vesta was celebrated in early June. At all other seasons the Storehouse was kept shut, but on 7 June it was thrown open to all married women, and for seven days they crowded into it barefoot. Then it was closed again. But first it had been carefully purified. The refuse was thrown into the Tiber or removed elsewhere, probably after storage in the deep pit that has been found beneath the shrine. This hole must have contained some pretty gruesome material, such as the ashes of the calves torn by attendants of the Chief Vestal from the corpses of thirty-one pregnant cows slaughtered and cremated on 15 April every year. Six days later the ashes, mixed with blood, were poured onto heaps of burning straw over which people jumped in a weird ceremony of purification.

When these performances had all taken place, the Storehouse was at last ready to receive the new grain: though it could still only be stored and eaten after elaborate ritual precautions. The traditions from remote antiquity which centred upon the Storehouse of Vesta were very numerous. It housed, for example, a jar containing the blood from the head of a racehorse which was decapitated and sacrificed to Mars every October.[9]

But above all the shrine cherished the sacred symbols and pledges of the power and eternity of Rome. Nobody knew what they were, and nobody knows to this day, because they were only seen by the Vestal Virgins and the Chief Priest; and for generation after generation the secret was kept. But it was said that the emblems were seven in number, and that they were preserved in a large earthenware urn. They were believed to include the sacred Palladium, an effigy of

Pallas Athene (Minerva) which, according to one popular version of its story, had been rescued by Aeneas from the flames of Troy and brought to Italy.[10] It had stood for the luck of Troy, but this link had ended when Troy was no more, and now the image represented the good fortune of Rome, and was one of the most potent guarantors of its safety. Indeed, this statue was so holy that the Chief Priest Lucius Metellus was said to have gone blind when he rescued it from a fire in the temple. But an even more dangerous moment came under the irregular emperor Elagabalus (AD 218–22). For, desiring to make his own

Coin of Elagabalus showing the procession of his god.

Syrian god the principal divinity of Rome, he wanted to marry that outlandish deity to Roman Vesta. With this shatteringly untraditional idea in mind, he proposed to carry off not only the sacred fire, but the jar containing the Palladium – so that Minerva could be united with her eastern husband in his new Roman shrine. But the Vestal Virgins claimed later that they had tricked the emperor by handing over an empty jar.[11] This story came from the current belief that, in order to thwart such thieves, they kept two urns in the Storehouse, one containing the Pledges and one empty.[12]

THE HOUSE OF THE VESTAL VIRGINS

The Virgins who guarded the shrine and all its antiquarian rituals lived a few yards away, in the House of Vesta (Atrium Vestae). Although the fine brickwork has been stripped of nearly all its marble facing, it is

Above: From the ruined House of the Vestals the view now lies open to the Record Office (Tabularium).
Overleaf: The House of the Vestals.

still possible to form a good idea of what the house looked like in the first and second centuries AD when it assumed its present form.

The most extensive feature of the building was its great colonnaded courtyard which can now only be imagined from its ruined remains. The courtyards of private houses, uncovered or with a central opening over a rain-water tank, had already been adorned with Greek colonnades since c. 300 BC. The courtyard of this House of the Vestals beside the Roman Forum was surrounded by a portico of forty-eight columns, of which the remains are now sparse. The centre of the open space contained a garden. Three cisterns for the reception of rain-water can be seen, and in the centre there remains the outline (now largely covered) of an octagonal structure which may have been a small formal wood or thicket, the symbolic survival of some ancient grove. Under the pavement, which dates from the empire, there remain traces of its predecessor of the Republican epoch.

At the short north-western end of the court are the remains of a kitchen (with fireplace), a dining-room, and vestibule (not easily accessible today). Just outside – nearly opposite the door of Vesta's round temple – stands a chapel which, as has been said, contained a statue of the goddess. At the opposite extremity of the courtyard is a broad central chamber which corresponds to the living or reception room in private houses, but was perhaps used here as a kind of sacristy. With access to this central hall, adjoining it on either side, are six smaller rooms, formerly lined with marble. This may have been used for one of the most important functions of the building, which was to serve as a safe deposit for public and private documents, including wills. In 45 BC, the year before he was murdered, Julius Caesar deposited his will with the Vestal Virgins, and this is where it was lodged. The employment of the Vestals' house as a safe deposit is no doubt one of the principal reasons for its large size.

51
The Roman Forum
Michael Grant
Weidenfeld & Nicolson 1970
246mm deep

51
The professional, publishing-as-a-business product, is seen here. It is typical of the academically respectable, semi-popular, integrated book of the 1960s and 1970s, but better designed than most. Well-produced – cloth binding, good maps and plans, printed endpapers, sixteen pages of well-printed colour – and designed by Gerald Cinamon, it suffers from the flat grey black-and-white printing characteristic of early offset. This is particularly regrettable, since most of the photographs were specially commissioned.

This and the previous example were both printed abroad (in Italy), a frequent practice from the 1960s onwards, partly because some Italian printers had organised their business to specialise in the printing of heavily-illustrated books. Other countries followed suit, and from the 1980s large numbers of books, especially those lavishly illustrated in colour, were and are well and economically printed in the Far East.

And so the crowd surged round and cremated Caesar's body just across the Forum, on the platform subsequently incorporated in his temple (p. 93).

Later, Antony invested the New Rostra with a further lurid distinction, for it was on its walls that he and his fellow-triumvirs, Octavian and Lepidus, displayed the lists of those who had been proscribed and sentenced to death. One of them was Cicero, and after his execution it was here that his severed head and right hand were exposed to public view. Antony, it was said, roared with laughter when they were first shown to him, and people declared that his wife Fulvia, who had previously been married to Cicero's arch-enemy Clodius, spat in the face of the dead orator and pierced his tongue with a hair-pin.

Caesar, Antony and the emperors who followed were all agreed that the Assemblies of the People should not retain any shadow of power or even nuisance value. Yet they could still be exploited for spectacular imperial purposes, being summoned, for example, for Augustus' ceremonial adoption of Tiberius as his son.[4] The main use of the New Rostra was for magnificent solemnities of this kind. For example, when Augustus died, an oration in his honour was delivered from this platform by the younger Drusus, son of the new emperor Tiberius who had already addressed the people from the Temple of Caesar where the body was lying in state.

Nero also held a particularly splendid ceremony on the New Rostra, in honour of a visiting king of Armenia, Tiridates.[5] Two years later, when Nero's downfall and death were at hand, he imagined that he might again go into the Forum and mount the Rostra and beg the people to forgive him or at least send him into honourable retirement. And after he was dead, his supporters secretly, at night, adorned the Rostra with images of him, and the texts of his decrees.

The sort of occasion which the emperors liked to stage at the place is also illustrated by two sculptured reliefs found a few yards away and now lodged in the Senate-house. They were once thought to belong to a separate Tribunal of Trajan, and they are generally known as Trajan's Plutei (balustrades) or Anaglypha (bas-reliefs); but it has instead been suggested, with a good deal of probability, that they formed the balustrades surrounding the platform of the New Rostra. One of them shows an emperor, who is, in fact, probably Trajan's successor Hadrian (AD 117–38),

addressing the people from this platform. In front of him is a seated statue of Trajan, to whom a woman, perhaps Italia, presents two children, one in her arms and one led by the hand. The panel refers to Trajan's endowment schemes for poor children, which Hadrian evidently extended. The other relief shows Hadrian standing on the dais while men bring him a heap of tablets, which he is giving the order to burn. The allusion is to his annulment of fifteen years' accumulation of debts to the state, amounting to 900 million sesterces, which was perhaps the rough equivalent of 45 million pounds – an event also commemorated by his coins (AD 118).

Both pieces of sculpture show backgrounds including interesting sketches of buildings in the Forum. They also depict a sacred fig-tree which had been miraculously transferred to a site nearby, where it grew, as its successor grows today, alongside an olive and a vine. Next to the tree is to be seen, on each of the

reliefs, a statue of the mythical Marsyas, which stood in ancient times beside the fig, olive and vine. He is best known as the musician who came to a bad end because he unwisely competed with Apollo, but here the reference is to a different thread in the tradition, according to which his name also stood for the free-

Detail of relief on p. 115; Italia presents a child to Trajan. In the background is probably the Basilica Aemilia.
Opposite: Statue of Marsyas (carrying a wineskin and standing beneath a fig tree) which symbolizes the freedom of the citizens of Rome.

Then came the Basilica Aemilia (179, first called 'Fulvia et Aemilia') and the Basilica Sempronia (170, later Julia) of which the ground plans, but unfortunately all too little else, can still be seen flanking the Forum on each of its long sides.

The original Basilica Aemilia (NE of the Forum) was another internally colonnaded, oblong hall. Its nave was probably taller than the side aisles; if so, the upper walls of the nave, rising above the aisle roofs, were lit at this high level by rows of small windows anticipating the clerestories of Romanesque and Gothic churches. In 159 BC the Basilica was furnished with Rome's first reliable timepiece, a water-clock, which was a considerable improvement on the sundials used previously.

When the building was reconstructed just after its centenary in 78 BC, it was given a colonnade outside as well as in – or rather two, for one was placed on top of the other. The coins which indicate these features confirm that, in accordance with a custom borrowed from the Greeks, shields were attached to the horizontal courses between the upper and lower colonnade.[13] It is also clear from the coins that the lower of the colonnades was Doric and the upper one Corinthian; and the same sketches seem to indicate that the short ends of the Basilica were crowned by gables or pediments.

The coins do not, however, suggest that there were any round arches between these external columns: they formed colonnades, not arcades. It was evidently when the building was again lavishly rebuilt by another member of the Aemilian family (55–34 BC), with

The Basilica Aemilia as restored by Marcus Aemilius Lepidus (78 BC), on a silver *denarius* issued not long afterwards.
Right: Reconstructions of the Basilica Aemilia: above, first to fourth centuries; below, fifth to sixth centuries.
Opposite: Drawing by Giuliano da Sangallo of the marble facade of the Basilica Aemilia in the sixteenth century. Vatican Library.

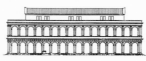

funds initially supplied as a political bribe by Julius Caesar, that the concrete-cored circular arches were added, so as to make an enormous two-storeyed arcade backing on the Basilica's outside wall, of which a good deal still survives. Henceforward, if not earlier, the New Shops were incorporated in the outer gallery between arcade and wall. It was probably at the same time that an additional aisle or ambulatory was added to the interior on the side farthest from the Forum, bringing the building to its final dimensions of 308 by 79 feet. Corresponding to the two external storeys were superimposed internal colonnades consisting of Ionic and Corinthian columns of black, red and white African marble, and green and white *cipollino* from Euboea. The ceilings were still flat and made of wood. A large, two-storeyed frontal portico was erected on the short side facing the Senate-house.

After a fire of 14 BC, the Basilica Aemilia was sumptuously restored once more under Augustus, who incorporated a chapel in honour of his grandsons Gaius and Lucius beside the New Shops (SE). Another restoration was undertaken by Tiberius on the two hundredth anniversary of the Basilica. At one of these stages, the frontal portico was adorned with an elaborate frieze.

Part of the rich relief sculpture of the interior of the building, probably dating from the time of Augustus, is still to be seen on the spot, while other portions are preserved in the Forum Museum. Executed in the vigorous, plastic manner of late Greek (Hellenistic) art, it includes various scenes from Roman legend, including the story of Aeneas and his escape from Troy to be the legendary ancestor of Rome, and the rape of the Sabine women by Romulus' men.

WYCLIFFE HALL AND EGGLESTONE ABBEY

deep, shaded course of the Tees, rocks brought down by torrents, and all overhung by trees—which would have called forth his usual response of patient, loving observation and delighted recording of detail but, although he was working in his largest sketchbook, he dashed down only a few quick notes of the river channels, a few rocks brought down by the Greta, and the suggestion of a few trees. We can imagine Turner now, narrowing his eyes as he peered out under the dripping brim of his hat. It was raining. He had been on his own now for a week, and he had the prospect of another couple of weeks of the same to come. He was cold, wet and depressed. He packed up as soon as possible and beat a retreat to the inn.

Thursday 1 August

The new day brought a new month and restored Turner's spirit. His first destination was Wycliffe Hall, about two miles downstream from the meeting of the waters. He made the required drawing (Ill. 66) straight away while the weather was fair enough for him to note the 'calm' water, and to enjoy the elaboration of details, including riverside cottages and a horse and cart passing by in the lane (Ill. 67). The riverbanks particularly impressed him, and he took a more distant panorama of the house, and some other sketches in which the house is but an afterthought. He concentrated rather on the rocky bluffs and hanging woods and the small meadows trapped in bends of the river.

These sketches of Wycliffe, which took up the first part of the morning, contain no indication of the girls chasing geese who appear in the foreground of the finished watercolour (Pl. 11). Turner may have intended this finished scene to be allegorical. Wycliffe Hall was reputedly the

birthplace of John Wycliffe (1324-84) the reformer and translator of the Bible. Many years later, John Pye, who had engraved the watercolour, recalled that when he had remarked to Turner that 'the geese are large'. Turner replied 'They are not geese, but overfed priests.' Turner increased the intensity of light over Wycliffe's house and told Pye that it indicated the symbolic light of the Reformation. Wycliffe's followers are driving away the geese-priests. This might seem fanciful, were it not for the long and serious inscription Turner added to one of the engraving proofs, describing Wycliffe's achievement.

Turner's finished compositions are as much pictures of his mind as literal records of places. 'Always paint your impressions,' he advised, but not the impressions of the eye so much as those of the imagination. The significance of place for Turner was a synthesis of many different elements: literary, historical and artistic associations, allegorical and symbolic details, natural effects, characteristic incidents, and his recollections of actually being there. The associations are a necessary part of the way he worked. As he looked at his sketch he could remember the sounds of cackling geese and girlish cries, a horse-drawn cart trundling down to the river and the sunlight flinting on the 'calm' (written on the sketch) water, but he was searching above all for significance. As he floated the washes over his paper, associations crowded round, and those that surfaced in his picture are those that conveyed to him most vividly the particular spirit of the place.

From Wycliffe Turner returned to Greta Bridge and walked directly from there to his next site, the tiny church of Brignall, about a mile from the inn along the banks of the Greta. 'O Brignall Banks are wild and fair, And Greta woods are green,' Scott had sung in *Rokeby* (III.xvi), and it was particularly these woods and banks that fired Turner's imagination. Brignall church was 'as small in its best days as churches among the North Country mountains and moors are wont to be', though most of it was carried off to help build a new and larger church at the top of the hill in 1834. It stood quite alone in a little meadow by the river Greta enclosed on all sides by hills and woodlands. Turner was delighted by the seclusion.

He began sketching on a hill to the south, looking out over the church. Once again, his first impression proved to be the most compelling, for after exploring the site, he returned to it to make the detailed study for Longmans. The result was one of the most poetical of all the *County of York* series. The watercolour itself was destroyed by fire in the last century but the engraving (Ill. 68) recorded it with special sensitivity. Turner diminished the already tiny church to give special emphasis to the river banks. His studies of rocks and trees prompted, in Brignall Banks, one of the most loving and meticulous of all his pictures of riverbanks, including in the foreground a further sign that he knew the poetic associations of the scene 'where twixt rock and river grew, a dismal grove of sable yew'.

Turner's studies at Brignall took three hours, and it was well into the afternoon by the time he set off for Egglestone Abbey. Little remains of the monastery buildings, though the greater part of the nave and chancel walls of the cruciform church still stand. The north transept has fallen, but was still there in Turner's day. It is the setting above all which makes a visit to this site worthwhile. The stream foams and rattles past the ruins through thick greenery to tumble into a gorge.

Egglestone is only two miles from Greta Bridge and, as Torrington related, 'Makes a grand object from which to see the ... [Rokeby] house, and well brought in is the ruin of Egglestone Abbey; to which (after my full

66

67

66. *Wycliffe on the River Tees near Rokeby.*

67. *A continuation of the sketch illustrated as Ill.66. The pony cart became the main theme of the finished watercolour (Pl. 11) appearing at the centre of the composition about to ford the river.*

68. *Brignall Church, engraved by S.Rawle. Described by Ruskin as the perfect image of the painter's mind at this period', this is the only record of the watercolour, which was destroyed by fire about a century ago. It is also one of the few records of the church which was demolished when a new one was built at the top of the hill in 1834. The landscape, however, is largely unchanged with still, silent woods growing up from the banks of the River Greta.*

70

52

In Turner's Footsteps
David Hill
John Murray 1984
238mm deep

52

Produced (or 'packaged') by Breslich & Foss, designed by Peter Bridgewater, and still suffering somewhat from the printing (Turner's subtle and delicate work is not easy to reproduce), nonetheless this account of the artist's 1816 tour of Northern England is a fine piece of book-making. Avoiding the 'this is a photograph taken from Turner's viewpoint' treatment, although such photographs are discreetly included, the author, carefully analysing Turner's sketchbooks, imaginatively re-creates the tour, and has us sharing the artist's experiences. 'For notes such as this he was oblivious of the weather, jotting them on to the tiny pages of the pocket book with the rain dripping off his hat on to the page, staining the paper and making it cockle. In contrast, he worked in the composition books seated under the shelter of his umbrella and the only stains they show are from where he dropped them in the mud.' The reader is there, dripping alongside Turner. Excellent maps show the route taken and places drawn; the design, owing much to the disciplined Swiss school, holds together the disparate elements – text, drawings, paintings, maps, photographs, turning what could be a series of chaotic pages into a sort of orderly scrap book (see overleaf).

MARRICK PRIORY
TO RICHMOND

47

48

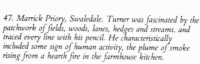
49

50

at Grinton, before crossing the Swale bridge and heading downdale to the priories of Marrick and Ellerton.

The church of St. Andrew at Marrick had been rebuilt only five years before out of the materials of the original twelfth-century Benedictine priory which, like Jervaulx, had been destroyed by the dissolution of the monasteries. Four years before the nuns were forced to abandon their home, however, a rich and very beautiful maid-of-honour named Isabella Beaufort arrived at the gates seeking sanctuary. Henry VIII wished to marry her but she, with commendable foresight, had no desire to be his queen. The prioress admitted Isabella and kept her in hiding, permitting her to correspond with her lover, Edward Herbert. When at last the priory was closed, Herbert rode up to Marrick, bore Isabella back to Somerset and married her.

Turner lost no time in deciding on the best viewpoint, and dashed off only a couple of quick notes before settling down on a bluff immediately downstream to record the view up Swaledale to the fells he had crossed an hour or so before. The priory is set on its own promontory amongst a patchwork of fields, woods, hedges and lanes, and in his drawing (Ill. 47) is punctuated by the new church tower rising from a farmyard, with smoke rising from a hearth fire in the farmhouse kitchen where dinner is being prepared in the late afternoon. As in all the sketches, there is little or no indication of weather. The finished watercolour (Pl. 5) is a magnificent study of billowing clouds and filtered sunlight dropping on different parts of the view.

On the opposite bank of the river Ellerton Priory lies about a mile downstream, and communication between the two convents was established over stepping-stones. Turner forded the river but discovered that little of the old

47. Marrick Priory, Swaledale. Turner was fascinated by the patchwork of fields, woods, lanes, hedges and streams, and traced every line with his pencil. He characteristically included some sign of human activity, the plume of smoke rising from a hearth fire in the farmhouse kitchen.

48. Richmond Bridge and Castle with Yorke House to the left. Turner had already visited the site in 1797 and engraved the subject on his memory on that occasion by sketching it and by painting it later in about 1799 (Ill. 50). He was satisfied that it was sufficiently unchanged in 1816 to use the early sketch as the basis of a new watercolour (Ill. 49).

49. Colour study of Richmond Bridge and Castle, made in c.1818.

50. Richmond Bridge and Castle, 1799.

60

One can visualise only too clearly this same subject treated as an academic plod. Had it been printed letterpress, this would probably have been its fate. But offset printing encouraged a more flexible and imaginative conception. The text, empathising with Turner, reproduces for our discomfort the rain, the cold, the poor roads, tired horse, wet and muddy clothes stuffed into a rain-soaked saddlebag. His sketches, ranging from a few scribbled lines with notes, to carefully-detailed drawings, are shown alongside the text, together with watercolour studies deriving from them (made later in the studio) and, in some cases, the final worked-up watercolours.

51

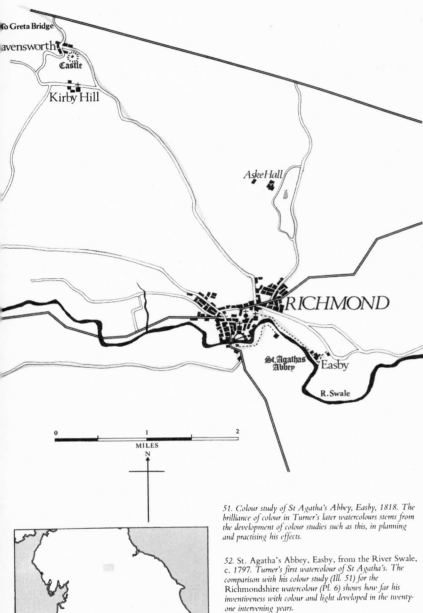

52

51. Colour study of St Agatha's Abbey, Easby, 1818. The brilliance of colour in Turner's later watercolours stems from the development of colour studies such as this, in planning and practising his effects.

52. St. Agatha's Abbey, Easby, from the River Swale, c. 1797. Turner's first watercolour of St Agatha's. The comparison with his colour study (Ill. 51) for the Richmondshire watercolour (Pl. 6) shows how far his inventiveness with colour and light developed in the twenty-one intervening years.

Cistercian nunnery remained worth sketching. Instead, he found a viewpoint further along the valley on the road to Downholme. From here he could record the whole stretch of Swaledale towards Ellerton and Marrick, though the sketch he made covers an angle of about thirty degrees, an unusually small proportion for Turner of the total view available. The priory itself was about a mile and a half away. Its details were barely visible. The angle of view, the foreshortening of distances and the visibility of the priory buildings draw the eye into the composition with an immediacy that demonstrates very vividly the way in which the artist used his eyes, and in which he drew sense and significance out of the raw material of landscape that he encountered.

Turner's first sight of Richmond, capital of Swaledale, was of the great Norman tower of the castle rising above the Swale, with the slate-roofed town clustered around and the whole plain of north Yorkshire spread out beyond. He stopped to commit this to memory, catching the clouds sweeping across the sky and the distant Cleveland Hills in shadow. The subject deserved longer contemplation, but for the moment he was keen to press on to the town. It was nineteen years since he had last sketched at Richmond and his first thought was to revisit the site of one of his early sketches.

The view of the bridge and castle, with Yorke House to the left, taken from a point on the left bank just upstream from the bridge, had formed the basis of a watercolour made about 1799 (Ills. 48 and 50). Although Yorke House was demolished in 1824, the view remains unchanged today except for the growth of trees, and Turner in 1816 found it exactly as he recalled it from 1797. He made a quick sketch in the pocket-book

61

131

APPLEBY

and he dismounted to give his horse a breather. He put up at the first roadhouse he found, at Dufton. An inn can never have looked so inviting.

Sunday, 4 August
After his hard slog the day before, Turner had to take it easy, if only for the sake of his horse. A strong horse could manage twenty to twenty-five miles a day regularly, but only over good ground. 'Nine hours making eleven miles' over the highest fells in Yorkshire was enough for any animal and Turner spent Sunday morning quietly. As he rode into Appleby around lunch-time he had to turn over eight pages of the pocket-book, still damp from the rain where he had stopped on High Cup Nick now more than 1500 feet above him.

He took a few sketches of the town and then pressed gently on south over the Maulds Meaburn and Bank Moors to the Lune valley at Tebay. Although the road commands spectacular views of the Lakeland hills to the West, Turner did not pause to record them. Only as he came over Orton Scar did he find himself confronted with a view that was, simply, too good to resist. He made the sketch on one of the now dried four pages in the pocket-book (Ill. 79). Between Tebay Fell on the left and Roundthwaite Common on the right, he could just make out the line of the Kendal Road and the site of his next commissioned drawing, the Lune Gap.

77

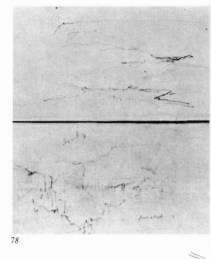

78

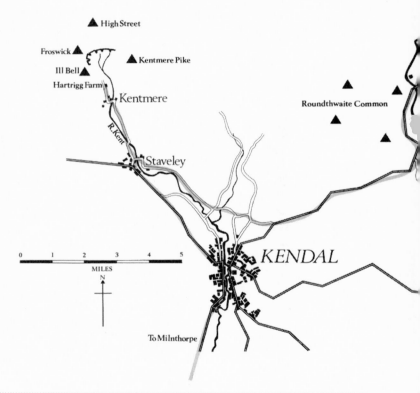

76

The immediacy of this approach produces an understanding of the artist's working methods (and his character) that would not have been possible had it been merely a routine assembly of images and facts. Turner, one feels, would have approved.

From Cauldron Snout

PPLEBY

R. Eden

▲ Maulds Meaburn
Moor

Scar

R. Lune

Langdale Fell

79

80

81

2

77

The valley of the Lune offered one of the few easy passages through the Westmorland Hills for Anglo-Scottish traffic. About a mile south of Tebay, the road crosses the marble-smooth gorge of the young river Lune, in Turner's day spanned at this point by two bridges. The northerly one replaced a medieval structure which had presumably now become unsafe. Turner devoted a page in the smaller composition book to this site (Ills. 81 and 82), choosing, as usual, to record his first impression as he rounded the bend in the road from Tebay.

This is a peculiarly satisfying sketch. The elegant twin bridges provide a landmark of human ingenuity amidst the bare fells raked by early evening sunlight. Human presence in a landscape, and man's achievement in direct and vital contact with the environment, are favourite themes with Turner. The Lune Farm and its bridges

77. High Cup Nick, near Appleby.

78. Two views of High Cup Nick. Despite the fact that Turner had just struggled across the bogs from Cauldron Snout he still had enough energy to sketch the view looking towards the Lake District mountains and 'Hellvelyn'.

79. The view from Orton Scar towards the Lune Valley and the 'Road' to Kendal, Orton Church to the right. Note rain-staining.

80. View from Orton Scar of about 70 degrees. Note the way that Turner seems to compress this view in his sketch (Ill. 79), and exaggerates the apparent height of the hills.

81. Lune Bridge, near Tebay.

82. Lune Bridge and Farm near Tebay. Turner almost always sketched his first impressions, whether of the surprise view coming over Orton Scar from Appleby, or as here, rounding a bend in the road from Tebay. The nearer bridge survives, as does the farm (almost completely unchanged), but otherwise there have been dramatic changes.

A more recent book (1996) by the same author, but for a different publisher, shows how easily things can go wrong. It covers Turner's earlier tour of 1797. Much of the text almost takes the form of a mapless guidebook instead of a diary, and the earlier concentrated day-by-day empathy is missing. It is more lavishly produced but on the whole, despite the use of a paper less sympathetic to drawings and watercolours, no better printed. The careful balancing act of the earlier book has not been appreciated, and large, often full-page, strongly-coloured photographs overwhelm Turner's delicate drawings and watercolours. The publisher or the designers have allowed bookshop impact to take precedence over respect for the artist's work and regard for the reader or even the real subject. Turner, one feels, would have been dismayed.

53

In Turner's Footsteps would have been difficult to achieve – and probably would never have been conceived – in its present form without the freedoms allowed by offset. The Eyewitness Travel Guides of eleven years later required – and exploited – a further advance in technology, being designed and created on the computer screen. The jigsawing together of images and type seen here is pushing technique, design principles and printing technology to somewhere near their limits, while still respecting the practical needs of the reader.

Dorling Kindersley concentrate on the popular end of the market. The guides exhibit many classic DK character-istics. The captions to the high-quality illustrations (drawings, maps and photographs) are frequently augmented with items of particular note pointed out as if by a lecturer's stick. There are numerous canny space-savers – symbols, time charts (or 'timelines'), colour codings and so on; boxes highlight 'Star Features', 'Visitors' Checklist', 'Tips for Drivers', related items and 'Story Boxes'. There are lists of 'Sights at a Glance', 'Getting Around', 'See Also'. 'Top Sights' are each given two or more pages. Although making no attempt to compete with the exhaustive detail contained in Blue Guides, these are serious books even if the information has been pre-digested for easy assimilation.

Perhaps somewhat less convenient for on-the-spot use than Blue Guides, Michelin or the admirable and well-thought-out Rough Guides, they are a down-market version of Collins' Companion Guides, in that, like them, they are designed to be of interest before and after a visit, as well as during it.

The book designer's structure and ideas – never the *only possible* solution, no matter how intensely the problem is analysed – will usually be triggered off by the subject and nature of the material. A house editor may contribute considerably to the organisation of the author's text, and the printer advise on production matters. But the *scheme* of a book can be provided by, for instance, a publisher (one man) enabling an author and an artist to visit Corsica; or several people co-ordinating to produce a book such as this guide. The two examples could hardly be more different: an inspired idea, the uncertain outcome of which could easily have failed, or the dogged accumulation and integration of assorted material to achieve a clearly-envisioned concept. They are almost a paradigm of the changes in publishing over the last fifty years: from a kind of artistry to a business operation. Books like the guides require teamwork worthy of film-making, and the credits almost resemble those endlessly rolling after a film. Only the Catering Crew and Best Boy seem missing.

The problem is not so much researching the material, but, for books such as these, editing the text down to bite-size chunks. Moreover, there is a budget and a finite number of pages. The product, not the text, comes first. The preliminary design is done at an early stage, illustrations, photographs and maps planned in, and authors told how many words they can have for each page or paragraph. Close liaison throughout is essential – for instance, discussions with illustrators or cartographers as to what can be shown, and how. First ideas may not work out in practice.

Books of this kind, with their shrewd marketing approach, would have been almost inconceivable twenty-five years ago. The Automobile Association and Reader's Digest, and packagers such as George Rainbird, produced some of the earlier examples; guides to the country-side, natural history, town walks, gradually spreading their net wider as they trawled the seas of popular publishing (DIY, gardening, aquarium fish, and for all I know, jam-making and cactus-growing). Large runs and foreign language editions allowed the use of full colour throughout (how different from the Odhams Press books on the countryside, around 1950, poorly printed on poor paper in black-and-white only; but they seemed wonder-ful, well-illustrated books at the time). Exemplary illustrators, cartographers and diagram designers could be afforded. The design of such books, a special skill, is carried out nowadays on computer screens – unlike the old techniques (which, as a designer set in my ways, I still use) of drawing board, layout paper, pencil and typescale, galley proofs and Cow Gum. The layout, with boxes, coloured panels, photographs caged-in with rules, endless variations of type measure, text run around pictures, and no space left unfilled, is not my style – it seems strangely old-fashioned to me; but I must admire it in the case of these guides. Perhaps because of the restricted format, they are more disciplined than many mass-market books (including others by this publisher). There is some fussy post-modern detailing such as dropped initials and small caps for entry openings – a device sometimes useful for typographic signposting, but here superfluous – and the equally unnecessary use of larger cap initials of words in caps. But these guides are highly professional and, despite the PoMo details and the intentional busyness of the pages – giving the impression in a bookshop that they are packed with information – readability is never really lost sight of.

As is normal nowadays with books in the popular genre, production is spread world-wide. In the case of *Ireland*, type-setting was done in Britain, origination in Singapore, printing in Italy.

53
Eyewitness Travel Guides: Ireland
Lisa Gerard-Sharp and Tim Perry
Dorling Kindersley 1995
200mm deep

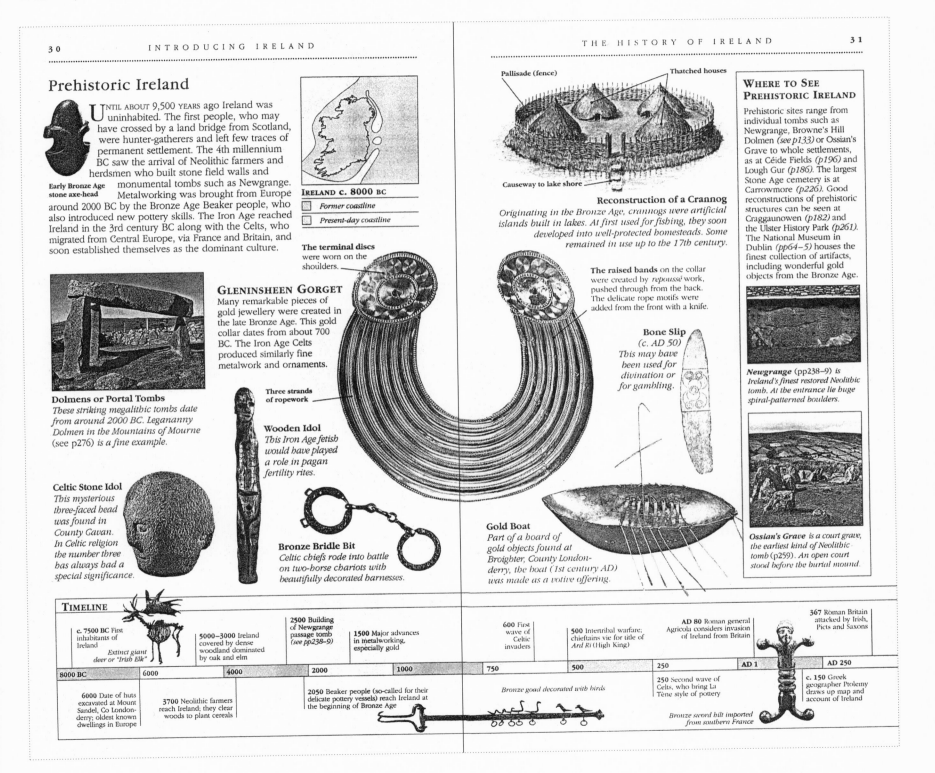

Prehistoric Ireland

UNTIL ABOUT 9,500 YEARS ago Ireland was uninhabited. The first people, who may have crossed by a land bridge from Scotland, were hunter-gatherers and left few traces of permanent settlement. The 4th millennium BC saw the arrival of Neolithic farmers and herdsmen who built stone field walls and monumental tombs such as Newgrange. Metalworking was brought from Europe around 2000 BC by the Bronze Age Beaker people, who also introduced new pottery skills. The Iron Age reached Ireland in the 3rd century BC along with the Celts, who migrated from Central Europe, via France and Britain, and soon established themselves as the dominant culture.

Early Bronze Age stone axe-head

IRELAND c. 8000 BC

- *Former coastline*
- *Present-day coastline*

Dolmens or Portal Tombs
These striking megalithic tombs date from around 2000 BC. Legananny Dolmen in the Mountains of Mourne (see p276) is a fine example.

Celtic Stone Idol
This mysterious three-faced head was found in County Cavan. In Celtic religion the number three has always had a special significance.

The terminal discs were worn on the shoulders.

GLENINSHEEN GORGET
Many remarkable pieces of gold jewellery were created in the late Bronze Age. This gold collar dates from about 700 BC. The Iron Age Celts produced similarly fine metalwork and ornaments.

Three strands of ropework

Wooden Idol
This Iron Age fetish would have played a role in pagan fertility rites.

Bronze Bridle Bit
Celtic chiefs rode into battle on two-horse chariots with beautifully decorated harnesses.

Reconstruction of a Crannog
Originating in the Bronze Age, crannogs were artificial islands built in lakes. At first used for fishing, they soon developed into well-protected homesteads. Some remained in use up to the 17th century.

Pallisade (fence)   Thatched houses

Causeway to lake shore

The raised bands on the collar were created by *repoussé* work, pushed through from the back. The delicate rope motifs were added from the front with a knife.

Bone Slip (c. AD 50)
This may have been used for divination or for gambling.

Gold Boat
Part of a hoard of gold objects found at Brighter, County Londonderry, the boat (1st century AD) was made as a votive offering.

WHERE TO SEE PREHISTORIC IRELAND

Prehistoric sites range from individual tombs such as Newgrange, Browne's Hill Dolmen *(see p133)* or Ossian's Grave to whole settlements, as at Céide Fields *(p196)* and Lough Gur *(p186)*. The largest Stone Age cemetery is at Carrowmore *(p226)*. Good reconstructions of prehistoric structures can be seen at Craggaunowen *(p182)* and the Ulster History Park *(p261)*. The National Museum in Dublin *(pp64–5)* houses the finest collection of artifacts, including wonderful gold objects from the Bronze Age.

Newgrange (pp238–9) *is Ireland's finest restored Neolithic tomb. At the entrance lie huge spiral-patterned boulders.*

Ossian's Grave *is a court grave, the earliest kind of Neolithic tomb (p259). An open court stood before the burial mound.*

TIMELINE

8000 BC	6000	4000	2000	1000	750	500	250	AD 1	AD 250
c. 7500 BC First inhabitants of Ireland *Extinct giant deer or "Irish Elk"*	**5000–3000** Ireland covered by dense woodland dominated by oak and elm	**2500** Building of Newgrange passage tomb *(see pp238–9)* **1500** Major advances in metalworking, especially gold		**600** First wave of Celtic invaders	**500** Intertribal warfare; chieftains vie for title of *Ard Rí* (High King)	**AD 80** Roman general Agricola considers invasion of Ireland from Britain	**367** Roman Britain attacked by Irish, Picts and Saxons		
6000 Date of huts excavated at Mount Sandel, Co Londonderry; oldest known dwellings in Europe	**3700** Neolithic farmers reach Ireland; they clear woods to plant cereals	**2050** Beaker people (so-called for their delicate pottery vessels) reach Ireland at the beginning of Bronze Age	*Bronze goad decorated with birds*			**250** Second wave of Celts, who bring La Tène style of pottery *Bronze sword hilt imported from southern France*	**c. 150** Greek geographer Ptolemy draws up map and account of Ireland		

Christ Church Cathedral ⑧

Arms on Lord Mayor's pew

CHRIST CHURCH CATHEDRAL was commissioned in 1172 by Strongbow, Anglo-Norman conqueror of Dublin *(see p34)*, and Archbishop Laurence O'Toole. It replaced an earlier wooden church built by the Vikings in 1038. At the time of the Reformation *(see p36)*, the cathedral passed to the Protestant Church of Ireland. By the 19th century it was in a bad state of repair, but was completely remodelled by architect George Street in the 1870s. In the crypt are monuments removed from the cathedral during its restoration.

★ Medieval Lectern
This beautiful brass lectern was hand-wrought during the Middle Ages. It stands on the left-hand side of the nave, in front of the pulpit. The matching lectern on the right-hand side is a copy, dating from the 19th century.

The Lord Mayor's pew is usually kept in the north aisle, but is moved to the front of the nave when used by Dublin's civic dignitaries. It features a carving of the city arms and a stand for the civic mace.

Great Nave
The 25-m (68-ft) high nave has some fine early Gothic arches. On the north side, the original 13th-century wall leans out by as much as 50 cm (18 in) due to subsidence.

★ Strongbow Monument
The large effigy in chain armour is probably not Strongbow. However, his remains are buried in the cathedral and the curious half-figure may be part of his original tomb.

The bridge to the Synod Hall was added when the cathedral was being rebuilt in the 1870s.

Entrance

Chapel of St Laud
The casket on the wall contains the heart of St Laurence O'Toole. The chapel features original medieval floor tiles.

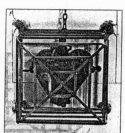

The Lady Chapel is used for Eucharist celebrations and is the chapel of the St John Ambulance Brigade.

★ Crypt
The cavernous crypt contains several oddities, including this mummified cat and rat, found in an organ pipe in the 1860s.

Stairs to crypt

Crypt

The foundations of the original Chapter House date back to the early 13th century.

Romanesque Doorway
Leading to the south transept, this ornately carved doorway is one of the finest examples of 12th-century Irish stonework.

STAR FEATURES

★ Strongbow Monument

★ Crypt

★ Medieval Lectern

TIMELINE

	1240 Completion of stone cathedral	**1600** Shopkeepers rent crypt space		**1689** King James II of England worships in cathedral	**1983** Cathedral ceases using Synod Hall
1038 Construction of original wooden Viking cathedral		**1541** King Henry VIII alters constitution of cathedral			

1000	1200	1400	1600	1800

1172 St Laurence O'Toole and Strongbow commission the new stone cathedral	*Meeting between Lambert Simnel and the Earl of Kildare (see p35)*	**1742** Choir participates in first performance of Handel's *Messiah* **1487** Coronation of 10-year-old Lambert Simnel as King of England	**1871** Major rebuilding of the cathedral begins, including Synod Hall and bridge

View across the harbour to Wexford town

Irish National Heritage Park 25

Road map D5. Ferrycarrig, Co Wexford. **from** Wexford in summer. **053 41733.** mid-Mar–mid-Jan: daily. 25–26 & 31 Dec.

BUILT ON former marshland near Ferrycarrig, just north of Wexford, the Irish National Heritage Park is a bold open-air museum. Trails lead visitors through woods to replicas of homesteads, places of worship and burial sites. These provide a good introduction to the country's ancient history (see pp30–31), and the section which deals with the Celtic period is particularly interesting. Other highlights include the Viking boatyard, complete with raiding ship, and a 7th-century horizontal watermill.

Sign of a popular Wexford pub

Wexford 26

Road map D5. Co Wexford. 15,000. *Crescent Quay (053 23111).*

WEXFORD'S name derives from *Waesfjord*, a Norse word meaning "estuary of the mud flats". It thrived as a port for centuries but the silting of the harbour in the Victorian era put an end to most sea traffic. Wexford's quays, from where ships once sailed to Bristol, Tenby and Liverpool, are now used mainly by a fleet of humble mussel dredgers.

Wexford is a vibrant place, packed with fine pubs and boasting a varied arts scene. The town's singular style is often linked to its linguistic heritage. The *yola* dialect, which was spoken by early settlers, survives in the local pronunciation of certain words.

Wexford retains few traces of its past, but the Viking fishbone street pattern still exists, with narrow alleys fanning off the meandering Main Street. Keyser's Lane, linking South Main Street with the lively Commodore pub on Paul Quay, is a tiny tunnel-like alley which once led to the Norse waterfront. The Normans were responsible for Wexford's town walls, remnants of which include one of the original gateways. This houses the **Westgate Heritage Centre**, which traces the history of Wexford. Behind it lies **Selskar Abbey**, the ruin of a 12th-century Augustinian monastery. King Henry II is said to have done penance here for the murder of Thomas à Becket in 1170.

Wexford also has several handsome buildings dating from a later period, including the 18th-century market house, known as the **Cornmarket**, on Main Street. The nearby square, the **Bull Ring**, is notable only for its history: it was used for bull-baiting in Norman times and was the scene of a cruel massacre by Cromwell's men in 1649.

Wexford Opera Festival, held in October, is the leading operatic event in the country. Aficionados praise it for its intimate atmosphere – both during performances and afterwards, when artists and audience mingle together in the pubs: the Centenary Stores off Main Street is a favourite, though the Wren's Nest, on Custom House Quay, is better for traditional music.

Westgate Heritage Centre
Westgate. **053 46506.** Jun–Aug: daily; Sep–May: Mon–Sat. 25 & 26 Dec.

ENVIRONS: Skirting the shore just east of the town is the **Wexford Wildfowl Reserve**. It covers 100 ha (250 acres) of reclaimed land and is noted in particular for its geese: over a third of the world's entire population of Greenland white-fronted geese winter here between October and April.

The mudflats also attract large numbers of swans and waders, and provide a rich hunting ground for birds of prey. The birds can be viewed from a number of hides and an observation tower.

Wexford Wildfowl Reserve
Wexford. **053 23129.** daily. at weekends.

Johnstown Castle 27

Road map D5. Co Wexford. **053 42888.** to Wexford. **Gardens** daily. 24 & 25 Dec.

Façade of Johnstown Castle

JOHNSTOWN CASTLE, a splendid Gothic Revival mansion, lies amid ornamental gardens and mature woodland 6 km (4 miles) southwest of Wexford. In state hands since 1945, the house now functions as an agricultural research centre. It is not open to the public, but it is possible to visit the **Irish Agriculture Museum**, housed in the castle's farm buildings. Reconstructions illustrate the work of a wheelwright and other traditional trades.

The real glory of Johnstown Castle are the grounds, from the sunken Italian garden and ornamental lakes to the woodlands and shrubberies. Azaleas and camellias flourish alongside an impressive array of trees including Japanese cedars, redwoods and Scots pine.

Hidden among the dense woods west of the house lurk the ruins of **Rathlannon Castle**, a medieval tower house.

Irish Agriculture Museum
Johnstown Castle. Apr–mid-Nov: daily (Sat & Sun pm only); mid-Nov–Mar: Mon–Fri. limited.

Saltee Islands 28

Road map D5. Co Wexford. **from** Wexford to Kilmore Quay: Wed & Sat. **from** Kilmore Quay: Jul & Aug (weather permitting). **053 29684.**

THESE ISLANDS off the south coast of Wexford are a haven for sea birds. Great and Little Saltee together form Ireland's largest bird sanctuary, nurturing an impressive array of birds, from gannets and gulls to puffins and Manx shearwaters. Great Saltee is particularly famous for its colonies of cormorants. It also has more than 1,000 pairs of guillemots and is a popular stopping-off place for spring and autumn migrations. A bird-monitoring and research programme is in progress, and a close watch is also kept on the colony of grey seals.

The two uninhabited islands are privately owned, but visitors are welcome. Boat trips are run in fine weather from **Kilmore Quay**. These leave in late morning and return mid-afternoon.

Kilmore Quay is a small fishing village built on rare Precambrian gneiss rock – the oldest rock in Ireland. Pretty thatched cottages nestle above a fine sandy beach and the harbour, where a moored lightship houses a **Maritime Museum**. The boat's original fittings are just as interesting as the exhibits.

Maritime Museum
Kilmore Quay. **053 29655.** Jun–Oct: daily (pm only).

Vast crescent of sand and shingle beach at Rosslare

Rosslare 29

Road map D5. Co Wexford. 1,200. *Ferry terminal, Rosslare Harbour (053 33622).*

ROSSLARE REPLACED Wexford as the area's main port after the decline of the original Viking city harbour. The port is so active today that people tend to associate the name Rosslare more with the ferry terminal for France and Wales than with the town lying 8 km (5 miles) further north.

Rosslare town is one of the sunniest spots in Ireland and draws many holidaymakers. It boasts a fine beach stretching for 9.5 km (6 miles), lively pubs and an excellent golf course fringed by sand dunes. There are good walks north to Rosslare Point.

ENVIRONS: At Tagoat, 6 km (4 miles) south of Rosslare, an old farmhouse called **Yola Farmstead** contains displays of traditional crafts such as thatching, glass-blowing and bread- and butter-making.

Yola Farmstead
Tagoat. **053 31177.** May–Sep: daily.

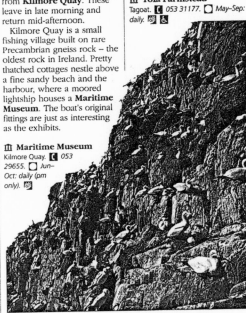
Colony of gannets nesting on the cliffs of Great Saltee Island

139
Section through west wall
1 Built-up felt roofing on 50mm (2in) Styrofoam insulation on 50mm (2in) concrete slab on steel decking
2 Double-glazed skylight with aluminium mullions
3 Reinforced concrete ring beams
4 Roof truss
5 Heating cables
6 Artificial lighting
7 Steelwork to skylight
8 Double-glazed curtain wall with aluminium mullions
9 Perimeter beam with tracks for insulated curtain on underside
10 Sound, projection and light rooms
11 19mm (¾in) diameter steel suspension rod
12 20 × 20 (8in × 8in) steel curtain wall bracing
13 Globe light fittings mounted round 56 (22in) diameter concrete column
14 Perimeter hot water fin tube radiation cabinet
15 Lobby
16 Steel spandrel panel with Styrofoam insulation backing
17 Exterior glass canopy with aluminium mullions
18 Double-glazed interior canopy
19 19mm (¾in) diameter suspension rod
20 20 × 20 (8in × 8in) steel curtain wall bracing with 10 × 20 (4in × 8in) steel brace to concrete column
21 Street level

138
Corner detail. The pavement is sheltered by a glass canopy which runs round the building.

look down through windows along the mall onto the access ramps to the garage. Also contained in the central mall are the cloakroom, box office, theatre shop, and the restaurant which in summer can be opened through and onto the pavement. Barton Myers has created an internal street in the traditional sense: a multi-layered, linear space full of activity at all times of day from which open off recreational and living areas. This is in dramatic contrast to the banality of Edmonton's Civic Centre itself, where public buildings such as an art gallery

and a library stand as separate entities, unrelated to each other, to the space surrounding them and to the people using them.

The back of house accommodation includes dressing rooms for fifty people, a green room, board room, a large rehearsal room and various workshops. Lorries can negotiate a ramp to the rear of the building up to workshop level from where assembled sets can move through a 6.5m (21ft) high acoustic lock into the wings.

The main structure of the building is a reinforced

140
Theatre lobby. The visitor moves through a complex series of spaces before reaching the auditorium.

110

111

54

Decorative Art and Modern Interiors
Maria Schofield
Studio Vista 1980
275mm deep

54

Back in 1980, this book was initially designed on layout paper, on a drawing board, followed by proofs and paste-up. The Dorling Kindersley books are 'picture-led'; but while the illustrations here play a major part, the pages describing each building were carefully developed by editor/author and designer working together. The choice of pictures was mutually agreed, and text allotted its natural space.

Nearly thirty years separate this book

from the Swiss book on exhibitions [44]. Although the subject and the elements are much the same, its appearance is very different. Yet much of the design thinking has grown out of that earlier book. A strict grid holds all the elements in place. Text, plans and elevations, photographs, captions, headings: all are thereby related; but pages are less full, less busy; headings larger. Fewer but larger pictures make for greater impact.

As with most heavily-illustrated books today, co-publishing was essential to

achieve all this. The selection of international examples, desirable in itself, was also intended to ensure international sales (at least four language editions were printed). And larger sales allow more lavish use of colour. Many of these developments are partly the result of increasing competition, compared with thirty years ago. Salesmen believe he who shouts loudest (and most colourfully) gets more sales. But here, unlike the 1996 Turner book previously mentioned, the subject is not compromised.

60
Plan of the completed
phases I and II
1 Public entrance
2 Main arena
3 Subsidiary sports halls

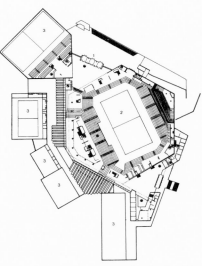

61
The main arena. The tubu-
lar steel perimeter supports
are articulated to allow for
movement in the space
frame. Circulation runs between the columns and the
external curtain walling.

would become a recognisable landmark, standing
out from the surrounding banal office blocks. The
large scale of the main stadium and the amenity of
the site, which borders the river Loire, provided
them with a very good opportunity to achieve their
purpose.

One of the major problems was to ensure good
visibility for each member of the crowd of 5000.
This was obtained by adopting an hexagonal plan
for the seating around the oblong arena. Spectators
are seated on steeply raked tiers which are concentrated in tapering wedges on the long sides of the
arena.

Covering the hall is a space frame 2.5m (8ft 2in)
deep constructed from tubular steel equilateral
triangles with 3.3m (10ft 6in) sides. This form of
structure allows a clear span of 80m (262ft) with no
intermediate supports obstructing vision lines. The
rigid frame is supported on thirty-six inclined
tubular steel posts of varying height placed immediately behind the rear row of seats and with
movable joints at the bottom and top junctions.

86

A Duplex House
Tiburon, California, USA

Architects
**Callister, Payne
and Bischoff**

Project Associate
Joseph O. Newberry

Photography
Carla de Benedetti

The village of Tiburon clings to the base of a
Californian cliff which drops steeply into San
Francisco Bay. Houses jut out from the waterfront
road and their foundations are often well beyond
the water edge.

This house was designed and built for two
separate families. One unit is a mirror image of the
other, separated by a 2.5cm (1in) gap for acoustic
privacy but using a common foundation system.
The site for the house was a particularly challeng-
ing one: the cliff is unstable along this stretch of
coastline and the edge of the public road required
support. To give the house a secure footing, reinforced concrete piers 60cm (2ft) in diameter were
constructed up to 2.4m (8ft) deep into the bedrock,
six of them below the high-water mark. A network
of 30cm (1ft) wide by 60cm (2ft) deep concrete
ground beams connect the pier heads on the slope
of the cliff and consolidate the earth. Circular
concrete columns 45cm (18in) in diameter rise
from the submerged piers to support a series of
laminated timber beams which carry the timber
framework of the house. The road is at the upper-
most level of the site, so the garages have been
placed at the top of the house. Descending two
external flights of stairs down either side of the

107
Plans: (above) street
level and mezzanine
(below) main level and
lower level.
Key to plans and section
1 Entrance
2 Solarium
3 Hearth room
4 Kitchen
5 Sun deck
6 Master bedroom
7 Bathroom
8 Dressing room
9 Bedroom
10 Workshop/mechanical
11 Lower deck
12 Gallery/study
13 Garage
14 Entrance gate
15 Fern garden

105
View from the entrance
balcony out across San
Francisco Bay. The house
extends over the water; a
section of the supporting
structure can be seen
through the balustrade.

106
Section.

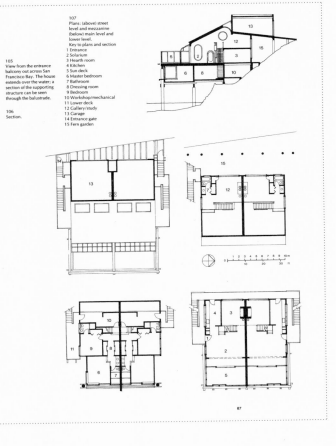

87

37 Bajokwe
Congo-Kinshasa
Standing figure of a man
13½in (34cm)
1969 Af9 5

38 Bakuba
Congo-Kinshasa
Standing figure of a woman
11½in (29cm)
1908 Ty164

39 Bakuba
Congo-Kinshasa
Squatting figure of a man
24¼in (54cm)
1909 12–10 1

This very fine carving (lately in the Eric Bedford collection) is of the type recently identified by Mlle Bastin as representing a Lunda chief whose name was Chibinda Ilunga in the early days of Lunda and Bajokwe history. The Lunda had built up a considerable empire some 300 years ago or more under their king Mwata Yamvo, and they employed the Bajokwe on more or less menial tasks such as carving figures for their use. In fact, it is said that all the carvings formerly attributed to Lunda are really Bajokwe works. This is one of the finest extant versions of the subject.

This, like the next piece, is part of the magnificent collections formed between 1907 and 1910 among the central Congo peoples by Emil Torday at the request of the British Museum. It is described as a house charm of the Bangendi subtribe.

This is the most famous of all Bakuba statues, being the representation of the king who is most celebrated in their traditions, Shamba Bolongongo, ninety-third king in the traditional list, who reigned early in the sixteenth century (and according to recent research may very well have come into the Bakuba country from outside and usurped the throne). Most important innovations in Bakuba culture, which is indeed higher than that of the surrounding tribes, are attributed to Shamba, and he is said to have made a journey to the west to fit himself for the kingship. Precisely at this time it appears that the Bakuba were in contact with the Kingdom of Kongo, whence they learned to make fine embroideries in a closely related style. One of his most celebrated innovations was the introduction of the game of skill called *lela* (Arabic *mankala*) as a way of eradicating games of chance; this is commemorated in the *lela* board which is carved in front of him. Shamba is indeed the great culture hero of the Bakuba.

It is not quite certain that this statue is contemporary with Shamba, since it is possible that if the original portrait had decayed, perhaps about 1800, it would have been thought necessary exceptionally to make a copy of it. Only one such portrait was made during the life time of each king, and after his death it played an important part in effecting the transfer of his wisdom to his successor, who slept with it by his head for several nights. The piece was given to Torday for the British Museum by King Kwete Peshanga Kena in 1909.

55

The Tribal Image
William Fagg
The British Museum 1970
210mm deep

55

In 1970, however, bookshop impact was not foremost in publishers' minds, certainly not museum publishers. Yet this little catalogue, designed by Ron Costley, and entirely in black-and-white, makes a strong impression. The offset printing here, of considerably higher standard than the contemporaneous *Roman Forum* [51], has facilitated the dropping-out of all backgrounds; and the bold treatment, all figures standing up from the bottom of the page, creates an arresting display of images. The varied grouping on the spreads avoids any feeling of monotony this 'one-idea' treatment might have had. The restraint, even severity, of the captions (headings and commentaries all in the same size) play off against the images, allowing them to dominate. The simple concept has drama; but the drama is created by letting these wonderful images speak for themselves.

61 Sepik River Tribes
Northern New Guinea
Squatting figure of a woman
9¾in (25cm)
1936 7–10 171

62 Bosman
Sepik River, Northern New Guinea
Standing figure of a man
11¾in (29cm)
1936 7–20 83

63 Torres Straits Islands
South coast of New Guinea
Figures of a woman and a man *in copula*
10in (25cm)
+2,500

64 Fly River Tribes
Southern New Guinea
Standing figure of a man
15in (127cm)
1906 10–13 41

In 1936 the British Museum received the most generous gift of a large number of works of art collected in the New Guinea area during the recent voyage of the late Lord Moyne, who had carried out a great deal of valuable research work in many areas which had previously been un-represented in the Museum's collections. This small figure is at once one of the most delightful and one of the most powerful of the sculptures which he brought back with him on his yacht *Rosaura*. Its precise purpose is not known.

This is another of the proceeds of Lord Moyne's expedition and is a particularly good example of the best Sepik River style, especially in the treatment of the frigate-bird attributes which are highly charac-teristic of the area. The Bosman tribe are in the delta of the Ramu River about twenty miles eastward from the delta of the Sepik itself.

Sir Augustus Wollaston Franks was the Keeper of Antiquities in the British Museum for most of the second half of the nineteenth century, and was one of the greatest of all the benefactors of the Departments into which the Department of Antiquities has subsequently divided. In the case of Ethnography, there was a long period, especially in the seventies and eighties, when his name appeared as donor of a very high proportion of the acquisi-tions of this Department from all sections of the world. He had a fine unprejudiced eye for sculpture from areas such as this in which the opinion of his day would not have admitted that sculpture could exist. The figure was described as a 'god of procreation' (the masculine presumably subsuming the feminine) and it is said to have been used for love magic. One is reminded, though with a reversal of roles, of Tibetan bronzes representing a god with his *sakti*.

This piece, which is from the important collection given by Major W. Cooke-Daniels in 1906, appears to come from the Papuans at the mouth of the Fly and is said to be an agricultural charm used in the gardens. It is probably made from the root of a mangrove to judge by its charac-teristic curved form. No explanation is evident for the turning of the head to the right, unless it is to show the vigilance of the image in watching over the safety of the crops.

22 Ijo
Niger Delta, Nigeria
Standing figure of a man
38¼in (97cm)
1952 Af26 1

23 Ibo
Eastern Nigeria
Standing figure of a man
6¾in (17cm)
1950 Af45 380

24 Ibibio
Eastern Nigeria
Standing figure of a man
10½in (27cm)
1914 6–16 15

This figure was collected by John Main, an engineer stationed in the Delta, between 1891 and 1901, and was presented in 1952 by his son. There is no documenta-tion which would show what the figure represents. The top hat suggests a chief, but could simply be a way of doing honour to a familiar or protective spirit.

The styles of art of the western and eastern Ijo prescribed so precisely what figures and masks should look like as to leave little room for individual variations, but there is always room for the subtler forms of artistry.

This remarkably monumental miniature wood carving was given to the Museum by P. Amaury Talbot with the great collec-tion which he made between 1907 and 1916 but unfortunately failed fully to document. It is probably from the Owerri area and is of a kind used in the magical curing of certain diseases.

This beautiful little figure was collected by P. A. Talbot in the Eket district before 1914, since when such old-style Ibibio carvings have become exceedingly rare. The somewhat benign appearance may well belie the purpose for which such pieces were used by the *Ekpo* and *Idiong* Societies.

In the next decade, museums and galleries began to realise they were sitting on a goldmine: the marketing in various ways of their holdings. These included photographs and transparencies for art books and magazines, replicas, postcards, posters, calendars, guides, and diaries. The museum shop became essential. Simultaneously, major exhibitions, usually sponsored by commercial firms, spawned large-format, fully-documented, lavishly-illustrated catalogues, often surprisingly good value, especially when bought at the exhibition. For these productions were conceived in a way that gave them life-after-closure, available, often in hardback only, at a higher price, in high street bookshops as well as the museum. (A major growth industry – art history – both created the demand, and supplied writers to satisfy it. Exhibition catalogues are at the popular end of the market; scholarly texts on, often, obscurely specialised subjects are at the other.)

The conception and design of exhibition catalogues – now usually sold at the exit, being too cumbersome to carry around – built on lessons learned in the production of the integrated book. Exhibit descriptions and illustrations (often of every exhibit) are welded together. The well thought-out Constable exhibition held at the Tate Gallery in 1991 had a magnificent catalogue weighing 2.5 kg – far removed from the slight affairs of the 1940s and 1950s. All paintings and many drawings were reproduced in colour, and commentaries for major works extended over three or four well-packed pages. The erudite text of such catalogues is partly fuelled by a fear of professional assassination by rival art historians. You might say these catalogues were damage-limitation exercises. Nonetheless, they are often exemplary productions.

56

Good Citizen's Furniture
Annette Carruthers and Mary Greensted
Cheltenham Art Gallery and
Museums/Lund Humphries 1994
265mm deep

25* Cabinet of drawers

Designed by Ernest Gimson and made at Daneway by Ernest Smith, around 1903-7. Handles inside made by John Paul Cooper and outside by Alfred Bucknell.

Mahogany carcase veneered with ebony, walnut and holly. Inside of the doors veneered with quartered mahogany. Drawer fronts veneered with whitebeam and cupboard doors of solid mahogany. Exterior fittings of wrought steel and interior handles of silver.

The piece was badly damaged by a bomb blast in the Second World War and the small separate stand is not original. The table-type stand was beyond repair and was discarded, though a small part of a drawer survives, and a handle. During reconstruction some original material from the back was moved to the front, new doors were made for the interior cupboards, quartered mahogany was simulated by paint techniques for the inside of the right door, and the new stand was made. Missing areas were made up to match.

$14\frac{3}{8} \times 24\frac{7}{8} \times 11\frac{1}{4}$ (365 × 632 × 285)

Purchased in 1970 from Edward Barnsley for £50 with a 50 per cent grant from the V&A Purchase Grant Fund. 1970.213

Design: CAGM 1941.222.591, unsigned and undated on paper watermarked 1902.

Record: CAGM object file, photographs with inscriptions by EWG and SHB, 'Table Cabinet 2' × 1' £35'.
CAGM 1941.226.240, photograph with inscriptions by EWG.

Edward Barnsley was given this piece by Russell Gimson, in the hope that he would be able to repair the damage (Fig.102). Barnsley believed this was impossible and it was stored in an attic for a long time. It came to the Museum contained in a carrier bag and was reconstructed by Alan Morrall, the Senior Technical Officer.

From the inscriptions on the photographs in the Museum's files, it seems likely that the cabinet is the one shown at Debenham and Freebody in 1907, for sale at £28. 10. 0. This had a small base and handles on the sides, but it appears that a table stand was later made for it and the side handles removed, probably in an attempt to make it saleable. The prices given on the photographs are £35 on its own and £70 with the stand. The fact that Sidney Barnsley's writing is on these suggests that the cabinet was unsold at the time of Gimson's death, when several members of the family bought items from the executors.

Fig.101 **Cat.25** *Cabinet of drawers on a stand now destroyed, from Gimson's photograph collection.*

The cabinet belongs in a series of elaborately decorated pieces beginning with a cabinet on stand made by Kenton & Co in 1890-1, which is now in the Musée d'Orsay in Paris.[1] Like Ashbee, Gimson was partly inspired by Spanish *varguenos* (see Fig.86) and the seventeenth-century type of spice cabinet with small drawers. Two boxes in the collections of Leicestershire Museums display similarities of shape and proportion, and all owe something of a debt to an Indian travelling box in the V&A, of which Gimson had a photograph (Fig.12).

In an interview, Ernest Smith remembered that he had to use veneers of slightly

Fig.102 **Cat.25** *The cabinet when it first arrived in the Museum.*

Fig.103 **Cat.26**

different thicknesses and he wanted to sand them off level but was not allowed, so each of the 500 to 600 pieces had to be cleaned of glue individually. Gimson explained to him that he had been to a castle where the floor had been partially repaired, beautifully level, but when the sun shone, the new area looked dead. The old part was worn and waving and looked beautiful, so he thought he would have these little bits of wood uneven to catch the light.[2]

See Col. Fig.57.

1. Illustrated in L. Lambourne, *Utopian Craftsmen*, London 1980, p.167.
2. EBET, Donnellan interview.

26 Two armchairs

Designed by Ernest Gimson in 1907 and made by Edward Gardiner in about 1907-30.

Ash and rush.

$35 \times 25\frac{3}{8} \times 18\frac{3}{8}$; h. of seat $17\frac{1}{2}$
$(889 \times 645 \times 467$; h. of seat $444)$

Given in 1988 by Mr John Crowder. 1988.336

Design: CAGM 1971.61.7 signed and dated Aug 8 1907.

These chairs belonged to the donor's father-in-law, B.J.Fletcher, Head Master at

the Leicester School of Art and then at the Birmingham Municipal School of Art. Fletcher is known for the designs he made for Harry Peach of Dryad (see Cat.43) and for his espousal of Arts and Crafts ideals. He lived at Daneway House for some years and acquired these chairs after the death of Squire James of Edgeworth, who presumably bought them direct from Gimson or from Gardiner.

This design was used for the platform chairs for a church hall at Wootton Fitzpaine in Devon which was commissioned from F.W.Troup by a Mrs Pass, and it is known as the 'Pass' chair. A high-backed version was made as the Chairman's chair. The platform chairs cost 25s each.

The shapely form of the splat is one also found in French country chairs.

27 Coffer

Designed by Ernest Gimson and made at Daneway, probably about 1910. Decorated with plasterwork which was probably executed by Gimson himself.

English oak with modelled decoration in gesso, four steel strap hinges inside, and a brass lock. Made of planks with cogged dovetails at the corners, rows of dowels fixed to arched ribs inside the lid, chamfered tenons on front and back, and butterfly-shaped double dovetails on the ends. Simple gouged decoration at each end of the lid and chamfered line below main front panel. Lock by Hobbs & Co.

$23\frac{7}{8} \times 49 \times 17\frac{1}{2}$ $(608 \times 1245 \times 443)$

Purchased in 1941 at the sale of Mrs Emily Gimson's effects, for £12. 10. 0 from the Friends Fund. 1941.42

Record: Sale catalogue of Hobbs and Chambers, Cirencester, 20.3.1941, lot 207.

The sale catalogue indicates that the coffer was in a bedroom in 1941.

Freda Derrick illustrated this piece in *Country Craftsmen*[1] and suggested that the gessowork would have been painted had Gimson finished it. She implied that he was working on the piece around the time that he died. Without evidence from designs or exhibition catalogues, the dating of this kind of simple oak furniture is fairly difficult. It cannot be assumed that because it is simple it is early, since dated designs exist for similar pieces from the middle of Gimson's career.[2]

The stylised decoration of plant forms is typical of Gimson's pattern design, based

Catalogues are also required for permanent collections, particularly those smaller regional museums holding important collections in a particular subject. The collection of Arts and Crafts furniture at Cheltenham is strong enough to provide material for a comprehensive catalogue.

The thorough research behind books such as this and the next two examples results in a mass of complex information. The designer's task is to organise that complexity and cloak it in simplicity and clarity. Here, following a review of the general background, each designer/craftsman and his circle is given his own section. Introductions are set in larger type, in two columns. Productions are then listed individually, each one illustrated. Apart from basic data, furniture requires a description of construction details. In this catalogue, such details were set in italic to distinguish them from background information, set in roman. Half-line spaces were also used to clarify the different kinds of information. Full references and bibliographic details were supplied for each entry.

Simplicity or Splendour, a companion on Arts and Crafts objects by the same authors, was produced in 1999. Together, these two volumes describe, in fully-researched detail, 375 items. Every one, from buttons to large wardrobes, was photographed by Woodley and Quick. Their careful and consistent work, of deceptive simplicity, gives the books uncommon unity. Gallery publications have come a long way since 1945; these two volumes, created by a modest-sized regional museum, are unusually fine examples of their kind.

57

The previous example was the catalogue of part of a museum's collection. This example is the catalogue of an artist's entire output of etchings – effectively a catalogue raisonné, although without the usual commentaries on the works. Included in it are a comprehensive introduction to the artist's life and work, and forty-eight full-page (often full-size) illustrations. For these, duotone printing was chosen, to convey the richness and density of many of the later etchings, as well as their technical brilliance.

The catalogue raisonné itself includes the basic information normally required by collectors. All the artist's etchings are illustrated, and every illustration has its particulars on the same spread. The illustrations are not always arranged in strict order: the overall effect of the pattern on the page was considered more important. But every spread has its own orderly structure. Because each illustration is one of three standard widths, a flexible vertical grid is automatically established. Horizontal alignments are contrived where possible.

In books of this kind, putting the text alongside or beneath each picture often produces a jumbled layout. Pulling out the pictures into an organised grouping displays them to greater advantage, and allows for a more lucid arrangement of the text. It also saves space.

57
The Etchings of Wilfred Fairclough
Ian Lowe
Ashgate Editions 1990
264mm deep

122. Venice Carnival, Make Up I
E. $8\frac{1}{2} \times 5\frac{1}{4}$
States 1/1. 1/2. 1/3
Exh: RE 1985 (71). RA 1986 (1405). New Ashgate Gallery, Farnham 1988. Bankside Gallery Christmas 1988

123. Venice Carnival, Paris in Venice
E. $5\frac{1}{2} \times 8\frac{3}{4}$
States 2/1. 1/2. 2/3
Exh: RE 1986 (94). New Ashgate Gallery, Farnham 1988

1986

124. Venice Carnival, Masks
EA $7 \times 4\frac{1}{2}$
States 2/1. 1/2. 2/3
Exh: RE 1986 (84). CCA Galleries plc Award £500 for the artist of the outstanding print in the Exhibition. Bankside Gallery Christmas 1988

125. Lucerne Fishmarket, Onlookers
E. $5\frac{1}{2} \times 9$
States 2/1. 2nd state, final proof
Exh: RE 1986 (158). RA 1988 (1178). Bankside Gallery 'Five Man Show' 1987 (150). Bankside Gallery Christmas 1988

126. Venice Carnival, Nozze
EA $7\frac{1}{4} \times 4\frac{3}{4}$
States 2/1. 2nd state, final proof
Exh: RE 1986 (50). RA 1989 (165). Bankside Gallery 'Five Man Show' 1987 (165). Bankside Gallery Christmas 1988

127. Lucerne Pike
EA $4\frac{3}{4} \times 10$
States 2/1. 2nd state, final proof
Exh: RE 1986 (174). Bankside Gallery Christmas 1988

1987

128. Lucerne Market, Flower Girl
EA $5\frac{1}{2} \times 8$
States 2/1. 1/2. 1/3. 1/4. 5th state, final state
Exh: RE 1987 (199). Bankside Gallery 'Five Man Show' 1987 (156)

129. Venice Carnival, Clown
EA 5×7
States 2/1. 1/2. 1/3. 1/4. 1/5. 6th state final state
Exh: RE 1987 (201). RA 1990 (244). Bankside Gallery 'Five Man Show' 1987 (161). Bankside Gallery Christmas 1988

130. Venice Carnival, Man in Black
EA $7\frac{1}{4} \times 5$
States 2/1. 1/2. 1/3. 1/4
Exh: RE 1987 (30). Bankside Gallery 'Five Man Show' 1987 (164). New Ashgate Gallery, Farnham 1988

122 124

123

125

108

144

126

127

128

130

129

set against a wall identical to Cottingham's traceried panelling of the choir. Two figures in academic dress survey the tomb while a cleric looks on from the elaborately carved choir stalls.

B12 (Fig.34)
Magdalen College Chapel, photograph of the west end showing Cottingham's stone screen and carved stone organ case and the 1855 organ, before the alterations of 1980
Photograph by Thomas, Oxford
Reproduced by permission of the President and Fellows of Magdalen College Oxford

The Bill of Works noted the fixing of the candelabra in the choir, gilt-bronze fittings attached to the choir stalls, of single branching stems with quatrefoil decoration and cusped ornament to the rims of the cups: this photograph shows them in place before their removal in later alterations.

The Chapel Account Book lists a payment to 'Mr Pratt' in 1833 when the furnishings of the chapel were being completed. The reference is probably to Samuel Pratt of Lower Grosvenor Street. Pratt was a well-known antiquarian dealer, cabinet-maker and upholsterer who made furniture and fittings, both ecclesiastical and domestic, to Cottingham's designs over a number of years. A.W.N. Pugin, in following Cottingham in his demand for the highest quality work, also used Pratt and other top craftsmen to execute his designs.

B13 (Fig.35)
Gilt bronze candelabra from Magdalen College Chapel, designed by L.N. Cottingham 1829; possibly made by Samuel Pratt of Lower Grosvenor Street, London
V&A Museum
(See also Jervis, S., 'Furniture Designs for Snelston Hall', V&A Album, 1984.) Gilt-bronze candlesticks impressed Summers, listed as coppersmith and brazier at Herbert's Place, Waterloo Road, in 1835. Jervis also notes the similarity to candlesticks illustrated in L.N. Cottingham's *Sale Catalogue* and listed as 'fine branches of brass with pickets, time of Henry V'.

B14 (Fig.36; Colour Plate 3)
Magdalen College Chapel, view of the west end showing Cottingham's stone chair case of 1829 and Julian Bicknell's carved wood case of 1985
Magdalen College Archive
Photograph by Thomas, Oxford
Reproduced by permission of the President and Fellows of Magdalen College Oxford

The interior of Magdalen Chapel has changed little since Cottingham's restoration. The light fittings were replaced

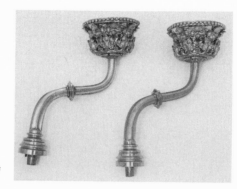

Fig.35 (Cat.B13) Gilt bronze candelabra, Magdalen College Chapel, 1829

Fig.36 (Cat.B14) West end of Magdalen College Chapel, 1985

with simple metal rods and plain glass light-holders. In 1855 a new organ by Gray and Davidson was installed with a case by J.C. Buckler which included 'the old work as far as practicable'. The installation of the organ proved a difficult task, for a bill itemises 'a second choir organ to suit the stone screen, as altered with new movements'; further modifications followed in 1866 and 1877-8. Gray

and Davidson's organ was recast in 1936, restored again in 1964, and finally removed in September 1985 to St Edmund's School, Oxford. All that remained was Cottingham's stone chair case. A new organ, built by Mander with a wooden case, designed by architect Julian Bicknell, to be in harmony with Cottingham's Gothic work, was installed in 1986.

Cottingham's work at Magdalen was greatly admired. James Ingram wrote in 1837 that 'though there may be as usual something to condemn there is much more apparently to admire, and whatever opinion may be entertained to the designs and fancies of the architect, it must be gratifying to behold, in aggregate, such accuracy and beauty of execution'.[20] It is hard to imagine what Ingram meant by 'fancies' but the accuracy reflected Cottingham's intention to bring a new standard of archaeological taste and knowledge to works of restoration. The detail and 'beauty of execution' shown at Magdalen is an embodiment of his *Working Drawings for Gothic Ornament* and a realisation of his instructions to architects in his *Plans etc of Henry VII's Chapel*, to study closely mediaeval precedents. Cottingham's surviving sketchbooks demonstrate his painstaking study of other mediaeval buildings in Oxford in preparation for his work at Magdalen, with architectural details drawn from St John's, Merton, University, Trinity, Magdalen and other colleges. Cottingham's work at Magdalen showed, too, a sensitive handling of the original fabric of the chapel, the use of good materials and a desire to restore by mending the decayed parts rather than by total renewal wherever possible, an instruction repeated throughout the *Bill of Works*. J.M. Crook has described the restoration of the Temple Church in 1840 – the removal of 'odious Wrenean overlayings of entablatures and fluted urns' – as an early landmark in the Gothic Revival, but Cottingham's complete transformation at Magdalen predates that work by eleven years. Clearly, too, his work predates the Ecclesiologists' principles and those of Pugin in his *True Principles* by some ten years. It is significant that Pugin was moved, in a letter of 1834 describing visits to Hereford and Lichfield Cathedrals where 'the villain Wyatt' had been at work, to invoke the language of praise when he came to write of Cottingham's work at Magdalen: 'At Oxford I was much delighted with the restoration of Magdalen College Chapel by Mr Cottingham which I can only say is one of the most beautiful specimens of modern design that I have ever seen and executed both in wood and stone in the best manner.'[21]

BIBLIOGRAPHY
Bill of Sundry and Artificers' Works etc., 1830, 31, 32, 33, agreeable to the Plans and Specs furnished by Mr Cottingham and Under his direction, Atkinson and Browne, Goswell St, London. Magdalen College Archives MS 735

88

58

L N Cottingham 1787-1847
Janet Myles
Lund Humphries 1996
239mm deep

58

A single, hitherto neglected, Victorian architect provides the subject for this catalogue/book. It has a complex structure. Following a lengthy examination of his life and work, the catalogue proper is divided up by subjects such as Church Restoration, Church Building, Domestic Architecture and Design. Within these subjects are some major entries such as, here, *St Alban's Abbey: Restoration 1832-3*, which themselves have an extended introduction. Such introductions are followed by descriptions of the (numbered) individual exhibits, with full data and further commentary. A bibliography

Bloxham, Rev. J. R., *The Archaeological Changes at Magdalen College*, Magdalen College Archive, MS 732

Buckler, J. G., *Observations on the Original Architecture of St Mary Magdalen College*, (pub. anon.) 1823

Colvin, H., *Unbuilt Oxford*, 1983

Cottingham, L. N., *Letters to Dr Routh*, Magdalen College Archive; *Letters to Fishmongers' Court*, 1832; Guildhall Library

Cottingham, L. N., *Five Notebooks of Drawings, 1828-34*, Avery Library, Columbia, Ref AA2620C82

Crook, J. M., 'Restoration of Temple Church', *Architectural History*, Vol.VII, 1964

Ferrey, B., *Recollections of A.W.N. Pugin*, 1861

Harper, J., 'The Organ of Magdalen College, Oxford', *The Musical Times*, May 1986, pp.293-6

Ingram, J., *Memorials of Oxford*, 3 vols 1837

Magdalen College Archive, *New Building Account Book*, 1829, CP2, 152; *The Book of the Chapel*, MS 824

Myles, J., 'L.N.Cottingham at Magdalen', *Magdalen College Record*, 1991

St Alban's Abbey: Restoration 1832-3

Cottingham's reputation was further enhanced by his repairs to St Alban's Abbey Church, which attracted praise not only on account of his scholarly and able work but also of his integrity in completing the work at a cost of £5700, one-third of the original estimate. Cottingham appears as a man of unimpeachable honesty in all matters of finance, of estimating costs and keeping of accounts, who always gave of his best efforts in his aim of restoring the Mediaeval even to the extent of working without payment to achieve this end. *The Gentleman's Magazine* reported the dilapidated state of the Abbey and described how, on 3 February 1832, 'a large portion of the wall of the upper battlement on the south west side fell on the roof below with such weight that it drove in the leads and timber and everything in its way, into the south aisle of the building'.[22] The writer called for active exertions to create a fund for its repair before 'this matchless monument, admirable for the sublimity of its design would be numbered in the ruins daily crumbling to dust'. J. C. Buckler illustrated this event in a watercolour drawing entitled 'South Aisle of the Nave of St Alban's Abbey as it appeared in June 1832', a melancholy picture which underlined St Alban's long history of increasing dilapidation through lack of funds and general neglect and was also a reminder of the Abbey's long and eventful history (Fig.37; Courtesy Hertfordshire Record Office).

The Abbey had grown from a shrine on the site of St Alban's Martyrdom outside the Roman city of Verulanium and reflected every development of architectural style from the great Norman crossing and

Fig.37 J. C. Buckler, 'South Aisle of the Nave of St Alban's Abbey etc', 1832
Line and wash 9½×7¼ in (24×18.5 cm)

transept of Abbot Paul de Caen, begun in 1077, to the Early English nave of Abbot John of Cella, the Decorated work of the fourteenth century, and Perpendicular additions by Abbot John of Wheathamstead in the fifteenth century. Cottingham described St Alban's as 'the very Alphabet and Grammar of English Architecture, containing the grammar of an art which the genius of a Jones, a Wren, and a Kent failed to imitate, but whose praises a Chaucer, a Shakespeare, a Milton and a Scott delighted to sing'.[23] Here Cottingham was alluding to the fact that previous architects had no concern for the Mediaeval; even such great ones as Jones, Wren and Kent had failed to understand the qualities of Gothic architecture. Cottingham here echoed Horace Walpole who, while alluding to the 'unrestrained licentiousness of that which is called Gothic', and criticised the Gothic of Jones, Wren and Kent, could then ask: 'Is an art despicable in which a great master cannot shine?' Walpole seemed not to be inclined to dismiss Gothic out of hand. Cottingham, however, went further in saying that by contrast the poets and writers had appreciated the Mediaeval; perhaps he saw himself

doing for the Mediaeval in architecture what the poets had done for it in literature.

By 1720 the building was in a serious state of disrepair and money was collected to restore the ceilings; a legacy was used to repair the nave and block up the west end of the aisles with brick walls. Between 1721 and 1724, when Nicholas Hawksmoor was called in to advise, several thousand pounds were spent and in an engraving of the Abbey to raise subscriptions, Hawksmoor wrote: 'Support this Venerable pile from being Martyred by ye Neglect of a slothfull generation', a sentiment echoed two hundred years later by Cottingham in his engraving to raise funds.[24] Very little was spent after 1724. As an early eighteenth-century historian of Herefordshire remarked: 'This noble Fabric, hath, since it became a Parish Church, wanted its Abbot's Zeale and Purse too for repairs.' Lewis Wyatt was called in to survey the Abbey in 1818 and again in 1827 and found the fabric in such a ruinous state that his estimate for repairs and 'improvements' amounted to an impossible £30,000.[25] Nothing was done and it comes to us as no surprise that the nave roof finally collapsed in 1832.

Cottingham, 'the able and learned restorer of Rochester Cathedral and St Magdalen's Chapel Oxford', was immediately summoned to make a report.[26] Previous reports of 1818, 1827 and the opinions of an unnamed architect in 1832 had advised the total removal of the nave transepts and roofs of the side aisles, removal of the spire, total renewing of fifty-one windows, taking down and rebuilding the clerestory and other such drastic measures.[27] At a public meeting it was stated that this restoration could not be carried out for less than £15,000. *The British Magazine* commented on this in an article on 'Repairing and Restoring our ancient Buildings':

'An appeal was made to the public upon the report of a gentleman utterly unknown to them as having any knowledge of the ancient Architecture of this country ... a wiser course is to resort to the advice of three or four of those architects who are known to the world as having made ancient buildings their study.'[28]

The report and estimate of £15,000 were unacceptable and Cottingham was then called in to make a survey. G. G. Scott, in his *Personal and Professional Recollections*, wrote that the nave roof had been declared unsafe and would have met with a similar fate as the nave of St Saviour's Southwark, 'but another architect, Mr Cottingham, let us give him all praise for the act, offered to guarantee the safety of the roof and to give his services gratuitously to save it, which he effected by inserting cast-iron shoes to the decayed beam-ends'.[29] The writer in *The British Magazine*, however, disapproved of the committee accepting Cottingham's offer:

---

completes each subject. In both this and the Cheltenham furniture catalogue, illustrations and descriptions are thoroughly cross-referenced. Lazy publishers avoid such nightmare editorial tasks.

This is more than a mere catalogue. Almost every fact seemed to send the

author off onto another line of investigation. The architect was a precursor of Pugin and Ruskin, a lover of genuine gothic, a hater of the scrape-and-rebuild school of 'restoration', a conserver who used archaeologically correct design in his work. To appreciate his importance it was necessary to contrast his views with the

prevailing architectural attitudes and building practices. Because of this wide-ranging text, space was severely restricted, and typographic intervention was kept as minimal as was consistent with clarity.

59

The Sculpture of David Nash
Julian Andrews
The Henry Moore Foundation/Lund
Humphries 1996
289mm deep

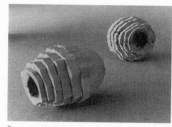

59

It seems ironic that the stylists of post-modern books should be working on computer screens to create a pastiche of Victorian or Edwardian idioms. That these are comparatively easy to achieve with computers does not make them desirable. But nor, to work in a truly late twentieth-century manner, need designers be self-consciously modernist. Both the previous example, which happens to be about a Victorian architect, and this next, about a contemporary sculptor, avoid stylistic tricks of any kind; yet both seem in sympathy with their very different subjects.

It is indicative of the 1980s and 1990s that many of my later examples are *about* artists, architects or craftsmen, but none are illustrated *by* artists. In the 1940s and early 1950s, the then equivalents of Freud, Hodgkin or Auerbach were asked to illustrate mainstream trade editions – Freud, in 1948, illustrated a limited edition of William Sansom's *The Equilibriad*. But the younger generation of today's artists would not, could not, illustrate such books. The changed status of artists and their relationship to the publishing world says much about that world, and art, today.

Although this present book is a less creative venture than those books of the 1940s, offset and its associated technology has enabled far higher production standards to be achieved than ever would have been possible, then, with letterpress. Half-tones can now appear on more sympathetic paper than high-gloss art, even though the range is somewhat limited. Text is crisp, blacks are black, a full range of tones can be achieved. Colour can be sumptuous without being crude or gaudy. Possibly because of the widespread use of silk- or satin-finish papers, type and images now seem part of the paper surface, integrated, with the kind of cleanliness and precision one feels ought to prevail in the computerised, technology-driven late twentieth century. It is a different effect from the heavily tactile impression of letterpress; but one which, I believe, could come to be prized in just the same way, as a virtue. The 'kiss impression' has always had admirers, even in letterpress.

The design, by Ray Carpenter, ultimately derives from the Swiss school. A grid keeps order, but is not obtrusive. Space is used positively, text detailing is careful and restrained, pictures are laid out in an orderly way, nothing is cramped. Stencilled chapter numbers gently relieve the serious layout.

This is not a coffee-table book. Its simplicity, subtlety and unadorned structural order are unfashionable. (The Utopian purist dreams of the 1920s, or even the 1940s, vanished long ago.) Such a monograph (one of a series from this publisher) does not rely on lavish full-colour photographs for effect (although sixteen pages of colour are included). The effect is achieved by fine printing, and the works themselves; the text illuminates these, the design presents them to us without fuss.

30 *Two Bonks in a Box*, 1971, ash and pine, 25 × 54 × 25 cm (10 × 21½ × 10 in)

he had recognised in Brancusi and in Giacometti, but had been unable to touch in his own work so far.

In *Bonks on a Rostrum* (1971) Nash constructed a formal wooden stand out of sections of pine which are effectively carpentered together. On the stand rests a separate presentation rostrum in three layers, and on the rostrum, almost as though they are being presented to potential purchasers in a shop window, are three separate rough 'bonks' of wood, the largest on the lower of the three levels, the smallest on the top. The whole piece is nearly six feet high, so the effect of the small round elements being formally presented to the viewer is very marked. The separation of the rostrum into three levels harks back to the several 'planes of distance' works that Nash had made at Kingston some four years earlier, while the formal, lectern-like structure of the whole piece is similar to Giacometti's *Four Figurines on a Stand* of 1950 which Nash had seen in the Tate Gallery's Giacometti exhibition of 1965.

With *Two Bonks in a Box* (1971) Nash appears to be attempting a totally contrasting method of presenting his carved pieces since, rather than being openly displayed, the two 'bonks' are closed in, shut away inside a box frame, like prisoners in a cramped cell. The use of a frame, or box, to enclose other objects is a theme he explored in a series of experimental works made in 1972 which are described separately below. *Two Bonks in a Box* also proved to be the seed which led to a major

work some sixteen years later when he was preparing a number of new sculptures for the *Viewpoint* exhibition held in Brussels in 1987: in *Plinth and Tomb* he made two enormous 'bonks' of solid oak, one of which is resting, almost concealed, inside a wooden box. The other is openly displayed on the top of a matching box, the two separate double-elements of the sculpture being placed in matching spaces within the gallery, for which they were specially made. This beautifully balanced piece seems to sum up the two methods of 'presenting' a work with which Nash was experimenting earlier, while also incorporating the element of a charred surface which he was to bring to a number of his sculptures in the 1980s.

The last work of this group, made over the winter of 1971/2, is *Sphere and Pyramid on Three Steps*, a small, very formal work, in which two 'bonks', or spherical elements, together with two small pyramid shapes, are displayed on a stepped base in the form of a ziggurat, rather like the 'step pyramid' of Saqqara. Images of the ancient Egyptian monuments had been very prevalent in the Press at this period in connection with the forthcoming Tutankhamen exhibition at the British Museum, which was much publicised. But Nash must also, in this piece, have been echoing the formal, geometric studies of spheres, cones and cylinders that he had practised in his drawing lessons at school, as well as reworking, once more, his theme of the three planes of distance.

31 *Nine Cracked Balls*, 1970/1, ash, 150 × 150 cm (60 × 60 in), largest diameter 40 cm (16 in)

32 *Nine Cracked Balls* in progress

33 Reed and grass tussocks, Vale of Ffestiniog

---

34 Step pyramid of Saqqara, Egypt

35 *Cosmic Geese*, 1971, ash, birch and beech,
3 elements: 6 × 16 × 6 cm (2½ × 6 × 2½ in);
7 × 12.5 × 7.5 cm (2½ × 5 × 3 in);
7.5 × 20 × 9 cm (3 × 8 × 3½ in)

36 *Plinth and Tomb*, 1987, oak and pine, each
76 × 169.5 × 104 cm (30½ × 68 × 41¼ in)

37 *Sphere and Pyramid on Three Steps*, 1971/2, pitchpine,
16 × 13 × 13 cm (6¼ × 5¼ × 5¼ in)

In all these early works, which form a distinct group within his œuvre, we see Nash moving more and more towards simplicity of form while engaging ever more closely with his material. Whereas he had earlier used pieces of wood to construct his works – the material itself being concealed beneath a painted surface – he was now working with and in the material, carving, cutting, chiselling and chopping his increasingly elemental forms. He made a large number of very basic carved shapes which were small enough to be held in the hand, varying the naturally spherical form that his chiselling produced by drawing it out into flanges or wings which, in turn, led him to christen them *Cosmic Geese* (1971). And it was precisely at this time that he noted, once more, the pile of carved 'bonks' which he had cut from the ash tree and then put aside, several months before.

To his surprise they had altered. Across the middle of each round wooden lump a wide crack had opened, so that the whole group looked like a series of grinning mouths sharing a joke with him. In physical terms what had happened was that the moisture in the green wood of the ash lumps had dried out, causing the grain of the wood to contract and open. In visual terms the effect was extraordinary, since the deep cracks, opening into darkness, gave the elements an effect of fullness and of life. It was as though they were calling out to him, and Nash's instinct was to say 'yes', and accept them. Laying them out on the floor of the chapel in three rows of

three, he found himself looking at a sculpture which combined simplicity of form and material with something of the rigour of minimalism, while still having a distinct vitality of its own. *Nine Cracked Balls* (1970/1) was to become a new starting-point in Nash's work, not only for the considerations already mentioned, but because it incorporated two new factors that were to become central concerns in his sculpture: the elements of time and of *change*, the second of these being dependent on the first. Had he laid out the nine balls as a work at the moment when he first completed them they would have appeared just as simple forms. By leaving them over a period of time, thus allowing the wood to dry out and the cracks to open, he reduced the level of his own intervention in the final shapes. The cracks, which are so prominent, have been produced by the movement and action of the material, not by the hand of the artist. This process, he realised, overturned the concept of the 'finished' sculpture with a surface which should remain intact, unchanged, from the moment the sculptor's tool left it. The piece could determine its own final form and surface which would not be pre-determined by the sculptor; the artist would become less dominant and the material would be allowed to speak with its own voice.

These principles would come to inform David Nash's work from now on, including sculptures of a very different kind that he would make over periods of many years. For the time being, he continued to experiment

60

Writing Home
Alan Bennett
Faber and Faber 1994
232mm deep

60

Although excellent typesetting can be found today, as my last few examples have shown, much of it is as bad, albeit often in different ways, as that which Tschichold found when he arrived in Britain in 1947. Double word spacing after a full point is no longer seen; but over-wide word spacing has reappeared; and now *letter*spacing can be – and often is – manipulated from line to line, sometimes into unreadability. Uncertainty about hyphenation has resulted in a reluctance to break words. Over-large type is often set solid or insufficiently leaded, rather than (more readably) set smaller and more generously leaded. None of this is the fault of the new technology – or only insofar as it has made typesetting seem easy. It must be added, however, that manufacturers, intent on pushing out an excess of type designs, have been somewhat miserly in their provision of small caps, non-lining figures and even (sometimes) ligatures: essential accessories (all of which can be seen in this example) for well-detailed text set in old face or transitional types.

While the 'modern' typography of the 1950s broke new ground in many ways, and was not without its detractors, it generally retained the basic decencies of typographic behaviour, usually, in fact, reinforcing them. Herbert Spencer, one of its leading practitioners, both in bookwork and the rougher commercial trade, drew up in the early 1950s comprehensive house rules for Lund Humphries, at that time printers *and* publishers. If these rules were to be generally followed today, standards would rise at a stroke.

This book shows that, given a knowledgable and persistent designer, good setting standards can be attained, and made to serve a careful design which, while generally traditional, has nonetheless a thoroughly late twentieth-century character. It has been read by tens of thousands of people; how many were even aware of its design? Ron Costley, Faber's designer, believes that designers

Russell Harty, 1934–1988

'I don't seem to be able to get started,' Russell wrote to me in 1966. He was a lecturer at a training college in Derby and at the age of thirty-two had just made his first foray into television, a catastrophic appearance as a contestant on Granada's *Criss Cross Quiz*. The only question he got right was about Catherine of Braganza. It was such a public humiliation that Myrtle, his mother, refused to speak to him, treating him, as he said in the same letter, 'like Ena Sharples treated the now late Vera Lomax'.

When he did get started, of course, there was no stopping him, and it was soon hard to recall a time when he had not been on television, though it was the capacity for provocative half-truths and outrageous overstatement that stood him in such good stead as a schoolmaster which now fitted him for a career on the small screen.

To me and his other close friends his career in radio and television was almost incidental. It furnished him with more stories, the cast of them more glamorous and distinguished and the attendant disasters and humiliations more public, but he never really altered from the undergraduate who had rooms on the same staircase as I did thirty-four years ago at Exeter College, Oxford.

He had learned then, by the age of twenty, a lesson it took me half a lifetime to learn, namely that there was nothing that could not be said and no one to whom one could not say it. He knew instinctively that everybody was the same (which is not to say they are not different), and he assumed instinctively that if a thought had occurred to him then it must have occurred to someone else. So by the time he got to Oxford he had long since shed youth's stiff, necessary armour, and the television personality who, in the last year of his life, introduced himself to a slightly mystified Pope wasn't very different from the undergraduate who invited Vivien

An Address given at St James's, Piccadilly, 14 October 1988

Leigh round for drinks. 'You can't do that,' I would protest. 'Why not?' said this youth off Blackburn market. 'They can only say no.' And if one had to point to the quality that distinguished Russell throughout his life it would be *cheek*.

While cheek is not quite a virtue, still it belongs in the other ranks of courage, so that even when he embarrassed you, you had to admire him for it – and, of course, laugh. It came out in the silliest things. He was one of the first people I knew who drove. It was the family car – opulent, vulgar, the emblem of successful greengrocery – and driving through Leeds or Manchester and seeing an old lady waiting at a bus-stop he would pip his horn and wave. She would instinctively wave back and, as we drove on, one would see her gazing after us, wondering who among her scant acquaintance had a large cream-coloured Jaguar. 'Brought a bit of interest into her life,' he would say, and that was as far as he got towards a philosophy: he understood that most people are prisoners in their lives and want releasing, even if it's only for a wave at a bus-stop.

He spent his life fleeing boredom, and he had no real goal beyond that. He had various romantic notions of himself, it's true – the country squire, for instance, though he was never particularly rustic; the solitary writer, though he hated being alone. Half an hour at his desk and he'd be on the phone saying 'Is the patch of wall you're staring at any more interesting than the one I'm staring at?'

'Private faces in public places', says Auden, 'Are wiser and nicer/Than public faces in private places.' For his friends he was naturally a private face, but for the public he seemed a private face too, and one that had strayed on to the screen seemingly untouched by expertise. That was why, though it infuriated his critics, the public liked him and took him to their hearts as they never did more polished performers. And yes he fumbled, and yes one wished he would reach for the right word rather than the next but two, and yes his delivery could be as tortured as his mother's was answering the telephone, but it didn't matter. That was part of his ordinariness and part of his style.

Still, television magnifies some personalities, but Russell it diminished, and people watching him saw only a fraction of the man. He once had to do a promotion for British goods in Bahrein. Flown there on Concorde with a party that included a beauty queen and a town crier, they sat down to a lunch of roast beef and Yorkshire pudding in a temperature of 110 in the shade. They all got on very well, except that after Russell had stood up and done his bit and sat down the town crier leaned over and said, 'I'll tell

Writing Home

ALAN BENNETT

ff

faber and faber
LONDON · BOSTON

Contents

should be invisible servants. (He has been described by an American designer as having zero tolerance for the arbitrary, the inconsistent, or the fanciful.) Although a very different kind of book from the previous example, the same kind of orderly thinking is behind it. Choice of typeface, type size, leading and margins; relationship of headings; the neat replacement of folio by footnote on page 48; the use of small caps (slightly sturdier than caps of an equivalent size) for the author's name on the title page; none of this has come about by accident. There is little to prevent any book consisting of text – history, essays, biography, novels, academic books or whatever – being of this standard.

The details of serious typography are contestable only within narrow limits. You could call them rules. More demanding is the analysis of content, the creation of a structure to clarify and unify this analysis, and the use of proportion, scale, space and texture within this structure. These, the architectural elements of book design, have perhaps become increasingly apparent during the last sixty years, as the concerns of serious architecture and serious typography have become more closely related (although book typography is unlikely to follow architecture into an equivalent of high-tech, deconstructive or organic design). The manipulation of these elements can be a logical process, or intuitive, or a combination of both. It will depend upon the personality of the designer, the requirements of the job, and the prevailing *zeitgeist*. So design is a somewhat nebulous process, seldom leading to the definitive, incontestable, solution. Consequently, unlike the more understandable contributions of author, publisher, editor, production staff and printer, design to many people seems a slightly mysterious add-on element, not always explainable. Most readers are unaware of it, and even publishers sometimes think it is dispensable. Strictly speaking, it is, just as poorly-cooked food can still keep you alive. Properly prepared books are more digestible. Although designers are always hoping for support and understanding, in their hearts, as they pursue their curious trade, they may be echoing the famous prayer of the Spanish Securicor robber, made while transferring the money to his own car. 'I'm not asking you to help me, God. *Sólo que no me jodas*'; which, loosely translated in a way acceptable to my publisher, means 'Just don't mess me around'.

Jackets then and now

Book design has been my main concern, but I also mention other changes in publishing. Nothing illustrates such changes better than the development of jacket and cover designs. The plethora of new titles, each fighting for attention in the bookshops, has resulted in a more aggressive style of jacket replacing the relaxed and often painterly approach seen in the 1940s and 1950s. Now, full colour is common, almost obligatory; paperback fiction is frequently advertised, not by the original spartan Penguin formula, but by pedestrian illustration in a banally realistic style. No lettering even begins to approach the quality or originality of that drawn by Barnett Freedman, say, or Eric Fraser. The most noticeable change, however, is the widespread use of photography, with, often, over-large lettering, positioned with little regard for the photograph itself, or the design as a whole. Even reproductions of paintings can be cavalierly treated.

Here, I try to highlight the changes with a small selection of jackets *then* contrasted with jackets *now*. As with the specimens of book design, I have chosen examples which I consider good of their kind, and of a higher standard than the average.

Should the jacket or cover design relate to the inside? Ideally and theoretically it should; in practice it rarely does. Of my examples, only three conform, and only one of them – significantly, a book on architecture – does so with any rigour. In art books or exhibition catalogues, the book designer is usually responsible for the totality, when at least some consistency can be achieved by the choice of typeface. But for most books, it has always been rare for the same designer to work on jacket *and* inside. The divorce between the two, while it may be regretted, merely reflects the necessity to recognise salesmen's prejudices. Understandably, they prefer to see not only something that has worked before, but also a more forceful image than any likely to be derived from the interior design. It requires a brave publisher to buck the trend.

Comparing the artists' jackets of the 1940s with those created by graphic designers in the 1990s, one can only regret that artists no longer involve themselves in bookwork. Even the very best designers' jackets – and those of Faber and Faber must be among them – seem bland in comparison. Faber's frequent use of Polish designer/illustrators, with their characteristic painterly imagination, does not entirely get over this problem. There have been some successful attempts to reflect the book's character in the illustration, but jackets are effectively small posters. From the 1930s to around the 1960s, the work of Tom Eckersley, F H K Henrion, Abram Games, Hans Schleger and others, all eminent poster designers, consisted almost entirely of visual puns. It was hard work, harder than producing a mere illustration, and far harder than fitting typography to a suitable photograph. But it was also more rewarding for the spectator. So we not only miss the painter's imagination, we also miss those unexpected associations producing an arresting, stimulating or provocative idea.

Writing as someone who is often asked to design the complete book, I know how much agonising there is, by both designer and publisher, over this packaging, or selling tool, even when the jacket is merely an assembly of uncontentious elements. It always seems to be regarded, perversely, as far more important than the inside layout. Well, if a book is not bought, everyone suffers, so The Market rules; although the gentler and, often, more creative approach seemed to work well enough in the 1940s and 1950s. Will sales by Internet change all this? Will we need anything more than an identifying title on the front? If bookshops are by-passed, significant savings could be made by a return to unlaminated one- or two-colour covers. Perhaps that early Penguin minimalism will become fashionable again. Personally, I would never buy a book without seeing it.

A cover by George Him (one half of the former design partnership Lewitt-Him) exemplifies the wit no longer seen today. In addition to the cover, the artist rewrote what he considered a rather pedestrian text, and designed the book as a kind of illustrated, heroic prose poem. 1958.
165mm deep

1 and **2**

The Poets Eye and *A Season in Hell* were both designed by the artists who illustrated the book; but while Craxton's design echoes his black-and-white decorative motifs, Vaughan employed a totally different style from the one he used inside. As an experienced jacket designer (and ex-commercial artist) he presumably realised that such a sombre style was unsuitable for the bookshop, even in 1948. Both jackets, although economically produced – Craxton's in two colours, Vaughan's in three – are, in their different ways, very effective. Having at least as much impact as any today, and far more style and originality, they come at the end of a tradition of artists able and willing to undertake commercial work.

The books are shown on pages 18-21 and 24-27.

3

The Fraser Darling jacket is number 6 in the amazing series of almost one hundred New Naturalist titles designed by Clifford and Rosemary Ellis. As far as I know, they were not painters, but their work (which also included pre-war posters for London Transport, Shell-Mex and BP) is entirely painterly in conception. For this series, they were always able to create a single strong image which summed up the subject. Three colours, with clever use of tints (could it actually be Zip-a-Tone?) were used. The rough edge to the horizontal title band subtly knits this into the image. Like the two previous jackets, this one is as forceful as any today (when a full-colour photograph would surely have been used. How boring.).

1
Frederick Muller 1944
210mm deep

2
John Lehmann 1949
223mm deep

3
Collins 1947
223mm deep

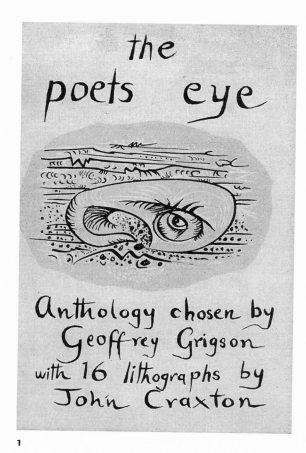

1

2

3

4

Kenneth Rowntree is a painter, a watercolourist in the English tradition and, like Eric Ravilious whose work is a little similar, was never loath to use his skills for commerce. He designed the cover of this King Penguin, which has twenty of his watercolours and three small black-and-white line illustrations. Representing the whole cover as a portfolio shows a Ravilious-like wit. The slanting rain depicted in the back illustration is a wry comment on Welsh weather.

Although less forceful than the previous three, the design is eminently suited to this elegant series. It is very English – whatever that unfortunate phrase may mean. Well, it means gentle, quiet, unassertive, witty, civilised. Perhaps it was more appropriate in 1948.

Like the graphic designers of the time – and one could, without insult, call him an honorary one – Rowntree took care to create an idea, rather than merely smack lettering over a painting. The problem of imaginatively encapsulating the contents has been solved with clarity, freshness and good humour.

The book is shown on pages 48–49.

5

Houses is also an 'ideas' solution. The series has, as a constant, the eye motif within a painterly white circle. This iris is always created by a relevant photograph, and the title lettering reflects the subject. (Goodness knows where that brick lettering came from.) Less entertaining than the previous examples, it makes a strong series image, using only a change of colour and black. The idea is perhaps a little hackneyed (maybe it was less so in 1947), but it has been done freshly and simply. The rough white background circle is an unexpected and effective element.

Today, that photograph would be full-colour, bled off. But would the idea of a cheap, simple propagandist series on visual education for Everyperson be accepted now? ('The aim of this series is to encourage us to look at objects of everyday life with fresh and critical eyes. Thus, while increasing our own daily pleasure we also become better able to create surroundings that will be a permanent pleasure.') Such a Utopian concept suited a time when hopes were high for a better and more pleasing world, but it does not seem to fit in with today's priorities. Even television attempts nothing seriously educational on everyday design.

4

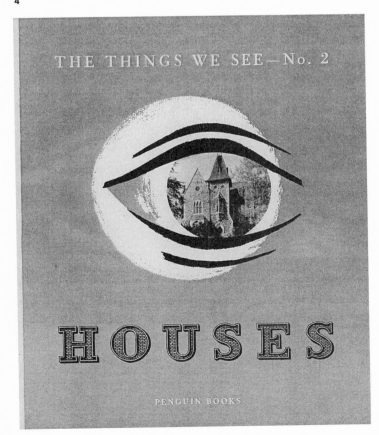

5

4
Penguin Books 1948
183mm deep

5
Penguin Books 1947
216mm deep

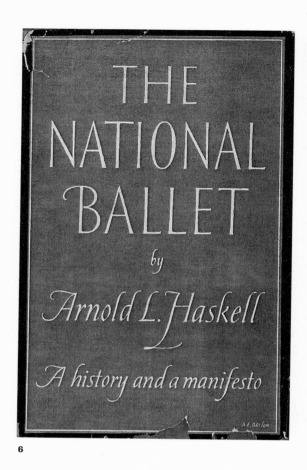

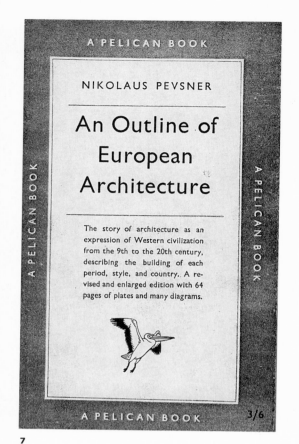

6

7

6

There is something a little sad about this jacket, although printed in a cheerful red and black. As a self-proclaimed manifesto it is strangely reticent. That elegance seems to be trying to give ballet a bad name. Post-Kenneth MacMillan, such effeteness would hardly be appropriate. No doubt a dramatic four-colour photograph, possibly with suitably dynamic typography, would be the current solution; but to our eyes today, this economical calligraphic jacket has a certain nostalgic appeal.

The book is shown on pages 40-41.

6

A & C Black 1947
Lettering by
A E Barlow
220mm deep

7

Penguin Books 1953
180mm deep

7

In his two-and-a-half years at Penguins, Tschichold not only attended to the typography of all books, he also designed or redesigned at least seven series covers. For Pelicans, a Pelican-blue border was devised, surrounding a white panel. This gave maximum flexibility for different lengths of title, short blurb, and so on. For one-line titles, the rules were closed up as necessary, the blurb set larger and/or opened out, and a third rule introduced between the blurb and symbol.

For about twenty years, Penguins (and Pelicans) had a devoted readership. Bookshops provided rows of shelves reserved solely for them; other publishers' paperbacks were bundled away elsewhere. With such a seller's market, this publisher had little need to develop a more forceful cover style.

8 and 9

Pentagram, responsible for all Faber and Faber jackets and covers, originally created a standardised title label, which was variable enough to cope with long or short titles, and title-led or author-led books. It was always carefully positioned in relation to the illustration. This was successfully used for many years, so successfully in fact that other publishers copied it. A freer typographic treatment was therefore introduced, while maintaining the carefully-chosen photographic images, or imaginative graphics. The sensitive typography refutes any idea that jacket designs have to be dumbed down for today's market. Using space in this way isolates the title from the surrounding clamour. In the bookshop, this restraint grabs attention.*

As part of the overall design approach, Faber's film, theatre, music and poetry lists, and certain authors too, are given their own style within the style. The Penguin variations, even at their peak, seem almost crude in comparison.

There is no visual relationship between jackets and inside design; but a common concern for quality, and a common feeling for the sensitive use of type and space, give all the books from this publisher a coherent image.

10

The sophistication of the spirited calligraphy seen in the third Faber book contrasts amusingly with the elegant such-good-taste lettering of *The National Ballet* opposite. Both are almost archetypes of their period, the later one reflecting the changed attitudes in this field since the work of Edward Johnston and his followers. Largely initiated by American and German letterers, the concern for regularity and perfection of individual letters has been replaced by a quest for free, vigorous forms and the creation of pattern for its own sake.

*No longer. In 1999, a change in marketing policy has resulted in Faber jackets losing this distinctive identity. It will be interesting to see whether this loss is compensated for by increased sales.

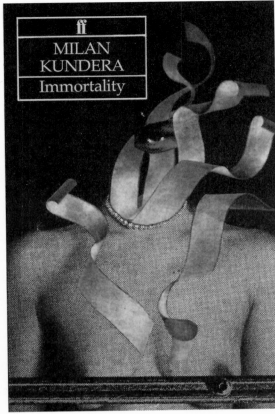

8

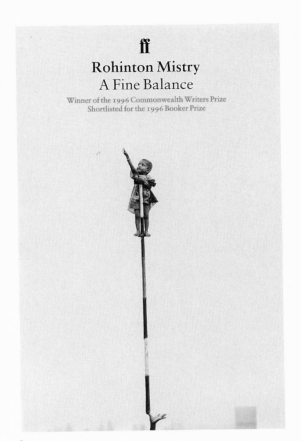

9

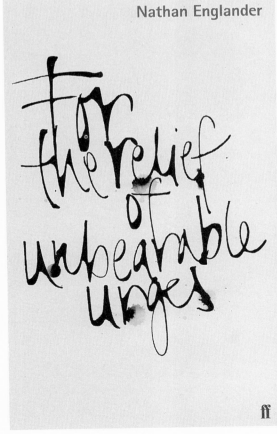

10

8
Faber and Faber 1991
Illustration by
Andrzej Klimowski
234mm deep

9
Faber and Faber 1997
Photograph by
Dario Mitidieri
198mm deep

10
Faber and Faber 1999
Lettering by
Lieve Cornil
216mm deep

11

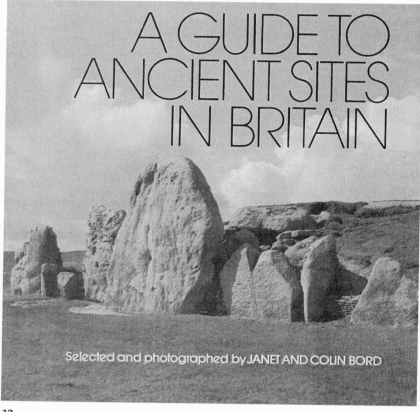

12

11
Lund Humphries 1996
280mm deep

12
Latimer 1978
204mm deep

11

A very different kind of lettering, although equally un-Johnstonian, is used on this exhibition catalogue. Intended to reflect lettering of the period, it was partly based on some scraps carved in a few of the ivories. It attempts to enliven the standard formula (fully-bled, full-colour reproduction of a painting) used for such volumes. So long as the lettering or typography is sensitively handled, and the picture is in the correct proportion, this formula can be effective. Here, more space at the top of the painting would have been helpful: the title crowds the head a little.

Of course, the lettering should have been smaller, and the ivory colour of it deeper. Moreover, backgrounds can be easily extended today during the origination process. I was the designer/ letterer. How often does one see the faults only after the job is printed.

12

Well-related to the full-colour photograph, the type, light in itself, has been carefully assembled into a strong block. The type style, although a sophisticated American late twentieth-century design, here none-the-less seems to reflect ideas of 'primitive barbarity', 'rugged antiquity' and the Noble Savage – ideas out of which grotesque letters originally grew.

Such allusive use of type shows a more knowledgeable approach than was common in jacket designs of the 1940s and 1950s. Then, graphic design as we now know it hardly existed. Although much was lost when painters no longer involved themselves with books, designers discovered subtle possibilities in the tools of their trade.

Gerald Cinamon designed both the book and the jacket, and chose not to attempt to relate one to the other, not even in type style. The book is shown on pages 90-91.

13

14

13

Ellipsis 3rd edition 1995
105mm deep

14

Dorling Kindersley 1995
214mm deep

13

This is an early title from a successful series of tiny guides to recent architecture (shown here actual size). Cover designs reflect the inside design, which is well-detailed throughout and strongly architectural. The vertical lines of type seem to contribute to this, as well as emphasise the modernity of the contents. The miniature size – a brave publishing concept – ensures the series is instantly recognisable, although the design is equally notable.

14

There could be almost no greater contrast than between *London* and *Wild Flowers* – yet both are characteristic of the 1990s. The hard-edge architectural layout of *London* is designed to appeal to its potential readership, just as the clutter, and over-large type, seen in *Wild Flowers*, is thought appropriate for its popular market. One hardly needs to look inside to know everything about its contents. Contemporary technology allows such a number of four-colour images to be included for almost no extra cost. So there is no attempt, not even a financial incentive, to create a single, symbolic image as was done for each New Naturalist title. (Would that more imaginative – and difficult – solution succeed in today's bookshops? Who knows – it never gets tried.) The design follows the well-established Dorling Kindersley formula; judged at the level for which it is intended, it has considerable appeal.

The book is shown on pages 84-86.

Conclusion

I write this in 1999. By chance, my story starts with the rise of the new (post-war) generation of typographers and book designers, and stops, as we near the end of the century, with the virtual demise of the kind of designer who chooses to work with paper and pencil.

Throughout my story, concerned typographers have greeted most new technical developments with groans; but once the capabilities (and limitations) of the new ways had been mastered, and engineers had to a large extent overcome designers' worries, these systems were found to have many advantages.

Today's major changes have pushed the drawing-board designer such as myself into history. Now, almost anyone, given a little mechanical training, can set type and produce pages of text (including illustrations, if need be). With no intermediary to misinterpret intentions, the operator now has unprecedented control over the output. But we are concerned with design, not output. So it is more important than ever that these users, whoever they may be, have an understanding not only of the machinery they are using but also of the craft they are practising.

Books score fairly badly as signifiers of social achievement. They stand apart from the disco-thud, designer-label culture of the beautiful people, with its consumerist priorities deliberately fostering discontent with our lot. Books can be judged by more permanent – and not necessarily Utopian – values. Let us assume, in this fast-changing world, that books have a future. In that future, they may be designed in many styles, using techniques far removed from the pencil, paper and drawing-board used for most of the examples I have shown. But however they are designed, and whatever the means chosen, there are what I have called basic decencies of typographic behaviour, refined over the centuries, which relate to the human eye and mind and the mechanics of reading. They are ignored at our peril. Or so it seems to me.